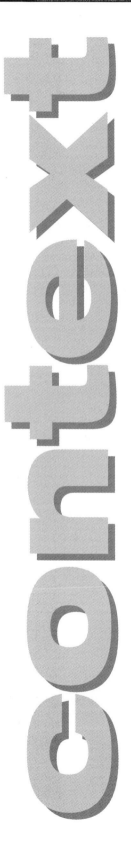

access to philosophy

context

An Introduction to

PHILOSOPHY AND ETHICS

Mel Thompson

Hodder Murray

A MEMBER OF THE HODDER HEADLINE GROUP

ACKNOWLEDGEMENTS

The front cover illustration shows a firefighter looking at the remains of the World Trade Center in New York after the attack on September 11th 2001. Reproduced courtesy of © Matt McDermott/Corbis Sygma.

The publishers would like to thank the following individuals, institutions and companies for permission to reproduce copyright illustrations in this book:

AP Photo/Emilio Morenatti/EFE, page 200; © Corbis, page 211; © Najlah Feanny/Corbis SABA, page 193; © Fukuhara, Inc./Corbis, page 34; Nomad Images 2002, pages 49, 110; PA Photos/EPA, page 62; © Pete Saloutos/Corbis, page 112; © Stocktrek/Corbis, page 27; R. Thompson 2002 (Nomad-Images), pages 41, 173.

The publishers would also like to thank the following for permission to reproduce material in this book: Duckworth Publishers and Professor MacIntyre for the extract from *After Virtue* by Alasdair MacIntyre (Duckworth, 1981); the extract from *The Coherence of Theism* by Richard Swinburne (Clarendon Press, 1993), and the extracts from *Is there a God?* by Richard Swinburne (OUP, 1996), reprinted by permission of Oxford University Press; Penguin for the extract from *Language, Truth and Logic* by A.J. Ayer (Reprinted in Penguin Books, 1990) Copyright 1936, 1946 by A.J. Ayer and for the extract from *The Myth of Sisyphus* by Albert Camus, translated by Justin O'Brien (Penguin, 1955) Translation copyright © Justin O'Brien, 1955; Routledge for extracts from *Why I am not a Christian and Other Essays on Religion and Related Subjects* by Bertrand Russell (Allen & Unwin, 1957).

Every effort has been made to trace and acknowledge ownership of copyright. The publishers will be glad to make suitable arrangements with any copyright holders whom it has not been possible to contact.

Note about the Internet links in the book: The user should be aware that URLs or web addresses change regularly. Every effort has been made to ensure the accuracy of the URLs provided in this book on going to press. It is inevitable, however, that some will change. It is sometimes possible to find a relocated webpage by typing in the address of the home page for a website in the URL window of your browser.

Orders: please contact Bookpoint Ltd, 130 Milton Park, Abingdon, Oxon OX14 4SB. Telephone: (44) 01235 827720. Fax: (44) 01235 400454. Lines are open from 9.00–6.00, Monday to Saturday, with a 24 hour message answering service. You can also order through our website www.hodderheadline.co.uk.

British Library Cataloguing in Publication Data
A catalogue record for this title is available from the British Library

ISBN-10: 0 340 87642 5
ISBN-13: 978 0 340 87642 8

First Published 2003
Impression number 10 9 8 7 6 5
Year   2009 2008 2007 2006

Copyright © 2003 Mel Thompson

Papers used in this book are natural, renewable and recyclable products. They are made from wood grown in sustainable forests. The logging and manufacturing processes conform to the environmental regulations of the country of origin.

Typeset by Servis Filmsetting Ltd, Manchester, UK
Printed in Great Britain for Hodder Murray, an imprint of Hodder Education, a member of the Hodder Headline Group, 338 Euston Road, London NW1 3BH by Martins the Printers, Berwick upon Tweed.

CONTENTS

PREFACE

Why the cover photo?

Why show the aftermath of 11 September 2001 on the cover of a book on philosophy and ethics? The fireman stands with his hands on his hips, looking up to survey the scene of devastation. Why has the world come to this? And slowly the answers unravel; slowly, because they are never simple.

They start, perhaps, with the acts of terrorists, and spread from there to attempt to understand what motivates those who want to give their lives – and take the lives of others – in gestures to highlight perceived injustice. If only one could see such people as mad, their horrific acts could be written off as the sad outcome of derangement. But commitment to a cause is not the same as madness, and so further questions have to be asked. What view of life is being attacked here? What is being affirmed or defended? What did America do – even before its wars on Afghanistan and Iraq – to cause such feelings of hate?

And so this act leads to a deeper questioning of the meaning and purpose of life, and the way in which people should treat one another. And questions of other injustices come up, and the Middle East, and values and lifestyles. One side fails to understand the other; each sees the other as blinded by prejudice.

And there stirs a deep sense that there must be some other way to organise our world and to resolve the disputes between its peoples. Warfare – whether by terrorist attack or conventional military force – leads to the same countless innocent victims. The pain on both sides is real, the blood is shed in equal measure, and all alike ask how it is that the world has come to this.

And from a consideration of the ethical, political and economic issues, there is a movement to deeper questions about the fundamental meaning and purpose of life. Where was God, or Allah, when the bombs and missiles fell on their targets, or the hijacked planes turned themselves into weapons? Why does he permit this to happen? Why was there no miracle to prevent it?

And the enraged weeping as the Iraqis bury their innocent dead, or the equally innocent who whisper 'I love you' into mobile phones, as they await their end high above Manhattan, challenge us to make sense of this life.

There is no greater challenge than to study and get to grips with philosophy and ethics, for it is the subject that goes deeper than all others, asking the fundamental 'Why?' and the equally fundamental 'What should I do?' In the routine of life, we can easily be distracted by more immediate and superficial preoccupations. Faced with moments of tragedy, we are forced to ask – as no doubt the New York fireman in the photo is doing in his own fashion, as he surveys the scene – 'Why has life come to this?'

For Students

It is important to remember that, at AS level and beyond, no single book can possibly cover all that is needed for the study of a topic in religious studies. One of the key skills that you need to develop, in order to do well at A level, is that of looking at a variety of ideas and arguments, comparing and evaluating them. In reading a book or extract, it is important to take into account the standpoint of its author, rather than simply taking everything that is said as though it were uninterpreted fact.

So, most importantly, this book does *not* claim to be all you need for preparing for AS examinations. In fact, if you simply learn all the details given here – perhaps getting all the names of thinkers organised into handy mnemonics that you can jot down at the top of your answer in the examination (and many candidates do just that!) – you will be guaranteed to do rather poorly. To do really well, you need to understand how to put an argument together, based on accurate information, and then add your own evaluation, but we will go into that a little later.

Hence, the task of this present book is simply to provide you with outlines or structures, setting out the basics of each topic, and suggesting the key things of which you should be aware. When you then set about further reading, discussion and essay planning, you will have a framework that enables you to appreciate the context of the ideas and arguments you are considering.

Additional information on some of the topics is available on my website **www.mel-thompson.co.uk** – so just log on and look at the 'Student Centre'.

For Teachers

In an ideal AS-level world, there would be time for all students to read a variety of books on each topic and to spend time discussing and comparing them, thus developing their critical and evaluative skills. But in reality, given the workload with which students have to cope, one of the key issues is the effective use of the very limited time that is actually available.

For any one topic, it is important that all students should gain an overall 'framework' or 'structure' of understanding. In other words, they need to know the key terms and ideas, the basic arguments and the names of the key thinkers associated with them. Once that basic framework is in place, additional reading will give substance and background to the ideas, and will enable students to develop their critical and evaluative skills.

When it comes to examination essays, some very able students demonstrate that they have done substantial reading, but they may not have appreciated its significance in the context of the topic as a whole. The result can be that an essay answer presents only one side of an argument, or shows that the candidate is unaware of the range of possible arguments that could be used. Seldom do such students do themselves justice.

At the other end of the scale, there are students who try to learn particular arguments by heart, and repeat them verbatim as soon as they see 'trigger' words in an examination question.

The aim of this book is to provide an overall outline of each topic within Philosophy and Ethics, with an indication of the issues to be considered, the most important arguments, and also notes on some of the most commonly encountered errors or misunderstandings. Hopefully, armed with such an outline, students can then use their time effectively in additional reading, setting such reading in an overall context.

This book attempts to set out arguments and information as clearly as possible, so that students can quickly absorb the basics and then move on to more substantial texts. It does *not* claim to be a comprehensive textbook for AS level Religious Studies – for no one book can possibly cover everything at depth, and (if it did) it would deprive students of the ability to develop a key skill in researching and comparing the approach of different authors.

Some of the material gathered here may be found in extended form in my other books on the subject, both in the *Access to Philosophy* and the *Teach Yourself* series, and in lecture notes on some of the topics, which are available in the 'Student Centre' of my website (**www.mel-thompson.co.uk**). It appears here in more concise form, in order to provide a viable starting point for AS level study. Other recommended books and websites are included in a 'Further Reading' section at the back.

The topics included here have been organised with particular reference to the AS examinations from OCR, but additional material has been drawn in, reflecting the needs of candidates taking examinations from Edexcel and AQA. In any case, there is a core of material in philosophy and ethics that is relevant to papers from all three examination boards.

Mel Thompson
May 2003

INTRODUCTION

1 Objectives at AS level

There is a progression from GCSE, through AS level to A2 level in terms of the degree of sophistication that candidates are expected to show in answering examination questions. It would be quite possible for the same question to be set at GCSE, A level or even degree level – what would be different for each of these levels is the way in which students would be expected to demonstrate their knowledge and skills at presenting an argument and justifying a point of view.

At GCSE, questions tend to explain exactly what they want you to do. So, for example, it is common for questions to end with a phrase such as 'Give reasons to support your answer and show that you have thought about more than one point of view.' At AS level the questions themselves will generally give you less specific instructions about how exactly you should present your answer. Your ability to construct an answer coherently, including what is relevant and excluding what is not, is an essential skill that is being tested. Your knowledge of the subject needs to be demonstrated; you should not leave the examiner to guess at how much you know.

Your objective at AS level is to demonstrate your knowledge of the facts and your ability to construct an argument.

First and foremost, therefore, examinations are about the ability to demonstrate and do justice to what you have learned.

There are two principle objectives that are tested at AS level:

▼ The ability to demonstrate knowledge of the subject.

▼ The ability to present an argument and to express a point of view.

It is not enough to write well and assume that the examiner will know that you have studied the material. You have to demonstrate, by the way in which you use information, that you understand it and can use it as part of your argument, or as an illustration of the point you are making.

And here the argument is important. A level is not a matter of memorising facts, but of being able to use your knowledge in arguing for a particular point of view. And, of course, to argue well, you need to be aware of the opposite arguments, and explain why you disagree with them.

Hint

Information you include in your answer will be credited if it is used either as **evidence** for something or as **an example** of something. In other words, it should form part of your argument. A list of correct pieces of information, however well expressed, is not the same thing as an argument, and will not gain you much credit.

Note

It is typical of questions at AS level that the first part will ask you to demonstrate your knowledge of the subject, and the second part will expect you to evaluate and present an argument for a particular point of view. Generally speaking, the first of these objectives potentially earns you two-thirds of the total marks for the question. It would, therefore, be most unwise to spend longer on the second part than on the first. We shall examine such things in the final chapter on examination technique. For now, as you take notes on the various topics, make sure you distinguish between the facts that you will need to understand and use in your argument, and evaluative comments, which you will use for expressing your own point of view.

2　Selecting and demonstrating knowledge

Many able candidates at AS level fail to do themselves justice because they do not take time to think about what information is relevant to answering the question. Thus, for example, once they see that a question is concerned with the Ontological Argument, they may simply reproduce, in as much detail as they can remember, all that they have been taught – ending up with a paragraph which attempts to link all this with the question. Not only does such an approach waste candidates' time – so that they are not able to present sufficient detail on the relevant material – but it also gains them no credit for having selected and demonstrated relevant knowledge.

Candidates should include *only* such material as contributes to answering the question. They should also be aware that a short answer does not necessarily score a lower mark than a long one. Irrelevant material is simply ignored by examiners.

In general, with restrictions in the time allowed in AS level examinations, the content base for questions is likely to be quite specific. For example, if a question asks about the Ontological Argument from Anselm, that is exactly what is needed – and little or no credit will be given for an exposition of Descartes, unless it is included in order to clarify or contrast with Anselm (and, if so, that must be explained if the material is to attract credit). Restricting syllabus content should help students to gain a reasonable knowledge in the limited time available, but only if they also learn to be selective in what they read and in how they present material in examinations.

Note

It is, of course, important to get to grips with the whole range of ideas on a particular topic; presenting such a range is part of the task of this present book. It is also useful for revision notes to list key thinkers and arguments. However, I would strongly suggest that candidates – perhaps working together as a group – discuss exactly what information is required to answer a range of sample questions. That way, they can get used to finding the quickest and clearest way of presenting answers, and to challenge and be challenged for irrelevance.

---

3 Sustaining a critical line of argument

This is one of the most important features of work at AS level. It is not enough to know the subject and to have a view of your own, you need to be able to argue the case for your view as clearly and coherently as possible.

A basic activity:

▽ Plan out the sort of answer you might give to a question – perhaps looking at the sample questions published by the examination board, or at a previous paper – and jot down the various points that you want to make.

▽ Then, between each of them, write 'AND', 'BUT', 'THEREFORE', 'SO', 'BECAUSE', 'WHICH IMPLIES THAT', 'WHICH CONTRADICTS WHAT', or some such connecting word or phrase.

▽ If you find that you have a string of ideas that cannot be connected up in that way, then it is unlikely that you have presented a clear line of argument.

Remember that when you are asked to 'examine critically', that does *not* imply that you should find only adverse comments. A critical argument is one that presents different points of view, evaluates them, and (probably) makes a judgement about them. If you are going to argue for one point of view, make sure you know why you are rejecting others, and – when appropriate – explain *why* you have made your particular choice.

Note

At the beginning of each chapter you will find a timeline of principal thinkers for the topics to be considered. As you put an argument together, check that timeline (either literally, or mentally if you are in the examination) for the thinkers that you want to include in your argument.

Remember, arguments move *forward* in time, not backwards. David Hume died in 1776, yet many examination candidates confidently describe him as criticising William Paley's argument about the design of the universe, which was not published until 1802!

Of course, it is perfectly valid to say that Hume's *argument* can be applied to Paley, but that is another matter. It may sound like a minor detail, but taking care over this can greatly improve your argument, and it shows that you have a sound grasp of the ideas and their context.

---

4 Looking at the context

Particularly for candidates who are going on to study Philosophy and Ethics at the greater depth required for A2, it is really useful to become aware of the context within which any one particular argument or theory has been put forward.

For example, utilitarian ethics developed at a time when democratic ideas were gaining influence in the political sphere, so it reflects a democratic respect for the welfare of individuals and their equal treatment. Similarly, Aquinas was seeking to expound traditional Church teachings at a time when Aristotelian philosophy had been rediscovered and was being taught in universities, so it is natural that he should use Aristotle's ideas in his writings.

It may not be necessary to include this information in a very specific examination answer (and indeed, as pointed out above, irrelevant material should be eliminated), but an awareness of their original context gives the most able candidates the edge, both in presenting arguments and in making connections.

5 Handling source material

Compared with subjects like History or English, you will find that less time is taken up in examining original source material in Philosophy and Ethics. The basic reason for this is that – for philosophy in general – the important thing is to grasp and be able to use the concepts and arguments that are being presented. The historical context within which the concept was originally set out is therefore of secondary concern, although in putting together your argument, you should be aware of it.

However, to do well, you should use one or more of the anthologies, and read some extended portions from original works. This has advantages:

▼ It gives you a 'feeling' for the kind of writing used. Some philosophers set everything out in logical sequence (e.g. Wittgenstein's *Tractatus*), others are more discursive (e.g. Descartes); some are densely packed, abstract and difficult to read (e.g. Kant), others can be quite entertaining (e.g. Bertrand Russell). Reading one of Plato's dialogues for the first time may transform your idea of philosophy – it can be lively, challenging and really quite down-to-earth.

▼ It enables you to set the argument in its historical context.

But how should you use that source material?

▼ By all means note down particularly important phrases or ideas, and be able to quote them where appropriate, *but* only do so if you are confident that you understand the context in which they appeared, and as a way of explaining the philosopher's argument.

▼ Remember: an isolated quote, without explanation, does not necessarily show the examiner that you have understood the argument. If you are going to use a quote in an examination, make sure that it is integrated into your argument.

▼ Linking a quote to an argument means that there is less chance that you will attach the wrong idea to the wrong person!

▼ In taking notes on a passage, try setting out the argument (perhaps in the form of a bullet list) and then show where any quote you are hoping to remember fits into that argument.

▼ Do not feel obliged to quote. 'I think therefore I am' may not be appropriate for absolutely every essay on Descartes! On the other hand, most students writing essays on Anselm's Ontological Argument might find 'that than which no greater can be thought' to be a useful starting point – although quoting it in Latin does not qualify you for extra marks!

6 Centre paradigms – and how to avoid them

When studying a topic, it is normal to go through the material systematically, taking notes from class discussions and from books, noting the main thinkers who have contributed to the topic and their lines of argument. By the time the topic is finished, you will probably have a good sequence of notes which you can read through.

When it comes time to revise, you may then decide to check through your notes and make a list of the main points. You go into the examination room confident that you can answer a question on that topic – say, the nature of religious language. You see a question on religious language and you know your luck is in. You rush at the answer, putting down all that you have learned, in exactly the right order – in goes Aquinas on analogy, Tillich on symbols, the via negativa, logical positivism, verification and falsification arguments, Wittgenstein and Flew. Both your memorised Wittgenstein quotes are included and so is an outline of Flew's parable of the gardener. You are confident that you have done yourself justice, that all the revision has paid off.

But a word of caution, you may not have done as well as you think . . .

The problem lies with the question. It may well have been specific to one aspect of religious language. It may also have asked you to evaluate how successful one approach is in communicating belief in God, or suchlike. Most of what you have included in your argument, although of general relevance, may not contribute directly to answering the question. You won't be penalised for including it, but it will have taken up valuable time, and given you the false impression that you have answered the question.

Sometimes, a majority of candidates from a centre fall into a trap that we can call a 'centre paradigm'. It may well be that all candidates from that particular centre have used the same set of notes, and they may even have been given a mnemonic to help them remember the names of scholars. In the examination, they all tend to reproduce the same essay, and it is seldom an appropriate answer to the question asked.

It is a particular danger in schools and colleges where the students and teachers are particularly keen – for the better the notes, the greater the temptation to keep closely to them in an examination essay. This is even more the case, of course, with examiner-marked coursework. Whole centres can produce what amounts to the same essay, with a few words changed here and there, but all in the same order and containing the same information.

To do yourself justice, learn the *arguments*, and why particular thinkers said what they did. Then, in the examination, only use those arguments that are appropriate for answering the question. More does not usually mean better when it comes to examinations. You will be judged on your ability to explain what you understand and to sustain a line of argument. AS level should not be seen as a test of your ability to memorise facts!

Hint

Why not reshape your revision notes?
- Put down the arguments and why they are important.
- Add the key points for and against.
- Make sure you know which scholars contributed to the argument.
- Check that you have a view on the matter! You may be asked about whether a particular argument or idea is valid or successful. Make sure you have something to say, and that you can argue your case.
- Then, know where you can find the scholars to back you up.

---

7 Thinking about connections

Inevitably, textbooks are divided up into chapters, sections and paragraphs, and the various arguments and ideas in philosophy and ethics are presented one after another. In practice, however, people who engage in philosophical or ethical debate need to move from one to another, picking out elements that are relevant for their argument.

So, for example, an argument about the existence of God might well involve one or more of the traditional arguments, but other arguments – for example about evil, or miracles, or religion and science – may also be relevant. These topics may have been studied in different modules or at different times during an A level course, but they may all link with one another.

A key to doing well in philosophy and ethics is therefore to learn the knack of spotting connections and then being able to draw them into an argument. From time to time throughout this book you will find 'Making Connections' boxes. These point out possible connections that the topic has with others. There are many more possible connections than can be included here, and noting them down as you study each topic will prove valuable.

Apart from anything else, the discipline of thinking about possible connections helps you 'place' a new argument or idea within the overall context of the subject.

One of the modules at A2 level is called 'Connections', and in it you will be required to show your ability to make connections across the modules you have studied at AS and A2 levels. It is difficult to revise for this paper, since there are many possible ways in which the connections could be explored, but if you have acquired the habit of noting down connections as you work through new material, you will have developed exactly the skill that the 'Connections' paper is designed to test.

ARGUMENTS FOR THE EXISTENCE OF GOD AND THEIR CRITICS

CHAPTER 1

POINTS TO CONSIDER

Can rational arguments ever prove the existence of God?

Do they show God's existence to be probable?

Do they show belief in God to be reasonable?

Is there any point in arguing about the existence of God? Some might claim that God can only be known personally, through some religious encounter or conversion experience, and that faith in God is not something that can be discussed rationally, nor generated as a result of an argument or proof. This is the distinction made between **natural theology** (knowledge of God through reason) and **revealed theology** (knowledge of God given directly to humankind through the action of God himself). But notice that these do not have to be mutually exclusive – it is quite possible to argue that God has in fact made himself known through revelation, but that it is also possible for human reason to frame valid arguments for his existence.

There are five basic types of argument for the existence of God:

1 arguments based on reason alone (Ontological Arguments)
2 arguments based on the fact that the world exists (Cosmological Arguments)
3 arguments based on particular features of the world (Teleological Arguments)
4 arguments based on the experience of morality (Moral Arguments)
5 arguments based on religious experience (Experiential Arguments).

Each has particular strengths and weaknesses, but each claims to show that it is *reasonable* to believe that God exists. Whether you find the arguments persuasive or not will depend on their logic, the evidence they present, and whether the kind of 'god' they argue for matches up with the concept of God that you consider it right to argue about. In other words, you might end up by saying – 'All right, this argument persuades me that there is indeed an "unmoved mover", but that's not what I mean by God.' If you do come to such a

TIMELINE

c.428–374 BCE	Plato
384–322 BCE	Aristotle
1033–1109	Anselm
	Gaunilo (a contemporary of Anselm)
1224–74	Aquinas
1596–1650	Descartes
1711–76	Hume
1724–1804	Kant
1743–1805	Paley
1806–73	Mill
1809–82	Darwin
1856–1939	Freud
1866–1957	Tennant
1872–1970	Russell
1907–94	Copleston
1911–90	Malcolm
1932–	Plantinga
1934–	Swinburne

conclusion, particularly in an examination answer, then it should be stated very clearly, along with your reasons.

In order to clarify exactly what it is that people are arguing about, we will therefore start by looking at concepts of God, and only then move on to consider the arguments.

POINTS TO CONSIDER

Individually, arguments may stand or fall, and some may seem to be more persuasive than others, but believers may claim that the *cumulative* effect of all five arguments is greater than that of each of them individually.

It is also perfectly valid to come to the conclusion that arguments alone cannot *prove* the existence of God, and yet to believe that God in fact exists.

Note: Arguments or Proofs?

Sometimes these five arguments are described as 'proofs' of God's existence. A proof is an argument that is sufficient to establish a fact. Clearly, those who put forward the arguments regarded them as proofs (since they thought that they were sufficient to establish the fact of God's existence), but those who challenge them do not. In this chapter we use the term 'argument' rather than proof. Arguments can be valid or invalid, and – if valid – their conclusions may be either certain or probable. In other words, you can present a perfectly valid argument that something is *likely* to be the case, without claiming that it is *certainly* the case.

1 Concepts of God

A basic dictionary definition of God: 'supreme being, Creator and Ruler of universe'.

This definition was further developed by R Swinburne in *The Coherence of Theism*:

[Reprinted by permission of Oxford University Press]

a person, without a body (i.e. a spirit), present everywhere, the creator and sustainer of the universe, a free agent, able to do everything (i.e. omnipotent), knowing all things, perfectly good, a source of moral obligation, immutable, eternal, a necessary being, holy, and worthy of worship.

Some elements in such a definition create problems and will need to be explored further. For example, how can God's omnipotence (ability to do anything) be compatible with the existence of evil, or his omniscience (knowing everything) with human freedom? We shall also look later in this chapter at whether God should be described as eternal or everlasting.

He may also be described as 'the greatest conceivable being', or as the sum of all perfections, which serve as the starting points for versions of the Ontological Argument.

All such attempts at defining what is meant by the word 'God' combine elements of the religious belief that come from the Judaeo-Christian tradition, with philosophical ideas, many of which are related to classical Greek philosophy. Believing in the existence of such a god is termed 'theism'.

a) The Judaeo-Christian Idea of God

i) As Creator

According to the book of Genesis, the world is created by God. However, the Bible is not a work of philosophy. It does not set out to prove that God exists, but simply describes God's relationship with human beings. In other words, it is written from within a situation of faith, and everything within it reflects a religious response, rather than a rational enquiry. So we should not expect the Bible to give a *systematic* explanation of how God creates. The usual interpretation of the Biblical account is that God first created the world in a formless state and then, over a period presented as six days, gave it form and structure.

Later thinkers were concerned that this interpretation would limit God in some way, seeing his creative power as dependent upon the material he uses. They therefore moved towards the idea that God created the world out of nothing (*ex nihilo*).

This is an important idea, because it suggests that God is not some external force coming in to work with pre-existing matter to shape or animate it, but that he is the absolute origin of everything. There is no independent material; no 'nothingness' out of which things can be made. Everything that comes into existence does so as a creative act of God. This represents the view of traditional Christian theology.

This idea is of fundamental importance for understanding the arguments presented in the Philosophy of Religion. If God creates as an external designer or manipulator of pre-existing material, then the question of God can be separated from a consideration of the nature and origin of the universe. However, if he creates *ex nihilo*, then he is both within and beyond everything that is created, as its origin as well as its designer.

ii) As Personal and Loving

In contrast to ideas of God that come as a result of philosophical argument, the image of God as presented in the Bible is one that speaks of him in personal terms, as establishing a relationship with people and as showing loving care towards them. In some passages, for example in the Book of Job, there is an examination of what the loving nature of God might mean in the face of suffering, but again this is not argued in an impersonal way, but as a challenge to understand the nature of a relationship with God. Hence, it is unreasonable to expect passages from the Bible to furnish philosophers with clear arguments about the existence of God. Rather, the Bible provides the images and models for understanding what religious people mean by 'God'. Therefore, arguments will only be relevant to the Judaeo-Christian tradition to the extent that they refer to a 'God' who is in recognisable continuity with the biblical tradition.

Note

When we come to examine ideas like Plato's 'Form of the Good' or Aristotle's 'Unmoved Mover', you should consider how these ideas compare with the traditional idea of God found in the Bible and continued in the Christian and other monotheistic traditions. A key feature is whether, for example, people can have a personal relationship with God, or whether 'God' is simply used as a theory with which to explain the nature of the universe. You need to consider what form of God is required for the various experiences related to religion (e.g. religious experience, prayer and worship) to make sense.

---

b) Plato

The ideas about God that developed within the western philosophical tradition were influenced by two strands within Ancient Greek philosophy. One comes through Plato and the other through Aristotle and the Stoics. In neither case does the Christian concept of God, as later debated, appear directly in the thinking of these philosophers, but the basic questions they addressed were hugely influential and set the agenda for many later debates.

However, in looking at Plato it is important to realise that the Greek philosophers did not discuss what would today be known as personal faith, or commitment to belief in God. Plato, Aristotle, the Stoics and others were considering the nature of the universe in order to find an ultimate point of explanation. The quest was to understand the universe, and the assumption was that human reason was created in such a way that knowledge of the universe was possible – in other words, life and the universe were considered to be fundamentally rational and comprehensible. This basic assumption lies behind much of Greek philosophy.

The wise understand the basic principles that underlie everything; this is what separates them from the mass of people who unthinkingly accept only what they know through immediate experience. This view lies behind the two aspects of Plato's work that we will consider here – his idea of the Forms and his analogy of the Cave.

i) The Form of the Good

Plato wrote his philosophy mainly in the form of dialogues, in which his teacher Socrates plays a key role. He shows Socrates' method of doing philosophy as one of debating the meaning of words (e.g. what is 'beauty', or 'truth' or 'justice'?). Thus we may ask the following:

▼ We may decide that many very different kinds of things are 'beautiful' (music, art, scenery, a person), and they can't all be beautiful in the same way, but what, therefore, do we mean by 'beauty' in itself? What is it that all beautiful things have in common?

▼ Why do we call different things 'beautiful', unless it is that we have some prior understanding of what 'beauty' is?

Plato's dialogues develop the 'Socratic method'. He works on the assumption that the meaning of a word corresponds to some permanent external reality. So, for example, 'justice' is not just a word used to bracket together certain events and situations. Justice actually exists in itself; it is a reality over and above any of the individual things that are said to be just. Indeed, individual things can be said to be 'just' only because we already have an idea of 'justice' itself. These general, abstract realities are what Plato calls '**Forms**'.

If we had no knowledge of such 'forms', meanings would be conventional only – what one person might call 'just' another might call 'unjust' and there would be no way to decide between the two.

The 'form' of something is thus its essential feature; it is what makes that thing what it is, and not something else.

The very act of thinking about, or communicating, reality requires abstract and general terms. It is amazing how fast young children pick this up. Show them a range of red things, and they quickly learn to select the common denominator and use the word 'red' correctly, as soon as they come across something else that is that colour.

Mediaeval thinkers who argued that such terms were merely names (for example, Abelard and William of Ockham) were therefore called '**Nominalists**'. Later, philosophers like Locke and Hume argued that all knowledge comes to us through sense experience. This approach is termed **empiricism**.

KEY QUESTION
Is there some 'essence' called 'redness' that inheres in these particular things, or is 'red' just a convenient way of categorising various objects that happen to be of that colour?

Why does it matter? Well, if you say that something is 'just' or 'beautiful' and I say that it is not, then we ought to be able to have a discussion about what constitutes justice or beauty. We may disagree, but we know that we are talking about general features of the real world.

But suppose we are forced to accept that there are *no* such permanent, abstract or general entities – 'suppose nothing is good or bad, but thinking makes it so'. Does that not mean (as Plato himself argues in the person of Thrasymachus in *The Republic*) that justice is whatever is in the interests of the stronger? '"Beauty", or "justice" is whatever I tell you it is!'

There can be no argument with this, unless you hold that there is some permanent meaning and essence of 'truth' or 'justice' to which something must conform.

So what about the theory of knowledge? How does Plato's idea of the Forms influence what we know and how we know it?

Plato divided the world into '**reality**' and '**appearance**' and our understanding of it is divided into '**knowledge**' and '**opinion**'. What we know of particular things is only 'opinion'; in other words, from my own experience, I gain partial information about the world, my understanding is limited, and therefore when I make a general statement based on that experience, it cannot claim to be absolutely correct, it cannot be true 'knowledge'. This must be so, according to Plato, simply because the ordinary things that are known through the senses are always changing, and therefore what we say about them now may not remain true for ever. For Plato, 'knowledge' is reserved for our understanding of the eternal realities – because the Forms alone do not change and can therefore offer certainty.

Is True Knowledge Ever Possible?

In science, we form hypotheses based on available evidence. No scientific law can ever claim to be 100% true, because it is always possible that we will find new evidence, or a new and better way of explaining the evidence we already have.

For example, it seemed obvious and true that light always travelled in straight lines, until Einstein showed that it was bent by strong gravitational fields.

For Plato there are two worlds (or, better, two very different ways of encountering the world):
▽ The changeable world that we encounter through the senses.
▽ The world beyond the things we experience through the senses: a world of 'forms' of which we can have true knowledge, and which is eternal.

He held that '**The Form of the Good**' was the highest of these forms, and that knowledge of the 'good' was the highest knowledge of which human beings are capable. It was, in effect, the ultimate explanation for everything.

In Plato's dialogues, Socrates challenges someone to explain the meaning of a concept and then tests it by introducing particular examples. This implies that knowledge is prior to experience, rather than the other way round. If experience came first, you would need to do no more than add up the sum total of experiences to gain true knowledge.

Plato believed that prior to our birth, our soul had direct knowledge of the Forms, and that we understand them now because we remember them. It is because we have this prior knowledge of 'beauty', 'justice' and so on, that we are able to use these words to describe our present experience.

MAKING CONNECTIONS

Plato uses this idea of knowledge as remembering, as a proof of immortality, arguing that the soul must have been in the eternal realm of the forms before its birth into this world.

ii) The Analogy of the Cave

In *The Republic*, Plato uses an analogy to illustrate the contrast between knowledge of reality and opinions about the individual things we experience.

He sees ordinary experience as being like that of prisoners, chained so that they can see only the back wall of a cave. Behind them is a fire, and in front of it people carry objects to and fro, throwing shadows upon the wall. Since they are all they ever experience, the prisoners assume that these shadows are all there is of reality.

If a prisoner were to escape and turn round, seeing first the fire and the objects being carried, and then going up to the mouth of the cave, he would be dazzled by the light of the sun. But that former prisoner would also recognise the difference between reality itself and the shadows on the wall of the cave, and might want to return and explain that difference to the other prisoners.

On returning, it is unlikely that the other prisoners would believe his account, nor would they see any reason to think that their everyday experience was nothing but shadows. They would think the returned prisoner foolish, because he no longer took seriously their interest in the shadows on the wall.

Thus, Plato contrasts the philosopher who, seeing objects illuminated by the sun (representing 'The Form of the Good'), understands and knows them as they really are, whereas the other prisoners, still stuck in their twilight world of change and decay, can do no more than form opinions about the shifting play of shadows.

iii) Implications of This for Religion

Consider the following features of Plato's view of reality:

▽ The 'real' world is not the one we see with our eyes, but an eternal world beyond the ever-changing world of our experience.

▽ Particular things have meaning and value only because they participate in the value of an eternal 'Form'.

▽ Reason takes priority over sense experience.

▽ The natural condition in which people find themselves is one of ignorance; they wait to be enlightened.

Clearly, if 'God' is identified with the 'Form of the Good', then he is not seen directly in the world of experienced things. On the other hand, it would suggest that 'God' is known implicitly, since, as the 'Form of the Good', he is the ultimate source of goodness, giving goodness to individual things.

MAKING CONNECTIONS

▼ Plato's cave links with the general issue of **epistemology** (the theory of knowledge), and in particular with the contrast between 'empiricists' (who hold that all knowledge is based on experience e.g. Locke) on the one hand and 'rationalists' (who say that knowledge starts with human reason e.g. Descartes) on the other.

▼ Plato's ideas here have implications for 'the problem of evil' (see page 61). If I say that any goodness in a human life is simply the participation of that life in 'The Form of the Good' (i.e. God), what am I to say about the origin and reality of evil? Augustine, who was influenced by Plato, therefore argued that evil was not a separate reality, but simply a privation of good.

▼ It suggests that science, and the whole process of gaining 'empirical' knowledge through the senses, will remain incomplete in its quest to reveal the truth about the world. It also suggests that reason should dictate how we interpret experience, rather than experience provide the basis of how we are to reason. This had profound implications for the religion and science debates of later centuries.

DEBATE
Be ready to argue whether particular things are more or less real than the 'forms' of which they are examples.

Since the world of our everyday experience is merely shadows on the wall of the cave, there is the tendency, in religious ideas influenced by Plato, to see fundamental spiritual reality as being 'elsewhere' and to downgrade human experience. Indirectly, this may lead to a 'compensatory' view of religion e.g. Augustine (influenced by Plato's philosophy) looked for an eternal and perfect *City of God* (the title of his famous book) to compensate for the fall of Rome.

This approach becomes possible if reality is eternal, known by reason to the enlightened few, and is not seen in the objects of experience.

Christian ideas about incarnation, along with humanism and Buddhism, try to focus spiritual reality in the 'here and now' world. Religion is about the truth of things as they are, exactly as you experience them. Buddhism, for example, has the cultivation of awareness of the present moment as a key feature of its spirituality – if you see clearly what is in front of you, you will respond appropriately. Humanists, too, want to see the potential for goodness in ordinary life, not with reference to some transcendent deity. Radical forms of Christian theology, including the 'death of God' theology, which developed in the 1960s and 1970s, saw the focus of Christianity shifting away from beliefs about a transcendent God and towards an incarnate idea of God in which the suffering Christ is seen in everything.

The other approach – which is represented in mainstream Christianity, Judaism and Islam – is to see God as being beyond the present changing face of things, but somehow underpinning it and giving it meaning. We have to look *beyond* this present world in order to understand God.

> **ISSUES:**
> To caricature Plato's influence on religion, one might argue that it makes a person 'so heavenly minded that they are no earthly use!' How might Plato's view of the Form of the Good influence ideas on ethical issues, or on the nature of human goodness?

Note

Many debates in philosophy can be traced back to Ancient Greece. Aristotle challenged Plato's view of the Forms. For Aristotle (as in modern science) experience forms the basis of knowledge – general terms come about because we categorise the things we experience.

---

c) Terms Used of God and Belief in God

It is not easy to give a definition of the word 'God' that would do justice to all of the elements that have contributed to the idea of God, but, using the definition provided by Swinburne (see page 10), we can say that:

▼ Belief that there is such a God is termed **theism**.
▼ Belief that there is no such God is **atheism**.
▼ Belief that we do not have enough evidence to come to a conclusion on the issue of whether or not God exists is termed **agnosticism**.

Theism is generally taken to mean **monotheism** – namely that there is one and only one God – as opposed to **polytheism**, which is the belief that there exist a number of Gods.

As we shall see later, most arguments assume that God both exists within and yet goes beyond the ordinary things that we can experience.

The 'existing within' element is called his **immanence** and the 'going beyond' is his **transcendence**.

Theism implies that God is both transcendent and immanent.

However, the belief that God is separate from the world, and that he is its creator although remaining external to it, is called **deism**. Notice that deism is incompatible with theism, since deism does not see God as involved with and encountered within the world, which is a feature of theistic belief.

At the other end of the scale, the belief that God is simply identified with the world is **pantheism** (meaning 'everything is God'). Notice that this is incompatible with theism, since it does not see God as transcending the world.

Panentheism, however, expresses the idea that God is within everything, although not identified with them. This is not incompatible with theism, since theism also claims that God is within everything, but most theists would claim that panentheism overemphasises the immanent aspect of God.

i) Eternal and Everlasting

Everything that exists within time has a beginning and an end, and passes through a process of change. It is constantly getting older, even if it does not appear to change physically. Such things are described as **contingent** – which means that they are limited, and dependent upon other things for their existence.

By contrast, God may be described as **eternal** or **everlasting**. These do not mean the same thing:

If God is *eternal*, he is outside time. It makes no sense to say that he grows older, and terms like past, present and future make no sense when applied to him. He cannot change (for that is a feature of existing within time), nor take an active role within particular actions (for to act is to make a difference to something within time and space).

If God is *everlasting*, he exists within a time frame, can intervene and act within the world, and has a past and a future. The difference is that his past stretches back infinitely, and his future stretches forward infinitely.

Note

Those who emphasise the idea that God is eternal, see him as transcending the world of space and time, as the God who creates the world out of nothing.

Those who emphasise the idea that God is everlasting, see him as active within the world, engaged in the unfolding of events.

ii) Key Words Describing the God of Classical Theism

▼ **Omnipotent** – all-powerful
▼ **Omniscient** – all-knowing
▼ **Omnipresent** – existing everywhere

The idea that God is omnipotent and omnipresent is related to the concept of him as a creator. It implies that there is nothing external to him, and no separate creation in which he is not involved, or over which he has no control.

The idea that God is omnipotent and omniscient is related to the problem of evil and suffering. If God can do anything and knows everything, why does he not act to prevent evil?

Getting the balance right in thinking about God

Thinking about the transcendence of God, one might say:

1 He is timeless.
2 He creates from nothing.
3 He cannot 'do' anything (because things only get done within space and time).
4 He cannot be a moral agent (for the same reason).
5 He can know everything past, present and future.

Thinking about the immanence of God, one might say:

1 He is within time.
2 He shapes and sustains the physical world.
3 He can act within the world.
4 He can be a moral agent, shaping events.
5 He can know the past and the present, but he cannot know the future (except if it is the inevitable outcome of things that exist in the present).

But traditional theism argues that God is *both* transcendent *and* immanent. Do you see the problem with this?

MAKING CONNECTIONS

Those studying the Old or New Testament alongside Philosophy of Religion may reflect on the implications of the image of God portrayed in the scriptures. Is an active and personally involved God compatible with the idea of God as eternal and unchanging, absolutely transcending events in this world of space and time?

ISSUES:
Is the God of philosophy compatible with the God of religion?
Do people need to believe in a God who can change his mind if prayed to, or intervene to help in time of trouble? If so, what does that say about belief in a God who has no 'parts of passions' and who does not exist within time?

2 The Ontological Argument

The Ontological Argument is based on a definition of the word 'God'. It claims that, if you understand 'God' in terms of that definition, then it is logical to conclude that he exists and that his existence is not just possible, but necessary.

a) Anselm v. Gaunilo

The argument was presented by Anselm (1033–1109) in his book *Proslogion*, written c.1080, and was based on the idea that God is *aliquid quo nihil maius cogitari possit* – 'that than which none greater can be thought'. His argument was challenged by a fellow monk, Gaunilo.

i) Anselm's Arguments
Anselm has two versions of the argument. The first is from *Proslogion*, chapter 2. This takes the form of a prayer in which Anselm considers the 'fool' in Psalm 14 who claims that there is no God.

The logic of the argument is as follows:
▼ God is 'a being than which none greater can be thought'.
▼ The atheist understands this definition, even if he does not understand that God exists.
▼ It is one thing to exist in the understanding, another to exist in reality.
▼ It is greater to exist both in the understanding and in reality, than to exist in the understanding alone.
▼ That 'than which none greater can be thought' cannot therefore exist in the understanding alone, or else something greater *could* be thought – namely that same thing existing *both* in the understanding *and* in reality.
▼ To claim that something 'than which none greater can be thought' did not exist in reality, as well as in the mind, is therefore self-contradictory.
▼ Therefore Anselm concludes: 'Without doubt, therefore, there exists, both in the understanding and in reality, something than which a greater cannot be thought.'

Key idea: Something is greater if it exists than if it doesn't; therefore, if God is the greatest thing that we can imagine, it is illogical to think that he does not exist.

Note: Faith Seeking Understanding

Mediaeval theologians believed in God anyway, but wanted to show that their belief was reasonable: in other words, their situation was 'faith seeking understanding'. But that did *not* mean that they were not asking serious questions, or challenging the meaning of religious ideas. They sought to show that religious belief was compatible with human logic.

Anselm presented the second version of the argument in chapter 3 of *Proslogion*; its logic runs like this:

▼ Something which *cannot* be thought of as not existing is greater than that which *can* be thought of as not existing.

▼ If 'that than which a greater cannot be thought' *could* be thought not to exist, it would not be 'that than which a greater cannot be thought' (because that would imply that one could think of something greater – namely, something that could not be thought not to exist).

▼ Therefore, to avoid self-contradiction, 'that than which a greater cannot be thought' must necessarily exist, and cannot even be thought of as not existing.

Key idea: Most things in this world are contingent (i.e. they can either exist or not exist, and depend on other things for their existence). However, 'that than which a greater cannot be thought' cannot be so limited. It therefore has necessary existence.

Note

Why did Anselm describe God as 'that than which none greater can be thought'? In an earlier book, *Monologion*, he spoke of degrees of goodness and perfection, arguing that there must be something that constitutes perfect goodness (God), which causes goodness in all else. Like Plato's idea of the Forms, which embody the perfection of what we see in a limited way in this world, Anselm sets God as the perfection of what we see as limited greatness among contingent beings.

---

ii) Gaunilo's Objection and Anselm's Answer

Gaunilo of Marmoutier argued 'On behalf of the fool' that Anselm's argument must be false, because it could equally well be used to prove that 'the perfect island' exists, which is clearly nonsense.

Anselm rejected this criticism. Essentially, he pointed out that an island is a limited thing, and you can always imagine better and better islands, but 'that than which a greater cannot be thought' is unique. If it could be thought of as nonexistent, it could also be thought of as having a beginning and an end, but then it would not be the greatest that can be thought.

Key point in assessing Gaunilo's objection:

Gaunilo's criticism applied only to Anselm's argument in *Proslogion* chapter 2, *not* to that in *Proslogion* chapter 3. Anselm's reply to him uses a key feature of the latter argument – namely that God's existence is not contingent but necessary, whereas the existence of an island, which is a limited thing, is always contingent.

In assessing Anselm's argument, remember that he took care to distinguish between ideas and reality, in a way that backs up his argument in *Proslogion* chapter 3. In chapter 4 of *Proslogion* he says:

> For we think of a thing, in one sense, when we think of the word that signifies it, and in another sense, when we understand the very thing itself. Thus in the first sense God can be thought of as non-existent, but in the second sense this is quite impossible. For no one who understands what God is, can think that God does not exist ... For God is that than which a greater cannot be thought, and whoever understands this rightly must understand that he exists in a way that he cannot be non-existent even in thought. He, therefore, who understands that God thus exists, cannot think of him as non-existent.

DEBATE

Be ready to argue whether or not you think that Gaunilo has shown that Anselm's argument is invalid. Also be prepared to say whether there are aspects of Anselm's arguments to which Gaunilo's criticism could not apply, and if not, why not.

For Reflection

It makes sense to discuss whether something that is limited exists or not, because either possibility can be imagined, and involves no self-contradiction. But it makes no sense to say that an unlimited being does not exist, because that would imply a limitation, and therefore be self-contradictory. One might argue that, by defining God as 'that than which a greater cannot be thought', Anselm was effectively defining him as a way that appeared to preclude the possibility of his non-existence.

---

b) Descartes v. Kant

Later philosophers, such as Descartes and Leibniz, also developed arguments of this sort. Descartes' version is particularly straightforward. The main criticism here came from Immanuel Kant, who attacked the logic on which it is based.

i) Descartes' Version of the Argument

In *Meditation* 5, Descartes argued that existence is a *necessary* part of the meaning of God, in the same way that three angles are a necessary part of the meaning of a triangle. He saw existence as a perfection, and therefore that God – a supremely perfect being – must have all the perfections, including existence.

He does not imply by this that our thought can determine what exists. He admits that:

> ... thought does not impose any necessity on things; and just as I may imagine a winged horse even though no horse has wings, so I may be able to attach existence to God even though no God exists.
>
> But there is a sophism concealed here. From the fact that I cannot think of a mountain without a valley, it does not follow that a mountain and valley exist anywhere, but simply that a mountain and a valley, whether they exist or not, are mutually inseparable. But from the fact that I cannot think of God except as existing, it follows that existence is inseparable from God, and hence that he really exists.

[Translation from *The Philosophical Writings of Descartes*, CUP, 1984, quoted in Brian Davies' *Philosophy of Religion*]

ii) *Kant's Criticism (given in his* Critique of Pure Reason*)*

▼ *If* you have a triangle, it must have three angles (i.e. to avoid contradiction).

▼ *But* if you do *not* have the triangle, you do not have its three angles either.

Therefore:

▼ *If* you believe in God, it is logical to think that his existence is necessary (rather than contingent).

▼ *But* you do not have to accept the existence of God in the first place.

Note

Kant distinguished between

▼ **Analytic statements** – which are true by definition

▼ **Synthetic statements** – which are only known to be true or false with reference to sense experience.

Statements about existence are synthetic; definitions are analytic. Descartes is trying to turn an analytic statement (about the nature of God) into a synthetic statement (about his existence).

Kant also argued that existence is not a predicate. In other words, you add nothing to a *description* of something (i.e. to its list of predicates) by saying that 'it exists'. By saying that something exists, you are simply saying that there actually is an example of that thing. There is no difference in the description of an imaginary football and an actual football – the only difference is that one exists and the other does not. So existence cannot be part of the description.

In general, it can be argued that statements of definition or logic are true of necessity (e.g. $2 + 2 = 4$ remains true under all conditions), but statements about existence are only validated by experience (there happen to be four things in front of me in two groups of two, but there might just as easily have been five in all). In other words, all existential statements are synthetic.

Note

Kant was the first to use the term 'Ontological' for this argument, but we have no evidence that he knew Anselm's writings. His criticism was probably based on reading Leibniz's account of it, but it applies equally well to Descartes' version.

---

c) Some Modern Debates

In spite of Kant's criticism, philosophers have continued to be fascinated by this argument, and there are a number of modern versions of it, which seek to overcome various problems raised by Kant and others. These may not be included in your AS level syllabus, but they do help to explain important features of the Ontological Argument.

In *Philosophical Review* January 1960, Norman Malcolm defended the Ontological Argument against Kant's criticism. His argument is that God's existence cannot be contingent (he cannot be the sort of being that might exist or not), since there is nothing that could cause him to cease existing if he does exist, nor cause him to start existing if he does not. Either of those last options would detract from the definition of God as either a being than which a greater cannot be thought (Anselm) or the most perfect being (Descartes). Therefore God's existence is *either necessary or impossible.*

But, Malcolm then argues that God's existence cannot be impossible (for if it were, then 'God exists' would be self-contradictory), therefore it must be necessary – in other words, God necessarily exists.

To appreciate the strengths and weaknesses of this argument, it is important to distinguish between **logical necessity** and **factual necessity**:

▼ If 'God exists' is logically necessary, then 'God does not exist' would be self-contradictory.
▼ If 'God exists' is factually necessary, it is not possible for there to be no God.

Malcolm's comment depends on this distinction. If the argument were about *logical* necessity, then he has a valid point; but most people consider the argument to be about *factual* necessity. However, what Malcolm is claiming is that existence itself cannot be considered a perfection (which is what Descartes and Leibniz thought) but that *necessary existence* (as opposed to contingent existence) is a perfection. Kant's criticism of the Ontological Argument also made this distinction: the necessity of a triangle having three angles is a *logical* necessity, but it is not *factually* necessary for there to be a triangle at all.

However, Malcolm makes the following important point in summing up what Anselm achieved in his argument:

> 'What Anselm did was to give a demonstration that the proposition "God necessarily exists" is entailed by the proposition "God is a being greater than which cannot be conceived" (which is equivalent to "God is an absolutely unlimited being").
>
> . . . once one has grasped Anselm's proof of the necessary existence of a being greater than which cannot be conceived, no question remains as to whether it exists or not, just as Euclid's demonstration of the existence of an infinity of prime numbers leaves no question of that issue.'

But that is exactly what Anselm himself was getting at in the 4th chapter of his *Proslogion* (see page 22).

The key issue to consider here is this: Do logically necessary truths refer to realities out in the world, or are they simply about our use of words? In other words, does 'God exists necessarily' simply indicate that, when you are referring to 'God', you are not thinking about some limited thing that might or might not exist?

Note: Exists?

David Hume pointed out, in his *Dialogues Concerning Natural Religion*, that you cannot define something into existence. You have to get outside your concept of something to say whether or not it exists.

Bertrand Russell's way of expanding on the word 'exists' might help here. In an example (given by John Hick in *Philosophy of Religion*), 'cows exist' means 'There are x's such that "x is a cow" is true.' In other words, to say that something exists is not to add to its definition, simply to point out that there are things to which the definition applies.

COMMENT

Malcolm ends his article (in J Hick, *The Existence of God*) with a comment referring to Wittgenstein's later understanding of the use of language – that its meaning is shown in the way that it is used, and is understood in the context of the group of people who use it in that way (just as every game has rules that are known to those who play it). All words have meaning in a context, and the context in which the word 'God' is used is that of religion. Hence the meaning of the necessary existence of God is one that makes sense chiefly to someone who is 'inside' that particular language game, in other words, it makes sense mainly within the language of religion.

MAKING CONNECTIONS

Do arguments about God only make sense in the context of religious belief?

This can be related to the criticisms of religion made by Feuerbach and Freud – since they see God as a projection of human consciousness.

It can also be related to the debate about language, and whether meaning is always related to use.

If the existence of God only makes sense within a religious community, what does this say about any form of religious ethics? Can you use the authority of God in order to support moral claims, if God makes no sense outside your religious group? Does that lead to relativism, where each religious group has its own gods and sources of authority, with no way of arguing for an overall, absolute or universalist ethic?

A further development in the Ontological Argument was taken by Alvin Plantinga. He uses a philosophical technique known as '**modal logic**', which is based on the idea of **possible worlds**. First of all, it is important to realise that this is a matter of logic, not astronomy! This is not speculation about whether there actually exist worlds other than our own, in which there might or might not be a perfect being. It is simply a way of looking at various logical possibilities.

Plantinga starts by using an argument like that of Malcolm – namely that the idea of God's existence is either impossible or necessary, and (since it is not self-contradictory) it cannot be impossible, so it must be necessary.

But he then goes on to consider a being with 'maximal excellence' (having all the perfections that Descartes wanted to ascribe to him) existing of necessity in one world. He then says that for such a being, its qualities are necessary, and therefore could not vary at all from world to world. Hence if a being with 'maximal excellence' exists in one world, it must exist in all possible worlds, and can therefore be described as having 'maximal greatness'.

But clearly, a being with 'maximal greatness' having 'maximal excellence' in all possible worlds, must indeed be what we call 'God'. Therefore God has necessary existence.

Although Malcolm and Plantinga's arguments give an interesting extra angle on Anselm's argument in *Proslogion* chapter 3 about God's necessary existence, my view is that both have a major flaw for a theist, namely that they can be used to prove the non-existence of God!

If God's existence is not contingent, then it is *logical* to say that it is either impossible or necessary. But – as pointed out above – logical necessary existence does not prove *actual* necessary existence. Hence, Plantinga's modal logic cuts both ways; on his theory, if God can be shown not to exist in one world, then he cannot exist in any possible world. Like Malcolm's, the argument shows that God's existence may be impossible or necessary – but (since logic cannot determine existence) it could be taken to show that, since the actual existence of a being with 'maximal excellence' cannot be shown to exist in all possible worlds, his existence is impossible!

3 The Cosmological Argument

Key questions:
▼ Does the universe offer an explanation of itself, or is its existence something which raises questions for us?
▼ Can the universe itself ever offer a *complete* explanation of itself, or does it look beyond itself for its explanation?

Figure 1 Looking out into space gives a sense of just how small the Earth is, and how fragile its thin film of life. It has also led both philosophers and religious people to ask fundamental questions about why anything exists, and whether it is possible to find an overall principle and explanation for the universe.

In its simplest form, the question is this: Why is there anything at all? Science can offer us explanations of things that are *within* the universe, but does the universe *as a whole* have an explanation?

The Cosmological Arguments set out to show that it is reasonable to look to an uncaused case, unmoved mover, an eternally existing being to uphold and sustain the changing and limited things within the universe.

If you believe that there is some sort of reason, cause or first principle, then you count yourself a theist. If not, then the world is self-contained, and needs an external explanation, in which case belief in the traditional God of theism becomes pointless.

In looking at the argument, we need to keep in mind that the relevant question to ask may not be 'Does this prove that God exists?' but 'What sort of "God" does this argument present? Does this argument point to the sort of thing that religious people mean when they use the word "God"?'

Note

It is important to be clear about the meaning of the terms 'contingent' and 'necessary'. These can be applied to the truth of propositions and also to beings.

A contingent proposition is one that might be true or might be false, and this depends on evidence; i.e. its truth is *a posteriori*.

A contingent being might or might not exist, or it might exist now, but will cease to exist at some future point, or did not exist at some time in the past, but has now come into existence.

A necessary proposition is one that is known to be true as soon as its terms are understood. (The Ontological Argument was concerned with whether there could be a necessary being, as well as necessary propositions.)

Now, in examining the Cosmological Arguments, we will be concerned with *whether contingent facts can point beyond themselves*, and therefore be used in an argument about the existence of God.

Note

Remember that *a priori* arguments are based on reason alone, not on experience. They are **deductive** (in other words, they reach their conclusions from the meaning of words and from their own logic) and they are **analytic** (in other words, they are arguments in which conclusions follow on from logical premises, without depending on any external information or experience).

By contrast, the Cosmological Arguments are **experiential** – based on experience. They are **inductive**, since the argument is built up upon evidence, and they are **synthetic**, in other words, the meaning is given with reference to external facts.

An important consideration here is highlighted by Ockham's razor, a principle which is expressed as: 'Entities are not to be multiplied beyond necessity.' Or, in simpler terms, 'always choose the simplest explanation'.

We may ask 'Do we need "God" as an explanation, or is there a simpler one?' And even if we decide that God is needed as an explanation of the fact that the world exists, do we need to ascribe to God any qualities other than those that are required for the purpose of causing the world to exist in the first place?

a) Greek Background

The ideas that lie behind the Cosmological Arguments come from Plato and Aristotle, both of whom considered the possibility of an unmoved mover. In *Timaeus*, Plato says:

> Now everything that becomes or is created must of necessity be cre-
> ated by some cause, for nothing can be created without a cause ...
> Was the world, I say, always in existence and without beginning? or
> created and having a beginning? Created, I reply, being visible and tan-
> gible and having a body, and therefore sensible; and all sensible things
> ... are in a process of creation and created. Now that which is cre-
> ated must of necessity be created by a cause. But how can we find
> out the father and maker of all this universe? And when we have
> found him, to speak of his nature to all men is impossible.

[From a translation by Jowatt, quoted in Paul Helm's *Faith and Reason*]

This sets out the cosmological question and also points to the question raised above, about how it is possible to say anything about the
'god' who appears as an uncaused cause or unmoved mover. Is such
an idea compatible with the God of traditional theism? That was, of
course, not Plato's problem, but it is important in assessing the validity of the Cosmological Argument.

In his *Metaphysics*, Aristotle comes to the following conclusion
about an unmoved mover:

> It is clear then ... that there is a substance which is eternal and
> unmovable and separate from sensible things. It has been shown also
> that this substance cannot have any magnitude, but is without parts
> and indivisible (for it produces movement through infinite time, but
> nothing finite has infinite power; and, since every magnitude is either
> infinite or finite, it cannot, for the above reason, have finite magni-
> tude, and it cannot have infinite magnitude because there is no infi-
> nite magnitude at all). But it has also been shown that it is impassive
> and unalterable; for all the other changes are posterior to change of
> place.

(*Book xii*)

The issue here is: Can such an unmoved mover really serve as the
'God' of theism?

b) Aquinas' Cosmological Arguments

Thomas Aquinas, probably the most important philosopher of the
mediaeval period, sought to reconcile the Christian faith with the philosophy of Aristotle, which had recently been 'rediscovered' and was
being taught in the secular universities of Europe.

Aquinas presented **Five Ways** in which he believed the existence of
God could be demonstrated:

1 The argument from an unmoved mover.
2 The argument from an uncaused cause.

3 The argument from possibility and necessity.
4 The argument from degrees of quality.
5 The argument from design.

The first three of these are Cosmological Arguments.

i) The Unmoved Mover

The first argument may be set out in this way:

▼ Everything that moves is moved by something else.

▼ That mover must also be moved by something else.

▼ *But* you cannot have an infinite chain of movers, or there would be no reason for movement to get started at all.

▼ *Therefore* there must be an unmoved mover, producing movement in everything, without itself being moved.

▼ This unmoved mover is what people understand by 'God'.

Aquinas was probably not thinking of physical movement, but of change in general – of things which are only potential becoming actual. (His own example was of fire causing something potentially hot to become actually hot.) His argument points to the fact that everything in the world changes, and then asks what could possibly start all those changes happening in the first place.

ii) The Uncaused Cause

The second argument is similar:

▼ Everything has a cause.

▼ Every cause has its own cause.

▼ You cannot have an infinite number of causes.

▼ Therefore there must be an uncaused cause, which causes everything to happen without itself being caused by anything else.

▼ Such an uncaused cause is what people understand by 'God'.

But can there be an infinite regress of causes? After all, the series of causes could be circular, or looped in a figure of eight. In that way, you could have an infinite number of causes, but never come to an 'end' or need a first cause. Everything could then be explained in terms of the one thing that causes it, without having to have an explanation for how everything started.

However, it is probably more realistic to think of a hierarchy of causes – each more general than the last – moving outwards until you come to a single overall cause, explaining all the others. Copleston, a twentieth century interpreter of Aquinas, takes this hierarchical approach to the sequence of causes.

In other words, to give a complete explanation of anything, you have to take everything into consideration. But how can that 'everything' be explained? That is the cosmological question.

Figure 2 As we think about the causes of any event, our mind moves outwards through both time and space, like ripples on a pond. In the end, the cause of anything is related to the cause of everything. The Cosmological Argument suggests that this process needs to be grounded in an uncaused cause

iii) The Possible and the Necessary

Aquinas' third argument follows from the first two:

▼ Ordinary things start to exist and later stop existing (in other words, they are finite, or contingent).

▼ Therefore at some time none of them was in existence.

▼ But something only comes into existence by being caused by something else that already exists.

▼ Therefore there must be a being whose existence is necessary and therefore not limited by time. That being is what people understand by 'God'.

In other words, we live in a universe that comprises finite, limited things. How could that universe and any of the things in it come about without being brought into existence by something that is *not* part of that finite world?

Note

Aquinas did not imagine that any of these arguments could *define* 'God'. He merely used them to point towards the sort of reality that people meant when they spoke of 'God'.

It can be argued that God cannot be proved to exist by arguments such as this, because his existence is beyond all human understanding. However, the arguments at least serve to show the sort of thing people speak of when they speak of God – not one thing among others in the universe, but that which is an explanation for the universe itself.

c) Some Challenges to the Arguments

There are serious challenges to the Cosmological Arguments, particularly from David Hume, and in the twentieth century, from Bertrand Russell, who debated the issues with Frederick Copleston on a radio programme in 1947.

i) David Hume

David Hume (1711–1776) was an empiricist; that is, he believed that all knowledge came from experience. He therefore argued that we understand that one thing causes another because we see them follow one another, and we therefore call the first 'the cause' and the second 'the effect'.

That works well enough for individual things, but in the case of the world as a whole, we have a unique 'effect', and we cannot observe its cause. In other words, we cannot get 'outside' the universe to see what the cause might be.

For Reflection

Our universe is all that we know. We may speculate that there could be other universes, but if we actually found that they existed, then they would become part of our 'multiverse', and Hume's point would still be valid, since we could not compare our multiverse with another! And so on . . . and so on . . .

---

ii) Bertrand Russell

Cosmological Arguments lead from the existence of the world as it is, to the idea of a God who is its cause or prime mover. But is it inevitable that the world has an explanation at all?

In his debate with Copleston, Russell took the view that the world is just there, it is a brute fact and does not need an explanation. Just because individual things have explanations, it does not follow that the world itself has one. Or to put it simply: just because every human being has a mother, it does not follow that the universe has to have a mother!

A similar conclusion could be reached through reading Wittgenstein's *Tractatus*. He argued that 'the world is all that is the case'. In other words, the world is everything that we can know and speak about. Yet religion tries to get 'outside' the world, to find a cause that is beyond what we can know through our senses.

The conclusion that Wittgenstein reached was not that some things (like the self or God) did not exist, but simply that they were outside the range of things that we could speak about, because speech was related to the world as we observe it, and these things were beyond observation. He therefore ended *Tractatus* with the famous statement 'Whereof we cannot speak, thereof we must remain silent.'

DEBATE

Be ready to argue whether or not the kind of god who is believed to exist as a result of the Cosmological Argument is an adequate object of worship for Christians.

Note

Wittgenstein was interested in mysticism, and knew the work of William James on religious experience. When he says that some things cannot be spoken about, he does not imply that they are unimportant, simply that they are beyond factual description.

MAKING CONNECTIONS

Think about how ideas like the 'uncaused cause' relate to the object of religious experience as described by James, Schleiermacher and Otto, as will be discussed in chapter 2.

---

4 The Teleological Argument (from Design)

The Argument from Design (also called the Teleological Argument) suggests that the world displays elements of design, with things being adapted towards some overall end or purpose (*telos* in Greek). Such design suggests that the world is the work of a designer – God.

a) Aquinas and Paley

The Argument from Design is the fifth of Aquinas' Five Ways. He argues that all goal-orientated activities are the result of intelligent planning and design. To use his own example; if you see an arrow flying through the air, you conclude that it has been shot by an archer for some purpose, simply because arrows do not shoot themselves.

In the same way, he observes, inanimate things seem to work together in the world in order to bring about a result. But this cannot be the result of their own nature, because they have no mind to direct their action. Hence, he concludes that they are evidence of the work of an intelligent designer.

Hume, who is famous for his criticism of this argument, presented it very clearly in his *Dialogues Concerning Natural Religion*, where one of his characters, Cleanthes, says:

> Look round the world, contemplate the whole and every part of it: you will find it to be nothing but one great machine, subdivided into an infinite number of lesser machines …
>
> The curious adapting of means to ends, throughout all nature, resembles exactly, though it much exceeds, the productions of human contrivance – of human design, thought, wisdom, and intelligence. Since therefore the effects resemble each other, we are led to infer, by all the rules of analogy, that the causes also resemble, and that the Author of nature is somewhat similar to the mind of man, thought possessed of much larger faculties, proportioned to the grandeur of the world which he has executed.

In other words, this argument is based on the analogy between machines (where we know there is a human designer) and the world.

Figure 3 Is a watch – or any other mechanism – adequate as an analogy for the way in which things work together in the world? Does it make sense to think of God as a watchmaker?

The best-known example of this approach is the 'watch' analogy used by William Paley in his book *Natural Theology*, published in London in 1807. He argued that if you came across a watch lying on the ground, picked it up and examined it, you would come to the conclusion that it was the work of a human designer. In the same way, he argues, various things in the world work together in a way that is even more complex than the watch, and it is therefore reasonable to conclude that the world must also be the work of a designer – God.

Note

The key features of Paley's 'Watchmaker' argument had already been presented by Hume. The difference is that Hume set them as part of a dialogue – putting them in the mouth of Cleanthes – and then followed on by giving his criticisms of the argument. It is clear that Hume himself supports the criticisms, rather than the original argument.

Since Hume was already dead, he did not personally attack Paley's argument, although his criticisms are relevant to our assessment of it.

Notice the details in his argument. Here he is considering and dismissing possible objections:

> ... when we come to inspect the watch, we perceive (what we could not discover in the stone) that its several parts are framed and put together for a purpose, e.g. that they are so formed and adjusted as to produce motion, and that motion so regulated as to point out the hour of the day; that, if the several parts had been differently shaped from what they are, of a different size from what they are, or placed after any other manner, or in any other order, than that in which they are placed, either no motion at all would have been carried on in the machine, or none which would have answered to the use which is not served by it.

> ... This mechanism being observed ... the inference, we think is inevitable, that the watch must have had a maker: that there must have existed, at some time, and at some place or other, an artificer or artificers who formed it for the purpose which we find it actually to answer; who comprehended its construction, and designed its use.

He makes some other important additions, anticipating challenges to the argument. He notes that his argument would not be weakened by the fact that he might never have seen a watch being made, nor having known an artist capable of making one. Nor is it necessary to understand *how* it is made (he gives the example of the turning of oval frames, most people don't understand how it is done, but that does not weaken the assumption that they are manufactured by someone who *does* understand).

He then adds an important point:

> Neither, secondly, would it invalidate our conclusion, that the watch sometimes went wrong, or that it seldom went exactly right ... It is not necessary that a machine be perfect, in order to show with what design it was made ...

MAKING CONNECTIONS

This point relates directly to the 'problem of evil', because natural evil – such as earthquakes and disease – can sometimes be taken as a sign that the world is not designed by a loving creator. See chapter 3.

He also points out that it is not necessary to understand the function of all the parts in order to see that it is an intelligent design, and he says that nobody would think that the arrangement of the parts of the watch might have come about by chance.

Nor is it enough to say that the watch was made by some 'principle of order', for he cannot understand what such a principle can mean, other than the intelligence of the watchmaker. Nor that the watch was formed because of some kind of 'metallic nature' in the parts that led them to come together automatically.

Finally, he rejects the idea that the mechanism was not proof of the working of a designer, but only a feature of our minds which make us interpret it that way.

Note

The philosopher Kant argued that space, time and causality were things that the mind imposed on its experience. Might it just be that our sense of design is something that we project on to a universe which has actually come about by chance? That is the argument that Paley is trying to guard against in his final point here.

---

i) Regularity and Purpose

Paley pointed to two different kinds of design in the world: **design *qua* regularity** and **design *qua* purpose**. Paley provides clear examples of each. For regularity, he points to the ordered movement of the planets. (The regularity of the world had been used by others – including Newton and Bacon – as a sign of God's operation.) To illustrate purpose, he points to the way in which an eye functions in order to achieve sight. He could not believe that such a delicate thing as an eye could have come about by chance, for it showed careful design in order to achieve its purpose.

b) Hume, Mill and Darwinist Challenges

i) Hume's Criticisms

Hume points out that, in order to argue convincingly that *this* world has a designer, it would be necessary to show that *other* worlds have designers – but since this is the only world we know, we have no reason to assume that worlds do, in general, have designers.

But even if it is conceded that there might be a designer, Hume has another criticism ready. A cause need only be proportional to its effect. So it is not valid to argue from this limited world and its supposed design to some infinite or perfect designer – the evidence just does not allow us to go that far.

He also points out that, since this is the only world we know, we really cannot tell whether or not it is particularly good. It may be the last of a whole string of worlds that were badly constructed, and may therefore be the result of having tried and failed many times.

In other words, we have no way of knowing how good the design of the world is, or of the relative ability of its designer, if it has one.

Hume raised three other objections to the design argument:

1   The world is more like an animal or vegetable than a piece of machinery – so we should not argue by analogy with human designers and their machines.
2   Our knowledge of the world is too limited to make judgements about it as a whole.
3   An animal could not live unless its various organs worked together as they do. In other words, if it did not appear to be well designed it would not be here for us to look at it!

Note

This last point is very important, because Hume anticipates the issues raised by Darwin and natural selection. An animal may appear well designed to survive in its habitat – but that is simply because it would have died out if it wasn't!

---

ii) Mill's Objections

J S Mill, writing in 1874 and therefore after Darwin's theory of natural selection had become known and widely discussed, presented a very serious criticism of the design argument. He observed that nature was fundamentally cruel, and that progress was made only at the cost of immense suffering. He pointed out that animals do naturally and freely what humans would certainly be punished for doing! The force of his argument is clear – if murder, rape and theft are quite 'natural' in the animal kingdom, then is it really possible to argue that nature is the result of an intelligent designer? As we shall see in the next section, the whole issue of natural selection is based on the fact that most organisms die out because nature does not regard them as favoured. Can we really believe that such a world is the product of an intelligent and loving designer?

MAKING CONNECTIONS

Mill's criticism of the Design Argument, and the suffering and death that enable new forms of life to appear through natural selection, may be related to the more general 'problem of evil'. How can an omnipotent God allow suffering – or in this context, how can an omnipotent creator have produced a world in which there is suffering and pain as well as beauty and elegant design?

The other obvious connection is between the Design Argument and religious language, and particularly with analogy. God as watchmaker, or as craftsman, is an analogy drawn from human experience of creativity. What are the limits of such language? Is it misused if taken literally? If so, is it wrong to think that God is a creator in any literal sense of that word?

iii) Darwin and The Origin of Species

Charles Darwin's theory of natural selection, as set out in his book *The Origin of Species* in 1859, is included here as a criticism of the Design Argument because it provided an alternative explanation for the appearance of design in living things, and one that did *not* need the help of an external designer.

Darwin argued that those members of a species whose characteristics were best suited to enable them to survive in their environment went on to breed. Those ill suited generally died off before doing so. This process of selection meant that whenever an advantageous characteristic appeared, those organisms who displayed the characteristic were able to pass it on to a proportionately larger number of offspring. In that way, Darwin demonstrated that a species could gradually evolve without the need for an external agency or designer.

Note

Darwin was primarily a scientist. He put forward the theory of natural selection only after extensive analysis of the differences between members of species, related to their environment, in order to explain the mechanism by which changes came about. He was also religious – even if rather unconventionally so – and his theory of evolution was not devised simply in order to discredit either the Design Argument or belief in God. It was the result of many years of careful scientific analysis.

There was no direct contact or debate between Paley and Darwin – they simply reflect two very different interpretations of the phenomenon of design in living things.

Since Paley was already dead, he did not criticise Darwin's theory, although his ideas may be contrasted with Darwin's.

The Teleological Argument had presented God as the designer and creator of the world. Each creature, it was argued, displayed a sense of design, and even parts of the body (e.g. the eye) were so perfectly organised to do their particular job, that there seemed no way to account for it other than as the product of the special action of God.

The theological problem posed by Darwin was that the theory of natural selection, if correct, could account for exactly the appearance of design that had previously been ascribed to the agency of God.

However, the fact that there is a natural explanation for the appearance of design does not necessarily invalidate the argument. It is possible to see natural selection as the means used by God for bringing about design – in other words, it becomes the instrument, rather than the agent of design.

DEBATE
Be ready to argue whether or not Darwin's theory of natural selection invalidates the Teleological Argument, or simply shows the mechanism used by God for putting his design into effect.

iv) The Impact of Genetics

Darwin's theory showed how species could develop, based on the fact that there were small differences between members of a species, some of which could be advantageous. What Darwin did not know was *why* there were these differences. We now know that the answer lies in the random mutations thrown up by the process of copying the sequence of genes. However, this does not radically alter the force of Darwin's perceived challenge to the Design Argument. What it does is to support his overall analysis of the process of evolutionary change.

Far more significant, from the point of view of arguments about whether species were all created separately or had a common evolutionary past, is the awareness of just how similar different species are genetically. A comparison of the genome of similar species can be used to show how long ago they diverged from a common ancestor. This has provided independent support for the original theory of natural selection by mapping out the process by which species branched off from one another over a period of time and also by showing the fundamentally interconnected nature of all living things.

v) The Anthropic Principle

The world is as it is because of a small number of physical constants, which have determined how it has developed. If any of them were different, even by a very small degree, the universe would not have developed as it has, and we would not be here contemplating it. This has led some thinkers to argue that a world so 'fine tuned' cannot be a matter of chance.

There are two forms of the Anthropic Principle:

1 A 'weak' form argues simply that, if the world were different, we would not be here. There are few objections that can be raised to this form. It does not say that the world *had* to be as it is, merely that it is as it is!

2 A 'strong' form argues that the world *had* to be as it is, in order for us

to be here. In other words, that there was some kind of built-in factor which made the development of human life inevitable. This is more controversial, but closer to the traditional Design Argument – since it makes the product of humanity a design feature of the universe.

This issue, which was originally presented by F R Tennant, has been discussed by both scientists and philosophers. It has been used to back up the general approach of the Cosmological and Design Arguments for the existence of God, by showing how appropriate the world is to be seen as the product of intelligent design. On the other hand, the 'weak' form can be seen as true but of no profound significance, whereas the 'strong' form, by appearing to make the design of the whole universe dependent upon the development of human life, can be seen as an improbable hypothesis.

c) Swinburne's Approach

Richard Swinburne uses the fact that the world is such that humans can develop within it as an illustration of what he sees as the nature of God:

> Like a good parent, a generous God has reason for not foisting on us a certain fixed measure of knowledge and control, but rather of giving us a choice of whether to grow in knowledge and control.
>
> It is because it provides these opportunities for humans that God has a reason to create a world governed by natural laws of the kind we find. Of course God has reason to make many other things, and I would hesitate to say that one could be certain that he would make such a world. But clearly it is the sort of thing that there is some significant probability that he will make.

[From *Is there a God?* OUP, 1996. Reprinted by permission of Oxford University Press]

He goes on to say that the orderliness of the world, as a theatre for humans, is not the only reason why God would have wished to create it that way. He points to the fact that an orderly world is a beautiful world.

In other words, Swinburne's approach is to assume that God is a loving and caring parent, and then point out how appropriate the present designed world is for achieving his purpose.

He summarises his argument thus:

> The argument to God from the world and its regularity is, I believe, a codification by philosophers of a natural and rational reaction to an orderly world deeply embedded in the human consciousness. Humans see the comprehensibility of the world as evidence of a comprehending creator.

[From *Is there a God?* OUP, 1996. Reprinted by permission of Oxford University Press]

In effect, by arguing that it would be appropriate for God to create a world like this, Swinburne is enhancing the *probability* that God exists. This builds on his earlier work, where he argues that the design of the world does not suggest that it is the product of mere chance, but that it must be a matter of weighing the probabilities involved.

Note: On Beauty

Swinburne sees the orderliness of the world as beautiful, and the appreciation of beauty is clearly an important aspect of human nature. But where does such appreciation come from?

This question was posed some years earlier by Tennant, who argued to the effect that human aesthetic experience – of art, music and so on – cannot be explained on the basis of natural selection, since it does nothing to promote survival. Therefore he suggested that it makes no sense to have a world which includes such things, unless it is the result of an intelligent, designing creator.

---

5 The Moral Argument

Kant believed that the traditional arguments for the existence of God did not work, because they could not prove the existence of anything that was *beyond* the phenomena that we experience. The idea of causality, which was central to the Cosmological Arguments, was – in Kant's view – something that our minds impose on experience, not something that we discover 'out there'. So, even if the mind was inspired by the idea of the wonder of nature, there was no way to argue from that to an 'uncaused cause' or designer beyond the world of our experience.

Rather than follow the traditional arguments, Kant starts from our sense of moral obligation:

> Two things fill the mind with ever new and increasing admiration and awe the oftener and more steadily we reflect on them: the starry heavens above me and the moral law within me.

[From *The Critique of Practical Reason*]

If God cannot be proved directly by looking at the 'starry heavens', Kant wants to see whether his existence is implied by our experience of morality.

a) Kant's Argument

Kant makes an important distinction between a '**categorical imperative**' and a '**hypothetical imperative**'. A categorical imperative is an unqualified moral demand, in other words 'you ought to do X', or 'it is right to do X'; it does not depend on the results of doing it. By contrast, a hypothetical imperative takes the form of 'if you want to achieve Y, then you should do X'.

In *The Critique of Practical Reason* Kant examined the presuppositions of a categorical imperative. In other words, he was asking 'If I sense a moral demand of this sort, what does that tell me about my beliefs?'

He argued that it showed three things (which he called the **postulates** of the practical reason):
▼ Freedom
▼ Immortality
▼ God.

The first of these is necessary because if you do not believe that you are *free* to do something, it makes no sense to say that you *ought* to do it.

The second is necessary because we naturally aspire to the highest good (*summum bonum*), in which virtue is rewarded with happiness. But that does not always happen in this life. So, if you respond to an unconditional moral demand, it implies that you sense that the highest good is achievable, even if that is beyond this life. An example of this might be a person who sacrifices his or her own life in order to save another person. If they feel they ought to do it, even if they lose their life in the process, it suggests that (in some form) they believe in immortality – not because they are looking for a reward after death (that would make the sense of morality depend on an expected good outcome), but simply through a sense that their own highest good lies beyond this limited earthly life.

The third follows from this. We do not find that virtue and happiness always come together in this world. Therefore, if you feel that you ought to do something, even if there is no guarantee that happiness will result, it suggests that you believe that there is a God who has ordered the world in a way that allows the highest good to be possible, and that your true happiness will lie in being virtuous and following your sense of 'ought'.

In other words, Kant is saying that you cannot prove the existence of God, but if you act morally, without concern for your own immediate benefit or happiness, it shows that you believe in a God who is able to make sense of such morality.

Note

These are 'postulates' or 'presuppositions', they are *not* necessary conditions. A postulate is something implied by what you do; you do not have to assent to it consciously first. In other words, we do not start to experience moral choice only *after* coming to the conclusion that we are free, immortal and that there is a God who will eventually enable virtue to result in happiness. Rather, these things are *implied* by the very act of feeling and responding to a moral demand. Responding to a moral demand does not make sense – according to this argument – unless in some way you believe in them.

Thus, you cannot wait until you are certain that you are genuinely free to act before you do anything (or you'd never move) – rather, by taking the decision to act, and taking it in line with what you see as your duty, you presuppose that you are free.

Some candidates answering questions on this treat Kant's 'highest good' as something 'out there', an ideal which we need to believe in before we can act morally. And the impression is sometimes given that if virtue and happiness do not actually come together, then the 'highest good' is impossible and his moral theory fails. But it's not like that. Rather, the highest good is what you decide by your own reasoning – you don't find it 'out there', you construct it and make it a reality by responding morally.

Kant also argues that, if you do in fact seek the highest good, it implies that you believe it is possible to achieve – that there is some ultimate purpose or end that can be achieved.

Note

In this argument, God is a **regulative** concept (part of our way of understanding the world) not a **constitutive** concept (one of the things out there in the world that we may be able to discover). This implies that God is a feature of the mind, and of faith. He is not something to be discovered in the external world of space and time.

MAKING CONNECTIONS

It is important to note how this argument for the existence of God related to Kant's moral theory. His moral theory (and the three forms of the 'categorical imperative', which are his criteria for saying that

---

ISSUE:

If you believe that there is an objective moral order – in other words, that there are absolute moral principles – it may be that the world is created by a moral being (God) or that morality is simply part of the way the world is, and therefore that it does not need a God to explain it.

This is rather like the problem with the Cosmological Argument. If the world has its own way of designing things (e.g. through natural selection), then no external designer is needed. Similarly, if moral sense can be shown to be a natural function (e.g. as a way that nature has of controlling behaviour that is likely to cause harm), then no God is required to explain it.

something is right or wrong) can stand on its own as a moral theory, quite apart from its use as a proof for the existence of God.

The connection, however, is that to follow Kant's moral theory, you believe that human reason is capable of understanding and regulating morality, and that implies that the world is a reasonable place – and thus links back to the proof for God's existence.

b) Other Approaches

Kant used the **postulates**, or presuppositions, of the experience of moral obligation as the basis for his argument. This implies that we have some deep beliefs that are shown to be the case when we face a situation of moral choice.

But we could equally well look at the situation of moral choice without thinking about postulates at all. If we have a sense of an unconditional 'ought', that implies that certain things have value, are ultimately worthwhile. If that were not the case, it would make no sense to feel any moral obligation. But where does that sense of value come from? A theist will believe that value comes from God, and will therefore see the sense of moral obligation as a kind of religious experience. If others share that sense of moral obligation, then it can become for them an indication that God exists. This approach is taken by Dom Trethowan.

Similarly, it is possible to argue that any sense of moral obligation amounts to responding to a command. But that command must come from somewhere. Hence we assume that there is a commander – God. That approach was taken by H P Owen.

Both approaches assume that we can argue from the fact that we have a moral experience to the existence of an external source of that experience: God. We need to be clear that Kant was not arguing in that way; for Kant, God is a *postulate*, not the conclusion of an argument.

Note: Autonomous Morality?

When we look at Kant's moral theory in chapter 8, we shall see that, with the forms of the 'categorical imperative', he presents a rational basis for morality – a set of basic principles upon which a moral system can be established. But it is possible to argue that, by doing so, Kant effectively neutralised his own argument for the existence of God, for if morality can be established by reason alone, then God is not needed.

c) A Psychological Alternative

Freud was generally critical of religion, which he saw as an infantile wish to have a father figure to protect you from the dangers of life, or as a way of getting rid of deeply unconscious feelings of guilt. (See page 66 for an outline of this.) Freud would therefore argue that your feelings of morality do not come from God but are there as a result of promptings from your unconscious mind. Moral obligation in an adult is the result of early training and experiences in childhood. In particular Freud was concerned with the issue of conscience and guilt.

It is difficult to prove that morality comes only from the unconscious, because the believer could reply by saying that it comes from God, but that God uses the unconscious as the vehicle for giving humanity morality. But it is equally difficult to argue that morality implies belief in God (which, effectively, is what Kant was doing) if there is a perfectly valid alternative explanation for it.

In a sense, Freud did for the Moral Argument what Darwin did for the Design Argument – he simply provided an alternative explanation for the phenomenon upon which it was based.

Note: Experiential Arguments

Arguments for the existence of God that are based on religious experience will be considered in the next chapter, since it does not make sense to consider them until examining the main features of religious experience.

However, you may want to refer back to the arguments in this chapter after having looked at religious experience, since it is possible that you will find that the argument from experience, even if not convincing in itself, may give added probability to the existing arguments.

Ask yourself: Does religious experience confirm the sense of purpose or design in the universe, or the sense of moral obligation? If it does, then it adds weight to that argument.

▼ ESSAY QUESTIONS

1 a) Explain Anselm's versions of the Ontological Argument.
   b) Does the criticism made by Gaunilo render them invalid?
2 a) Describe Kant's Moral Argument.
   b) Assess its strengths and weaknesses.

See the 'Further Reading and Websites' section at the back of this book for follow-up work on this chapter.

2

REVELATION AND RELIGIOUS EXPERIENCE

POINTS TO CONSIDER

Is religious experience a natural phenomenon, or does it depend on the existence of God?

How might religious experience influence ideas about the meaning of the word 'God'?

TIMELINE

1724–1804	Kant
1768–1834	Schleiermacher
1818–1883	Marx
1842–1910	James
1856–1939	Freud
1858–1917	Durkheim
1869–1937	Otto
1878–1965	Buber
1919–	Hare
1922–	Hick
1934–	Swinburne

There would be no religion if there were no religious experiences. Great religious leaders and founders of religions (e.g. Muhammad, Moses, Jesus, Buddha, Nanak, Isaiah) have all recorded powerful experiences which have shaped their lives, and which led them to teach and preach as they did.

Also, it is estimated that at least one in four people have an experience at some point in their lives which could be called 'religious', in the sense that we shall describe later in this chapter, even if they do not think of themselves as religious or are not practising members of a religion.

The special experiences that people might have – experiences that may change their lives dramatically – have some common features, and these have been examined by William James and others. But there are also experiences that are more usual and mundane but which may also count as religious – not that the experience is very different from that of many other people, it's just that some choose to see the religious significance of it.

Also, if people did not find that the experience of taking part in religious ceremonies, or practising meditation, or praying, gave them some new element in their lives, they would not continue to do so. So, the fact that religions exist at all means that they provide experiences that their followers find valuable. They take part in worship and feel 'uplifted' by it. They may feel inspired by readings from scripture, or ritual, or even the building in which the worship takes place.

People may also find that religion gives new depth to ordinary experiences – they may see something that is overwhelmingly beautiful, or they may be faced with the powerful moments of birth or death, they fall in love or fall ill. How they experience these moments may be influenced by their religious beliefs, but equally the experience may then reinforce those same beliefs.

We need to consider the main features of religious experience, including mystical and near-death experience, and then turn to see how these claim to give knowledge of God. Finally, we shall look at whether or not religious experience can provide the basis for an argument for the existence of God.

Note

In general, religious experience involves:
▼ a sense of wonder
▼ a sense of new insight and values
▼ a sense of holiness and profundity.
A religious experience involves the whole of a person – mind and emotions, values and relationships – and seems to touch the most basic and fundamental sense of being oneself.

Note

Kant took the view that human beings have only five senses, and that all that they know comes through one or more of them. Since God is not part of the phenomenal world of objects that can be apprehended through the senses, we cannot have any direct knowledge of him. He would therefore rule out religious experience as a way of demonstrating the existence of God, since whatever is experienced is part of this phenomenal world, and therefore is not God.

There are two general approaches to interpreting religious experience – the '**experiential**' and the '**propositional**':
▼ The experiential approach is concerned with the experience itself, and religious claims that arise from it are seen as filtered through the particular circumstances of the experience and the understanding of the person who has had it. It allows the experience to speak for itself, without trying to define exactly what is experienced.
▼ By contrast, the propositional approach is one that extracts from the experience certain definitive propositions, which are then claimed to be religious truths, backed by the authority and power of the original experience.

In general, the philosophy of religion tends to encourage an experiential approach, since the propositional approach does not allow the understanding of such an experience, or the tradition that springs from it, to be revised and enhanced by the experiences of others. In other words, propositional interpretations of experience tend to be a matter of 'take-it-or-leave-it', with little scope for interpretation.

This experiential approach gets round another problem. When Hume discussed miracles, he argued that the miracles of one religion could cancel out those of another – presumably on the basis that only one religion can be right, and that if two religions conflict and yet both claim truth, then there is no way to decide between them and judgement must be suspended. Now Hume (although not using the term, which is part of a much later debate) was effectively using an **exclusivist** approach to religious truth. An **inclusivist** would say that miracles in all religions can be considered on their own merits and evidence, and that they can all contribute to an overall view of the action of God, even though they come from different traditions.

John Hick (see particularly his *An Interpretation of Religion*, Macmillan, 1989) makes an important distinction between inclusivist and exclusivist traditions. An exclusivist religion thinks that it alone can offer truths that can help a person to get in touch with the supreme reality. An inclusivist approach – which is the one that Hick wants to take – sees all religions as attempts to point to a single spiritual reality, but that none of them can claim to have the whole truth, or to exclude the truths of others.

When we come to examine religious experience, therefore, we must think carefully about whether it leads to an exclusivist or inclusivist interpretation. If a person claims that the particular experience, perhaps Muhammad hearing and reciting the words of the Qur'an, offers a unique and infallible truth – so that the words of the Qur'an are believed to be the very words of Allah – then they will have a corresponding authority. On the other hand, an inclusivist might be happy to accept that the Qur'an contains valid religious truth, and that it is inspired, but not that it can claim truth in any absolute way.

Note

Experience comes first, religious beliefs in the form of creeds and dogmas come afterwards. In the end, what religion is about rests on the experiences that people have. The problem is that the Philosophy of Religion deals with words and concepts, not directly with experiences.

---

1 The Nature of Religious Experience

There are many different experiences that can be categorised as 'religious', but here we shall simply look at some of the main features of the experiences of individuals. In other words, we shall be looking at:

> the feelings, acts, and experiences of individual men in their solitude, so far as they apprehend themselves to stand in relation to whatever they may consider the divine.

(which is the way William James introduces the subject of his famous book *The Varieties of Religious Experience*). In other words, quite apart from the authority of scriptures, or creeds, or public acts of worship, we shall look in this section at those very private kinds of experience that people find life-changing, and which they describe in religious terms.

a) Features of Religious Experience

In his book *On Religion: speeches to its cultured despisers* (1799), Schleiermacher described religious experience in this way:

> The contemplation of the pious is the immediate consciousness of the universal existence of all finite things, in and through the Infinite, and of all temporal things in and through the Eternal.

In other words, religious experience – whether it is a particular moment, or a general way of looking at things – is a way of putting particular, limited things into a new and eternal perspective. They are related not simply to one another, but to the whole.

In *The Idea of the Holy* (1917), Rudolph Otto introduced the idea that religious experience may be an encounter with something powerful, uncanny, weird, awesome, but also attractive and fascinating. Something like the 'creeping flesh' sensation or the shudder of fear at the prospect of encountering a ghost, whether real or on the page or screen.

Otto described the object of religious experience as *mysterium tremendum et fascinans* – a mystery that is both awesomeness and fascinating. He spoke of this as an encounter with 'the numinous'.

Figure 4 Walking in the high Alpine pastures, with the Eiger in the background, evokes a sense of wonder, and of the insignificance of a single human life within such a magnificent setting. That new perspective on life is what Schleiermacher described as a key feature of religious experience. The sudden fear when faced with a mountain precipice might also evoke Otto's sense of the 'numinous'.

He also pointed out that it could not be described in ordinary language, since none of our words quite capture that special sense of something being 'holy'. However, the set of words that we use (e.g. good, loving, powerful) in our attempt to describe the holy are its '**schema**', and the process of grasping at words to express the holy is '**schematisation**'. Religious language is just such a schema.

In *I and Thou* (1937) Martin Buber argued that we have two different kinds of relationships: **I-It** and **I-Thou**. I-It relationships are impersonal; I-Thou relationships are personal.

For Buber the relationship with God was an I-Thou relationship. In other words, it was more like getting to know another person than getting to know scientific facts. He described God as 'the Eternal Thou', to be seen as present in every other 'Thou' that we encounter.

b) Mysticism

A mystical experience is one in which a person may sense the underlying unity of everything, going beyond all conventional barriers between the individual self and the external world. It can produce a very deep sense of joy, of 'being at home', of being at one with nature and of seeing a truth that cannot be put into words.

In *The Varieties of Religious Experience*, William James lists four qualities associated with religious experience, and particularly with mystical experiences:

1 Ineffability (they are quite different from ordinary experiences, and cannot be described using ordinary language)
2 Neotic quality (they do provide information of a kind – a knowledge that cannot be expressed fully, and may be called 'revelation')
3 Transiency (they don't last long)
4 Passivity (the person who has the experience feels that they are passive – they simply receive something that is offered – rather than actively bringing the experience about)

The person who has a mystical experience may feel suddenly caught up in a sense of the unity of all things, and with a sense that they 'belong' or are carried along by a stream of life. There is a sense of knowing something supremely important, but yet without being able to put it into words that even start to do justice to the experience.

Note

In a mystical experience, the distinction between the subjective self and the objective world is overcome: the person has an experience of something or some level of reality that is 'out there' in the external world, perhaps as permeating everything, but at the same time finds that he or she is absolutely at one with that external thing.

That makes it impossible to describe in any literal way, and it also makes it difficult to use as evidence in a discussion on the existence of God.

c) Near-death Experiences

Many people who have been very close to death (even to the point of being pronounced clinically dead) and have subsequently recovered, describe what are termed 'near-death experiences'. These are neither rare, nor limited to people who are religious.

Such an experience may include an awareness of floating above their nearly-dead body, looking down at the scene. The person may feel quite detached from whatever traumas are happening to the body – happy and comfortable. There are descriptions of people sensing that they are moving down through a dark tunnel towards some comforting light at the end. Sometimes, towards the end of such experiences, the person may sense that they have a choice, either to move forward into that welcoming place, or to go back and enter the body again.

How can such experiences be explained? One theory put forward is that they are brought about in a brain that is starved of oxygen, and that a 'near-death experience' is actually the experience of the brain shutting itself down.

What effect do they have? As a result of this experience, the person may find that they see life differently, have a new sense of values, are no longer worried about trivia, and – most commonly – that they no longer fear death. In that sense, whether they are conventionally religious or not, the experience acts like a religious conversion, since their lives can be changed by it. For that particular person, the experience has an authority that cannot be challenged. They may accept that it was to do with their brain being starved of oxygen, but that would not, in itself, invalidate the experience for them, because what they have experienced may be something that informs their whole life and outlook.

On the other hand, it is difficult to know how you could argue from such an experience to prove the existence of God or the immortality of the soul. The experience is just that – an experience. It does not come with a package of beliefs attached.

ISSUE:
You need to consider for yourself whether such 'near-death experiences' show that there is a God, and that people survive death, or whether they are simply a phenomenon associated with extreme situations, where the brain is about to cease operating. If the latter, does that imply that God is not involved?

d) Conversion

There are different forms of conversion. First of all, there is the dramatic conversion of someone who has an experience which totally changes his or her whole way of life. The classic example of this is St Paul on the road to Damascus. He changed from being a persecutor of Christians to being a Christian himself.

Then there is the more long-term conversion, when a person or a society gradually comes to accept the beliefs of a different religion. This does not depend upon any one special event or experience, but rather the cumulative effect of interpreting events and beliefs differently over a period of time.

In addition to this, there is a form of conversion where a person does not actually change their beliefs or loyalties, but becomes far more deeply involved in them. In other words, the conversion is in terms of the priority and value that the religion has for the person concerned.

William James, in *The Varieties of Religious Experience*, sees a conversion experience leading to:

▼ loss of worry
▼ truths that were not known before
▼ the sense that the world has objectively changed.

In other words, a person who has the experience of conversion may find that there is a change in their experience of the external world as well as a change in their own self-awareness. They see things differently as well as becoming more integrated and happy as a result.

Note

R M Hare used the term **blik** to describe a set of ideas by which experience is understood and judged. A paranoid may have a blik that everyone is out to harm him; a generous and sociable person sees people as potential friends with whom to share life. A conversion can be seen as a change of 'blik'; the facts of life remain the same, but the understanding and appreciation of them changes.

In assessing the validity of a conversion experience, it is appropriate to examine how the person subsequently behaves. Do they treat people differently or appear to think of themselves differently as a result of the experience? The validity of a conversion may be challenged if it appears to have made no difference.

e) Group Experiences

When people gather together for worship, they have a group experience. They listen together, pray together, sing together; and such group activities produce a sense of belonging to a community, and of being valued as a member of it. This is, in itself, an important part of religious experience.

The experiences that people have in connection with worship may often be induced. In other words, they are deliberately stimulated in order to create an overall effect. Those planning worship put together readings, pieces of music, the use of candles or special robes, perhaps, in order to express and make real a feature of the religion. Of course, a person may have an experience which is not the one that the person planning the worship intended – but nevertheless, the aim of worship is to create an environment in which certain ideas and emotions are expressed and celebrated.

Although such experiences are induced, that does not make them magic. You cannot guarantee that two people attending the same religious event are going to respond in the same way. A group experience can only be a valid religious experience for those taking part if the external actions (e.g. singing, dancing, listening to readings) actually touch upon the individual person's feelings, experiences and ideas.

> **KEY QUESTION**
> If it can be shown that 'religious' experiences can be generated by using particular music or dance or drugs, does that invalidate them?

2 Can Religious Experiences be Deemed Revelation?

Revelation is the term used for knowledge that is given through supernatural agency. In other words, it is used to describe situations in which religious people believe that God made something known directly. Revelation can come through events, people or through scriptures.

Religious experiences tend to be authoritative for those who have them, going beyond what can be known rationally. Revelation may therefore be claimed as something superior to the knowledge given by reason; it is experienced directly, not filtered through the limitations of normal human awareness.

Revelation is generally thought of as a gift from God – in other words that it is a moment when God chooses to reveal himself. However, when it comes to evaluating revelation, it will depend on one's idea of God, because without some idea of God it would be impossible to say whether any particular knowledge was a revelation or not.

Another Way of Looking at it . . .

The term revelation can also be used for the process of opening up something that is opaque, in order to reveal what lies beneath.

One can describe something as a 'real revelation' – meaning that it exposes a truth that was previously hidden. That second sense of the word 'revelation' does not have the same personal connotations or authority as the 'revelation' we are considering in this section. But it may still be relevant, since you might want to argue that opening up previously hidden levels of reality is exactly what religion is about.

Revelation raises problems for philosophy:

1 Knowledge can only be articulated using words that have a commonly agreed meaning – without that, it would not make sense. Once written down, a revelation is inevitably reduced to a set of propositions that can be assessed rationally. It is this last process with which philosophy is traditionally concerned, but it is not the same thing as exploring the moment of revelation itself. It always deals with an **interpretation** of that experience.

2 The power of the revelatory experience is such that the person concerned is unlikely to be dissuaded of his or her new-found knowledge by rational argument. For the person who has received it, the 'revelation' may be used to evaluate everything else. So if someone else tries to argue that the revelation is meaningless or wrong, the person who has received the revelation is likely to counter the attack by saying that such arguments only reveal the limitations of human reason. They may not be able to defend what they have experienced rationally, but for them it is authoritative.

3 Just because something is known through revelation, does not mean that it cannot also be known through the normal process of experience and reason. It is probably unwise, therefore, to dismiss the claim that something has been revealed, simply on the grounds that it was possible to know it anyway.

a) Revelation in Scripture

Members of the Jewish, Christian and Muslim religions may also regard their scriptures as a direct revelation of God. To some extent this is merely an extension of the original religious experiences that are recounted in the scriptures, and which led to the setting up of the religions in the first place.

However, once the scriptures are written down and accepted as authoritative, they take on a role of being revelatory in themselves. In other words, their every word may be regarded as coming directly from God.

The dilemma here is that everything that is written down uses words, and those words have to have a commonly accepted meaning.

Every scripture therefore reflects the words, meanings and ideas of the time in which it was written. It may be the result of what is believed to be a direct revelation of God, but once that revelation is written down, it is fixed and thereafter open to interpretation.

In assessing the revelatory nature of any scripture, it is therefore necessary to make a distinction between the form of words and range of ideas used to express the religious insight, and the basic nature of that insight itself.

One person may claim that the authority of scripture is such that the particular words and ideas used are absolutely the one and only final revelation of God. In that case, the person is likely to take a very literal interpretation of scriptures.

No less valid is the position which argues that all revelation has to be mediated through human words and ideas. Hence the scriptures can be taken in a non-literal, symbolic way, where that is appropriate, and need not be taken literally in order to preserve their authority.

MAKING CONNECTIONS

When looking at the nature of God (page 17f) we noted the balance between the **transcendent** and the **immanent** elements; God was both beyond and yet within the world. This reflects the nature of revelation. The transcendent aspect of God leads to an appreciation that something is revealed that is beyond normal human experience and understanding. The immanent aspect leads to an appreciation that all encounters with God have to be via some particular experience – and that leads to the use of words and ideas that come from the particular situation and person.

A balanced view is going to appreciate that the scriptures point beyond themselves to a transcendent reality – that is what gives them their authority. However, they are also written in a particular time and place, and the words they use are always going to introduce an element of interpretation and particularity.

One way of approaching revelation through scripture is to ask the following question:

What must this person have experienced to have written what he or she did, using the best available language and ideas of the day?

And this can be followed by a second question:

Using the best language and ideas available to me today, how might I express that same religious insight?

In that way, the authority of scripture (and the revelation on which it is based) is preserved, whilst avoiding the temptation to take scripture literally, with the risk that the revelation may thereby be restricted by the ideas and language of the past.

DEBATE
Be ready to argue whether or not religious experience can give proof for the existence of God, and – if so – what kind of God it might be able to prove.

ISSUES:
If someone claims to have experienced God, that claim is irrefutable. All you can say in response is that they are calling what they have experienced 'God'. What they have experienced may not be what others would choose to call 'God' but that does not detract from the fact that it has become 'God' for the person who has experienced it.

The issue is not the authenticity of the experience for the person who has had it, but whether it is valid to use that experience in a logical argument about the existence of God.

3 The Argument from Religious Experience

So far in this chapter we have been looking at different kinds of religious experience, and the authority that they have for religious believers. But the key question now is this: can any such experience be used as an argument for the existence of God?

We need to start by looking at some features of religious experience which may cause problems when it is used in a rational argument of this sort.

First of all, every experience involves the *interpretation* of sensations. There is the thing experienced, and the interpretation and understanding of what is experienced. The former is objective, the latter subjective. Things are experienced 'as' something. In other words, our minds take the information supplied by the senses, and attempt to make sense of it.

Religious experience must therefore include both the objective and subjective elements. The crucial thing, however, is to appreciate that, if God is beyond the limited, physical world of objects that are known through the senses, he cannot be experienced directly. There cannot be any set of sense data that corresponds to 'God' and to nothing else.

Hence, the problem with trying to put together an Argument from Religious Experience is saying how – if at all – those experiences that are important for religion can also be used as *evidence* in a rational argument for the existence of God.

Note

In *An Introduction to the Philosophy of Religion*, Brian Davies argued that, if it is possible that the claim to have experienced God is *mistaken*, it is only logical to accept that the claim might also be *correct*. This implies that knowledge of God through experience is at least *possible*.

But notice the presupposition of such an argument. It requires a prior knowledge of what God is. If you do not know what God is, then there would be no grounds for saying that an experience of him was either correct or mistaken. The most you could say is that the person has experienced what he or she calls 'God'.

If God is infinite, he cannot be located in a particular place, nor does he have boundaries. You cannot point to where God is not, if he is infinite. Yet all our experience is of particular things in particular places; they are known only because they have boundaries. Our senses divide reality up into segments to which we can give names: this is one thing; that is another.

So arguments about whether or not an experience is of God require a prior knowledge of what God is. In other words, since *all* experience involves interpretation (we experience 'as'), our prior understanding of 'God' will be used to interpret whether this experience is an experience of God or not.

Therefore, in order for religious experience to be part of a logical argument about the existence of God, there needs to be an agreed definition of what is meant by the word 'God'. Otherwise, there will be no way of knowing how the person is interpreting their experience.

a) James and Swinburne

In *The Varieties of Religious Experience*, William James took a psychological approach to his subject. He made no attempt to argue from his accounts of religious experiences to any supernatural conclusions but was simply concerned to examine the effect of religion on people's lives.

In effect, James is pointing to religious experience as a phenomenon that can have a profound effect on people's lives. In one sense, it is the ultimate argument, for it is self-authenticating for the person who has it. On the other, James admitted that it did not offer any logical proof of the existence of God.

James was particularly concerned with mysticism, and it is difficult to know how one would either prove or refute anything that a mystic said about his or her experiences. If what is being described is a state of mind, then it cannot be contradicted, any more than the honest claim to feel happy or unhappy.

Claims can only be proved true or false with reference to empirical facts that can be checked. When it comes to mystical experience, all rational thought is transcended. It is not a matter of thinking, but of encountering and knowing.

In fact, James did not speak of 'God' but of 'the spiritual' or 'the unseen order' or the 'higher' aspects of the world and the self. He was definitely against any form of dogmatic theology. Hence it is only in the most general of terms that James can be said to offer any kind of argument for the existence of God – it would be better to say that he simply points to the phenomenon of the experiences people have of what they feel to be a 'higher' order of reality. What he does hold to be important, however, is that human beings should establish a harmonious relationship between their earthly and higher selves – which he sees as able to fill people with happiness, love, humility and peace, all of which he sees as being very 'healthy minded'.

Swinburne pointed out that religious experiences are authoritative for the individual who has them, even though other people, hearing an account of the experience, may remain sceptical. What is clear is that the experience takes a person beyond the rational arguments.

Swinburne, however, is not arguing for religious experience to be conclusive proof of God, all he is saying is that you need to balance out the probabilities when it comes to belief. Unless one has reason to doubt the testimony of a witness, one should – on balance – accept it, unless it starts to conflict with other things that are known. By the same token, one should accept the testimony of those who have religious experiences, unless one has some reason to question what they are saying.

b) Challenges from Freud and Marx

Freud argued that religion was a sign of sickness rather than health – that it resulted from an infantile need, and that a healthy-minded adult should not need it.

But this was not new, William James spoke of the 'healthy minded soul' (the person who is naturally happy and positive) and the 'sick soul' (the person who is depressed and negative). To the 'sick' person, the 'healthy' soul is blind and shallow, and does not face the more uncomfortable realities of life; to the 'healthy' person, the 'sick' person is sad and unable to enjoy a normal life. James argued, however, that religion needed to engage with the wide range of negative things in life, so that people could benefit from life when encountering sadness and suffering of various sorts.

In other words, even if religious belief may appeal to people that have problems with life, that does not deny the value of the religion. Rather, it shows why religion is needed. James describes the positive aspect of religious experience as a process of moving from 'tenseness, self-responsibility and worry' towards 'equanimity, receptivity and peace'.

Freud noted parallels between religious behaviour and those of his patients who had obsessional neuroses, e.g. those who were continually washing themselves, yet never felt clean. He called religion a 'universal obsessional neurosis'. In other words, religious phenomena can originate in subjective human needs and neuroses, rather than coming from a God who is perceived as existing objectively.

However, this criticism is not necessarily valid. Just because religion may deal with the issue of guilt, for example, or the lack of a human father later in life, it does not follow that it has no objective basis for that religion.

Sociologists like Durkheim point out the social function of religion. It may mark particular stages in life and acceptance of an individ-

> **COMMENT**
> Aspirin may help to cure a headache, but that does not imply that aspirins are the product of headaches! Freud and Durkheim give reasons why people may be religious (to meet psychological or social needs), but that in itself does not disprove religion.

ual into society. It may be a way of holding a society together and giving it an identity and sense of purpose.

Similarly, political thinkers may take the Marxist view that religion is a social construct, devised by those with power to keep the working people in their place, with rules about obedience and promises of heaven after this life. Marx argued that religion was encouraged by those who exploited working people, in the hope that those who were oppressed now would look for some religious compensation in an afterlife, rather than attempting to improve their situation. In this way, religion was a harmful distraction from the real task of working people, which was to improve their material circumstances here on earth.

The issue here is whether such explanations of the phenomenon of religion and religious experience thereby invalidate any **propositions** that arise as a result of religion. In other words, we need to ask:

Does an explanation of religion in terms of politics or sociology or psychology thereby show that God does not exist?

Some Conclusions

We have seen that there are a great variety of forms of religious experience, and also a good number of different ways in which they may be 'explained away'. There is also the obvious fact that different religions present very different experiences and interpretations of religion, and this can suggest that there is no single or objective reality to which they all point.

We therefore need to take extreme care in moving from the 'experiential approach' to the 'propositional approach' – and it is the latter, of course, with which all arguments about the existence of God are concerned. Is it valid to try to prove the existence of God on the basis of this rich and ambiguous mixture of experiences?

Note

The philosopher Schleiermacher (in *Speeches on Religion*, 1799) welcomed the variety of religions on the grounds that no one tradition could possibly give an adequate idea of the divine. The same caution might be needed in considering religious experience as a basis for an argument about the existence of God. The experiences will be varied, and will be interpreted in the light of the thoughts and circumstances of the people experiencing them – they cannot therefore be used as the basis for a logically compelling argument.

We may conclude that the Argument from Religious Experience is not like the other traditional arguments for the existence of God. First of all, it depends on experiences which may not lead to propositions about God, or may not lead to anything that can be described literally.

Secondly, the experiences that form the basis of one person's conviction may not persuade someone else – the experience itself may be overwhelming, but that does not mean that it automatically leads to statements about God that all would have to accept.

Thirdly, religious experience can back up other reasons for believing in God. It may suggest that there is a balance of probability in favour of there being a God, even if it cannot demonstrate it logically.

But fourthly, an appreciation of religious experience points to exactly what is meant by 'the divine' or 'the eternal' or whatever lies at the root of religion. The other arguments for God may simply point to a particular form of words, a limited idea of what 'God' might mean. Religious experience, especially where it claims not to be able to provide a literal description of what is 'known' in moments of intense religious experience, is a good safeguard against making 'God' too small.

The argument from religious experience may therefore be interesting (in that it shows what people mean by 'God') and persuasive (particularly for the person who has the experience), but it is not a logically compelling argument.

▼ ESSAY QUESTIONS

1 a) Describe what Otto means by 'the numinous'.
   b) To what extent does this match traditional theistic ideas of God?
2 a) Explain some key features of mystical experience.
   b) Discuss the view that mystical experience cannot give factual knowledge about God.

See the 'Further Reading and Websites' section at the back of this book for follow-up work on this chapter.

CHALLENGES TO RELIGIOUS BELIEF

POINTS TO CONSIDER

Does the fact of evil and suffering make belief in a loving God unreasonable?

Can religion be sufficiently explained by psychology and social science?

Is religion healthy, or a neurosis, or an escapist fantasy?

1 The Problem of Evil and Suffering

TIMELINE

c.130–c.202	Irenaeus
354–430	Augustine
1224–74	Aquinas
1711–76	Hume
1770–1831	Hegel
1804–72	Feuerbach
1809–82	Darwin
1818–83	Marx
1856–1939	Freud
1858–1917	Durkheim
1864–1920	Weber
1872–1970	Russell
1875–1961	Jung
1922–	Hick

The fact of evil and suffering in the world creates a problem for those who believe in God. In its simplest form, it may be set out like this:

▼ God is all-knowing, all-powerful, all-loving and the creator of everything.
▼ Suffering exists in the world.
  Therefore
▼ God knows that there is evil (if he is all-knowing).
▼ God could prevent evil (if he is all-powerful).
  But
▼ He allows it to continue.
  Therefore
▼ Either he wishes evil to continue (in which case he cannot be all-loving).
▼ Or he cannot eliminate evil (in which case he is not all-powerful).

This argument is a strong one both from a logical and a psychological point of view. Logically, it seems impossible to reconcile a literal understanding of an all-loving and all-powerful God with the continuing existence of evil.

Psychologically, it is natural to ask for God's help in times of trouble, and his failure to intervene to overcome suffering and evil may therefore be a disincentive to continue to believe in him.

There are two particularly well-known approaches to this problem, the **Irenaean** and the **Augustinian**. These were outlined by John Hick in his book *Evil and the God of Love*. The first, from Irenaeus, argues that God permits evil for a good purpose. The second, from Augustine, claims that evil and suffering are not God's responsibility, and that he is therefore perfectly justified in allowing them to

Figure 5 The fact of human suffering as a result of natural disasters is the most serious challenge to the idea of the existence of a loving God. It may be argued that a God who fails to help in such situations is either indifferent to suffering, cruel, impotent or non-existent.

ISSUES:
One challenge to the Irenaean position concerns the amount of evil and suffering that is necessary in the world in order to achieve God's chosen plan. If learning and growth could take place with a lot less suffering than there is, then why does God allow this degree of suffering and evil?

DEBATE
Be ready to argue whether or not you think that the goal of becoming more like God is worth the suffering and evil that may be the opportunities for personal growth.

continue. Neither argument attempts to take the other two ways out of the problem – namely that either suffering is not real, or that God does not exist.

a) Irenaeus

Bishop Irenaeus held that God had created humankind in his own image (according to the Bible) but in order to develop more fully into the likeness of God, it was necessary for humans to face and overcome the challenges presented by life. Hence, suffering and evil are seen as opportunities to learn and to grow.

A more modern development of this argument is known as the free-will defence. This argues that, in order for humans to grow spiritually they need to have free will. But freedom implies that it is possible to choose to do evil rather than good. Hence, on balance, it is better to have a world in which evil is a real possibility, than to have one in which there is no real freedom to do anything other than choose the good.

For either argument, it is accepted that God is aware of and permits evil in order to achieve a greater good – namely the development of free human beings who are able to grow into his likeness.

In the end, according to Irenaeus, all will develop to the point at which they will be fit for heaven.

MAKING CONNECTIONS

This problem links with that of free will and determinism. Irenaeus and the Free Will Argument can only make sense if we are aware of ourselves as free agents.

b) Augustine

Augustine came to the problem from two different perspectives, one philosophical, the other based on the Bible.

He argued that evil was not a separate force over and above goodness. Rather, to call something evil was simply a way of saying that it lacked goodness (evil as a 'privation of good' is the usual way of expressing this). The world was full of finite, limited things. Their limitations prevented them from the perfect expression of their own natures. Therefore they 'fall short' of what they were designed to be, and hence participate in evil.

His second approach was to put the blame for evil on humankind, rather than on God.

Augustine pointed to the 'fall' of Adam and Eve in the Garden of Eden, and to the idea that all subsequent humanity are descended from them and therefore share in their sin and fall (through what is termed 'original sin'). Thus, moral evil (evil done through human choice) could be blamed on humankind, rather than God.

But what of natural suffering, unrelated to moral evil? Augustine followed the traditional story that some of the angels, led by Satan, rebelled against God. They too 'fell' and took all the created order with them. Therefore creation itself became a place of suffering.

According to Augustine, God will finally come to judge people, and will administer justice in accordance with how they have behaved, sending some to hell and others to heaven. Meanwhile, natural suffering is either sin or a punishment for sin (in the sense that it comes about in a world that is fallen, and therefore full of suffering).

Note

Augustine's argument that evil is only a privation of good can be related to other arguments in the philosophy of religion.

The fourth of Aquinas' Five Ways (see page 30) concerns the way in which we understand goodness and perfection, and moves from them to the idea of a source of goodness. In *Summa Theologiae* (Bk 1, Ch 1, 5:1) he describes goodness as **achieved actuality**. In other words, to be good is to express your own nature. This is seen most clearly in the idea of tools used by humans: a good knife is one that cuts well – it completes its nature by cutting well.

A version of this argument had also been presented by Anselm in his *Monologion* (and is related to the Ontological Argument – see page 20).

DEBATE

Be ready to argue whether or not you think that Augustine's view of natural evil as a punishment for sin is compatible with belief in a loving God.

ISSUE:

Bertrand Russell, in examining the claim that 'the universe has been shaped and is governed by an intelligent purpose', turns a sharp eye over the iniquities of humankind and comments:

The world in which we live can be understood as a result of muddle and accident; but if it is the outcome of deliberate purpose, the purpose must have been that of a fiend. For my part, I find accident a less painful and more plausible hypothesis.

[From *Why I am not a Christian and Other Essays on Religion and Related Subjects*, Allen & Unwin, 1957]

MAKING CONNECTIONS

This argument about falling short of perfection, and of being judged according to one's potential, can be related to the 'Natural Law' approach to ethics, where – essentially – moral choices are judged according to the degree to which the action being considered does or does not confirm to something's 'essence' or 'real self'.

c) Some Key Differences Between Augustine and Irenaeus

▼ Irenaeus makes God responsible for evil, while Augustine blames it on the 'fall' of angels and human beings.

▼ Irenaeus allows freedom in order that human beings can grow through moral choice, while Augustine sees human free will as responsible for the 'fall'.

▼ Irenaeus sees all people as eventually being prepared for heaven, while Augustine sees God judging people, who are to go either to heaven or to hell.

▼ Irenaeus sees evil as performing a positive role in God's purposes, whereas Augustine sees it as a sin or punishment for sin.

▼ Irenaeus sees suffering and evil as real, while Augustine sees them only as a privation (or 'lack') of good.

The Problem of Evil influences the ideas people have of God. So, for example, within the Christian tradition, Jesus on the cross is seen as an expression of God's willingness to suffer alongside his people.

This leads some theologians to point to a God who deliberately sets aside the attribute of omnipotence, and prefers to share in human life, with all its limits and suffering.

But can a suffering God still be God? This has always been an important question for Christian theology. How is it possible that an omnipotent God could take on human form in the person of Jesus? How can God suffer? Why should he choose to suffer?

One way out of this problem is to think of God as being in a process of change, as evolving towards the future, and engaged with the whole of the creation in that process. Notice that this places God within the world of space and time, engaged as an agent in the process of change. Looking at the qualities of God set out on page 18, choices need to be made, for a God who is engaged in the world cannot also be timeless or eternal.

Teilhard de Chardin is an example of a thinker who wants to show God as involved within and guiding the process of change within the world, reconciling his faith with the fact of evolution. He saw evolution rather like a pyramid, with the most basic atoms at the base, rising up through more and more complex forms. At the very top of the pyramid – and therefore the point to which convergent evolution was moving – was a point he called **Omega**. His argument was that God was to be found in that Omega point, the final goal of creation and the end of the process of evolution. With such an image, God does not have to have destroyed all evil and suffering in the present in order for the believer to claim that, in the end, he will be 'all in all'. Evil and suffering are just stepping stones in the forward march of evolution towards the point Omega.

2 Issues raised by Psychology and Sociology

In chapter 7 of *The Origin of Species*, Darwin argued that social activity could be explained by his theory of natural selection. Just as particular features of individuals enabled them to survive and breed, so ensuring that their offspring continued those features, so a society flourished and survived depending on the social behaviour and co-operation between the people living in it. Certain behaviour patterns were therefore beneficial for society as a whole.

He therefore argued that you could examine society (and thus also the moral and religious features it displayed) in a scientific way, looking at the role that beliefs and behaviour played in the way it worked.

Sociology and psychology are the sciences that examine human behaviour and try to give explanations for it – and that includes explanations of religion and morality.

> ## Note
>
> Psychology and sociology do not ask 'Is it true?' but 'What does it do?' Just because they provide an answer to the second question, it does not follow that the first is not also worth asking.
>
> If a sociologist argues that religion exists in order to hold society together, or a psychologist holds that religious belief is connected with guilt, that does not mean that what is believed is necessarily false. My reason for believing something is not the same as the truth of what I believe.

One possible explanation of religious beliefs is that they are fantasies or projections. This was not an idea that started with the development of psychology, but was discussed much earlier. The philosopher Hume argued that religion and religious principles were nothing but 'sick men's dreams', whereas Feuerbach saw God as a projection of all

KEY QUESTION
The main point to consider here is whether such an evolving God is true to the western theistic tradition, where God is seen as the omnipotent creator.

The more literal and definite your idea of God, the more difficult becomes the problem posed by the fact of evil and suffering.

DEBATE
Be ready to argue
whether or not
psychology and sociol-
ogy have given a suffi-
cient explanation of
religion, thereby ren-
dering God redundant,
and whether from a
psychological, sociolog-
ical or political per-
spective, religion is
harmful or beneficial.

that is best in humankind. On the face of it, Feuerbach's position
sounds very positive, with God as a projection of all that people most
admire in human behaviour. However, Feuerbach (perhaps influenced by his experience of religious people at that time) saw that it is
potentially harmful, because projecting everything that is good outwards on to the idea of a God, produced a general sense that humankind was degraded, because nobody can compare with that ideal projection. Hence, worship of God leads to pessimism about humanity,
and a general tendency to see the world as a place of sin and failure,
with the hope for perfection only in heaven after death.

Political thinkers also examined the role of religion. Marx
famously held that it was the 'opium of the people', numbing them to
the pain of their everyday situation, and offering them false benefits
in heaven, rather than prompting them to seek genuine benefits on
earth.

In this chapter we shall examine some of the main thinkers who
have contributed such psychological and sociological criticisms.

a) Freud

Freud developed psychoanalysis as a technique for dealing with
patients who came to him suffering from hysteria. Through the analysis of dreams and the free association of thoughts, they were encouraged to express feelings which had been locked away within the
unconscious mind, and which were therefore not recognised by the
patient, although they produced patterns of behaviour which seemed
bizarre.

Freud believed that each stage of life produced tensions. Those
which were not faced and resolved at the time could become buried
in the unconscious. Then, later in life, they came to the surface again
in the form of emotional or behavioural problems.

He examined patients who came to him with compulsive tidying
or washing routines. These he ascribed to a sense of uncleanness
that had been instilled into his patients during their childhood.
However much the adult washed or tidied, he or she still felt dirty.
He called such conditions **obsessional neuroses**. Freud's treatment
of such patients was based on the idea that once they could locate
the origin of their feelings of dirtiness, they would no longer seek to
counter them in the present, and would be free from their neurosis.

When he examined religion, Freud saw patterns in which people
confessed sins and went through elaborate rituals to ensure that they
were forgiven. In particular, he saw the meticulous detail in which
people followed religious rituals as similar to the compulsive
behaviour of his neurotic patients. He therefore suggested that relig-

ion was a **universal obsessional neurosis**, motivated by unconscious guilt.

In his early work, Freud examined the idea of the primal horde. In this, young men in a tribe, frustrated by not being given access to women by their dominant father, rise up and kill him. This sets up guilt, which they later seek to overcome by being obedient to a religious 'father' or God.

His basic assumption was that the early stages of humankind would be similar to the early stages in the life of individuals. Hence, childhood neuroses are paralleled out with his assumptions about the primal horde. Freud necessarily has the origin of religion in infantile experience, because he sees the infantile stage as the source of later neuroses. Hence, if religion is an unhealthy phenomenon, it is natural to identify it with a similar origin of neurosis – and therefore with some early experience of humankind. However, such a view of the origins of religion may be challenged. If it is taken away from Freud, however, it does not entirely demolish his argument about religion being an illusion, for the need for comfort in the face of the impersonal forces of nature can still give a good reason for mankind having developed the idea of God, even if there never was a stage during which a primal horde killed off their leader. However, like many of Freud's assertions, it is not possible to disprove the theory, simply because we do not have the sort of evidence that can be used decisively against it.

This part of his work is given little emphasis today, and is of secondary importance to the main thrust of his work, which is to see religion as essentially a projection of unconscious need. Therefore, in order to put Freud's criticism of religion into perspective, it is important not to focus on the early Totem and Taboo issue alone. Otherwise, a discussion of Freud is really little more than a consideration of nineteenth-century views about early human society. Freud's work on projection does not depend on the Totem and Taboo material.

In *The Future of an Illusion* (1927) Freud set out the benefits and problems he saw in religion (which is the 'illusion' of the title).

The benefits:

▽ The threatening and impersonal forces of nature are tamed to some extent, by being seen as conforming to the will of a loving and providential God.

▽ God provides the adult with the sense of protection that a child seeks from a human father.

▽ That the believer can hope to influence things that happen, by gaining God's help.

▽ That there is a sense of dignity from having a relationship with God.

▽ That religious teachings diminish the threat posed by death.

▽ That religion offers an explanation of otherwise inexplicable events.

But against these are set the problems:

▼ That faith is actually an illusion, based on what people would like to be true, rather than what is actually true.

▼ That religious rules and regulations, believed to come from God, may go against the personal needs and well-being of individuals, thus hampering their personal growth.

Freud describes religious ideas as:

> illusions, fulfilments of the oldest, strongest and most urgent wishes of mankind . . .
>
> Those who cling to them do so because of the comfort they bring, God taking the place of a benevolent father, needed later in life, where threats remain but an actual father is not there to help.
>
> . . . the terrifying impression of helplessness in childhood aroused the need for protection – for protection through love – which was provided by the father; and the recognition that this helplessness lasts throughout life made it necessary to cling to the existence of a father, but this time a more powerful one. Thus the benevolent rule of a divine Providence allays our fear of the dangers of life . . .

Religion is thus an illusion, created out of our adult need to find childhood comfort. But Freud is careful to define what he means by an illusion:

[From *The Future of an Illusion*, Penguin translation, quoted in *Faith and Reason*, ed. Paul Helm]

> An illusion is not the same thing as an error; nor is it necessarily an error . . . What is characteristic of illusions is that they are derived from human wishes . . . Illusions need not necessarily be false – that is to say, unrealisable or in contradiction to reality . . . Thus we call a belief an illusion when a wish-fulfilment is a prominent factor in its motivation, and in doing so we disregard its relations to reality, just as the illusion itself sets no store by verification.

Be clear about what Freud claimed. Freud called religion an 'illusion'. That is not the same thing as saying that its claims are not true. His term 'illusion' refers to the idea that religion is based on a projection of unconscious needs. 'God' offers security for the adult who has lost an actual father and wants a heavenly one by way of compensation.

Now, this gives an alternative reason for being religious, but it does not actually claim that religious beliefs are wrong. In other words, God may exist, even if the reason for wanting to believe in him is the desire for a substitute father.

Freud assumes that science is the only source of knowledge. Therefore religion must be no more than wish-fulfilment, since there can be no scientific (and therefore no objective) proof of the existence of God. He sees why humankind may have found it valuable to have such a projection in the form of God, but believes that reason will eventually prevail, and the projection will be recognised as such.

Freud's criticism is important because it implies that, if religion survives because it fulfils emotional and psychological needs, then a healthy and well-balanced person would not need religion.

Hence, Freud undermined religion in two ways:

▼ By suggesting an alternative reason for holding religious beliefs, which implies that they may not be correct, even if it does not show it.

▼ By suggesting that the motivation that leads to religion is essentially unhealthy.

b) Jung

In examining the work of Carl Jung, it is important to be clear about the following three things:

▼ His idea of the collective unconscious.

▼ His idea of the archetypes.

▼ The positive psychological role he gives religion.

Jung agreed with Feuerbach and Freud that religious beliefs were the result of projection from the unconscious, but – unlike them – he saw a positive and healthy role for such projection. In particular he pointed to the integrating effect that religious beliefs could have on people, particularly those who were older. Jung did not argue about whether or not God existed. His concern was to examine the idea of God in the mind of the believer and see what function it performed.

To appreciate his ideas about this, however, it is important to understand two of his key concepts: **the collective unconscious** and the **archetypes**.

The collective unconscious is Jung's term for the cluster of images (which he called archetypes) in the unconscious mind, which are found in many different cultures and eras, which provided a rich source of religious and other images. Through the collective unconscious, an individual is able to share in religious and cultural life, and through them can come to a deeper understanding of herself or himself.

The positive role that he gave to religion was in line with his general view of what psychology could offer people. Basically, as well as the collective unconscious, there is the individual unconscious which contains many repressed and unacceptable parts of the self (which Jung refers to as the 'shadow'). He also pointed out that

ISSUES:
Although Freud claims to be scientific, this has been challenged, particularly by Karl Popper who argues that Freud's scientific work is not open to falsification (i.e. whatever is challenged, Freud can devise an alternative explanation), and does not therefore satisfy the normal criteria of science.

In other words, Freud's claim that present neurosis is accounted for in terms of the frustration of infantile desires, may be no more scientific than the projection of early group neuroses, which he sees as the origins of belief in God.

DEBATE
Be ready to argue whether or not Freud was right to describe religion as an illusion.

people have to balance the male and female aspects (*animus* and *anima*), so that a man has to come to terms with a feminine side, and a woman with a masculine side.

According to Jung, in the first part of life a person tends to grow into an individual by repressing aspects of himself or herself that are unacceptable to the image of self that he or she is developing. However, during the second half of life, there is an opposite process, as people seek to come to terms with the repressed side of themselves and to integrate them. Religion, Jung believed, helped with that process of integration.

Therefore, Jung gives a very positive role for religion. However, his view of religion is not that of conventional western theism. Religion exists in terms of archetypes, which are projections of humankind's deepest fears and emotions. In other words, religion becomes part of human self-understanding. He does not start with a God who might or might not exist 'out there' in any way, but with a set of religious images which live on in the collective unconscious.

Notice that Jung's is a **naturalistic** view of religion. It is a phenomenon like any other, something that can be examined and whose place in the scheme of things can be assessed. This is not an approach which is concerned with the truth or falsity of religious propositions (e.g. the claim that God exists) but with the facts about what religion does (e.g. the beneficial or harmful effects of being religious). God is a psychological reality – i.e. he is something that is believed to exist, and that belief has an effect on the believer. Whether or not he is a physical or metaphysical reality (in other words, whether he 'exists' separately from people's belief in his existence) is quite another matter.

> **KEY QUESTIONS**
>
> Should religion regard Jung as a friend or foe?
>
> Is his view of religion compatible with traditional Christian beliefs?

c) Durkheim

Durkheim saw religion as having a positive, beneficial role in society; it was what society needed, but only because it was created by society, and was the expression of social values, morals and authority. For Durkheim, religion is a social phenomenon, not an individual one. Through religion, the individual participates in the values and self-understanding of the group or society.

Durkheim examined the function that religion played within society. He was therefore concerned with what religion *did* rather than with the truth claims that it made. In one sense, therefore, he held that all religions were true, but in another, that they were false – for they did not describe a transcendent reality, but were the expression of collective social realities.

Durkheim argued that religion had an important role in society. It provided a range of images and activities which enabled the community to come together and see themselves as having a common purpose and common values. Thus religion continues to be of value, because it integrates and strengthens the community as a whole, as well as individuals within it.

Rituals within religion are the method by which an individual expresses his or her identity with the group. In other words, a unified system of beliefs and practices is able to unite people into a single, moral group.

Durkheim gave religion a positive and moral role. It was not based on primitive fear of the unknown, or an attempt to use magic to ward off harm, but it was a celebration of unity and moral purpose within society. Whereas he sees spiritual power as impersonal, it is quickly taken and made personal, and people are able to use particular things (religious objects, even sacred animals, take on roles as totems – representatives of spiritual power) as a vehicle for harnessing the religious impulse into a positive social role.

But notice that Durkheim is not saying that there is actually an objective spiritual power – something outside the human realm which can change situations. Rather, that power is actually the expression of the group or society itself. What is important within community life is symbolised, and becomes the object of religion. In other words, the God of a clan is simply the clan itself. There will be many different forms of god or religion, but only because there are many different kinds of society or clan. There is no need for a separate, objectively existing God to explain the phenomenon of religion.

Something is called sacred because it is used as this sort of vehicle for social integration. This does not necessarily imply that the beliefs expressed through religion are wrong, but that the reason for holding them is social rather than metaphysical.

Durkheim himself seems to be suggesting that because it was the motivating force behind religion, in some way society itself was sacred. Most sociologists would not go as far as that, although they would point out the social benefits or hazards of religion.

In effect, Durkheim is saying that religion is good for society, in giving it a sense of purpose, unity and morality, but that the object of devotion – God – is something that society creates for that purpose.

ISSUES:

Durkheim saw God as a personification of the clan, and therefore as the vehicle for integrating its members. But does belief in God actually function in that way?

Does religion give society its moral sense, or does society's moral sense create religion? Religious believers tend to say the former is the case; Durkheim says the latter. If Durkheim is right, how can religion ever challenge a society, or go against its prevailing moral or social attitudes?

MAKING CONNECTIONS

Durkheim's argument that religion expresses the moral sense and values of society can link with ethics. One can ask if, for example, Utilitarianism, which explores what is to the benefit of the greatest number, is adequate for religion, or whether religion requires the more individual and absolute approach of Kantian ethics. If Durkheim is right, religion should promote Utilitarianism, and accept relativity in ethics – because everything, in the end, comes down to the values of particular societies.

DEBATE

Be ready to argue whether or not you think that Durkheim has adequately explained what religion is all about, and – if not – what is missing in his account.

d) Weber

Weber (1864–1920) took a different approach to religion from that of Durkheim.

▼ He was aware of the 'charisma' and power of religious leaders. He noted the way in which they can inspire and empower their followers. Hence religion can be evaluated in terms of the influence of individuals, not just in terms of its function of holding society together.

▼ He also recognised that religion could influence society, rather than society influencing religion. Features of the lifestyle and ethics of a religion coloured the whole of a society in which it was practised.

Notice that religion is being explained here as a phenomenon – something that can be examined and quantified. Sociology therefore acts like any other science and seeks to explain what it sees. It is not able to move from such observations to declare that any particular religious belief is either true or false.

Unlike Durkheim, Weber argued that although religion does not directly affect how society operates, it could provide ideas and attitudes that could influence social change. The example he gave was the way in which the Protestant work ethic was said to help the rise of capitalism. In the same way, socialism could be promoted by those who followed religious teachings about equality.

If Weber is right, then we should expect to see religious attitudes shaping the way in which society operates and the values it promotes. So, for example, Jewish religious views about being given land by God in the Scriptures might be related to present-day social and political issues about Israel and the Palestinians. Or Muslim ideas of jihad and martyrdom might provide a context for understanding how Muslim fundamentalist groups justify acts that are regarded generally as terrorism.

To take this approach does not imply that beliefs *automatically* lead to, or justify, political or military actions, rather that religious belief provides a context and stimulus, which is then taken up by those who have their own particular agenda. It is a recognition that society can be influenced and shaped by values, not just (as Marx suggested) by the distribution of material goods – a theory to which we will now turn.

e) Marx

Karl Marx argued that because human survival depends on the supply of food and other goods, the production and distribution of goods is the key to understanding society and how it changes.

From the philosopher Hegel, he took the idea that change comes as a result of a 'dialectic', in which one thing or situation (a thesis) produces an opposite reaction (its antithesis) and finally the two are resolved (in a synthesis). This process then starts over again, and so on. Hegel saw society developing in this way, and as moving in a direction that gave progressively more expression to what he called the **Absolute Spirit**. Some followers of Hegel, however, (generally called 'left-wing' Hegelians) saw the process of change as being within society itself, and not as an expression of an overall power or spirit.

Marx therefore took over from Hegel the idea of a development in the form of a dialectic, and saw it as describing the inevitable march forward of society. But since Marx held that material goods were at the basis of society, the theory he developed is called **dialectical materialism**.

Central to his dialectical materialism is the idea that there is conflict between the ruling classes who hold the wealth and control the means of production, and the working classes who sell their labour, and are largely alienated from the results of the work they do. His aim was that the working class should rise up and take charge of the means of production, thus putting an end to their oppression and establishing a classless society.

His main criticism of religion was that in the face of real oppression on earth, it offered spiritual blessings in heaven. People would therefore put up with their present suffering in the hope of a spiritual reward – using it like a drug to ease the pain of their situation:

> Religion is the sigh of the oppressed creature, the heart of a heartless world, the soul of the soulless environment. It is the opium of the people.
>
> The people cannot be really happy until it has been deprived of illusory happiness by the abolition of religion. The demand that the people should shake itself free of illusion as to its own condition is the demand that it should abandon a condition which needs illusion.

[From the *Introduction to the Critique of the Hegelian Philosophy of Right*]

Marx believed that religion worked to the advantage of the ruling classes. However, once working people united and took responsibility for their own welfare, overthrowing the existing class structure and removing the causes of oppression, religion would no longer be needed and would therefore wither away.

If Feuerbach was right that the projection of the best in humankind on to an illusory God led to a pessimism about humanity, then the only way in which people would realise their own self worth, and act in a positive way to improve their situation, was to abolish that projection. Hence the abolition of religion was, for Marx, the condition for human improvement.

Notice that, as with other criticisms of religion in this chapter, Marx is not really concerned with the truth or otherwise of religious beliefs. Rather he is concerned with the use to which people put those beliefs. Thus, rather than arguing whether or not people might survive death and live on in heaven, he is concerned with the negative effect that belief in heaven has upon people who need to improve their conditions here on earth.

DEBATE

Be ready to argue whether Marx's view of religion as 'the heart of a heartless world' should be regarded as a positive or negative view of religion.

Note

Marx saw religion as a tool of repression. He had little awareness of religion being used in a revolutionary way, or as a means of working for social justice.

In assessing Marx's critique of religion, it is important to keep that limitation in mind. His criticism is related to the religion of his day as he perceived it; it may not necessarily apply to religion in general.

General note

Sociology and psychology are sciences, basing their claims on the examination of evidence. Marx, too, saw his work as scientific, based on the observation of the nature of society, the class structure, and the process of social and political change.

All these disciplines therefore examine the *phenomenon* of religion and explore the part it plays within their whole area of style – as part of a psychological or sociological understanding of humankind.

Whereas religious beliefs attempt to express truths that may apply to all people at all times, and arguments in the philosophy of religion go beyond the prejudices and circumstances of particular people, the same cannot be said for the sociology or psychology of religion.

Hence the attitude towards religion and the conclusions about its function are closely linked to the experience of the particular thinker. Marx and Freud had particular views of religion based on their areas of study – whether as part of an ongoing process of class conflict and social change, or as an explanation of neurotic behaviour.

In assessing what they say about religion, one should ask which of their comments (if any) can claim to be universally relevant, and which are limited to the experience of the religion they encountered in their particular time and place.

▼ ESSAY QUESTIONS

1 a) What did Marx mean by describing religion as 'the opium of the people'?
   b) Do you consider this to be a positive or negative view of religion's role in life?
2 a) Explain what Freud meant by a 'universal obsessional neurosis'.
   b) To what extent is this an adequate view of religion?

See the 'Further Reading and Websites' section at the back of this book for follow-up work on this chapter.

CHAPTER 4

RELIGIOUS LANGUAGE

POINTS TO CONSIDER

Does language have to be literal in order to be meaningful?

Can 'God' be described, without ceasing to be God?

TIMELINE

1224–74	Aquinas
1711–76	Hume
1886–1965	Tillich
1898–1951	Wittgenstein
1902–94	Popper
1910–89	Ayer
1919–	Flew
1922–	Hick

Language is about communication. You might be able to mutter things to yourself, using words that are unique to you, but once you try to convey something to other people, you have to use words with an agreed meaning.

If religious language is going to communicate, we have to know how to interpret it, and that is not as obvious as it may at first appear.

1 Some Basic Features of Religious Language

Some kinds of language are very straightforward, for example, descriptive language. I might say: 'Buddhist monks wear orange robes.'

It is absolutely clear what I mean. The statement needs to be qualified, for example, by saying 'Some . . .' (because there are monks who wear red or black robes), but otherwise it is clear to everyone what is meant, and everyone knows in principle how to check whether it is correct – go and find as many monks as possible and check what they're wearing.

But a religious person might say: 'I have just seen a miracle.'

The truth of this is not at all clear. First of all, the person would need to say what he or she meant by 'miracle'. If the definition implied that the event could not be accounted for in the ordinary way, then it would be open to an impartial observer or scientist to check the evidence on which it is based. Two people could witness the same thing; one might call it a miracle, the other might not.

The issue of religious language was highlighted by the work of the **Logical Positivists**, early in the twentieth century. They insisted that the meaning of a statement was given by its method of verification. If you could give evidence to back up what you said, then that evidence was what your statement was all about.

For example: 'The cat is outside the door' is a statement that can be proved to be true or false by taking a look. The *meaning* of that statement, from the Logical Positivist point of view, is 'If you open the door and look, you will see the cat.'

The Logical Positivists argued that if you can't give evidence which would show a statement to be true, then that statement is meaningless.

Much of the modern discussion about religious language has come about because the Logical Positivists argued that it was meaningless. We shall need to look at the claims of the Logical Positivists in a little more detail, but first we need to be clear about some basic features of language.

a) Cognitive and Non-cognitive

Cognitive language is language that conveys information. **Non-cognitive language** may convey emotion, give an order, express hopes and fears, but it does not depend on external facts that can be observed and checked.

KEY QUESTION
How much religious language is cognitive and how much is non-cognitive?

The philosopher Hume argued that there were only two kinds of statement: those that gave matters of fact, and those that simply explained logic and meanings. In the theory of knowledge, philosophers who believe that all our knowledge starts with experience are called **empiricists**. Hume was an empiricist, and he therefore regarded the information we gain through the senses as the basic test of truth for all cognitive language. But is language just about conveying what we have experienced, or does it have other functions, especially in connection with religion?

b) Analytic and Synthetic Statements

An **analytic statement** simply explains the meaning of its terms; it does not depend on evidence. 'Red is a colour' is true in all cases and for all time. Once I know the meaning of the words 'red' and 'colour', the matter is fixed. It is therefore analytic. All tautologies are analytic.

'There is ice on the path outside' is a **synthetic statement**, because it can only be shown to be true or false with reference to evidence for or against there being ice on the path.

c) 'Believing In'

If you **believe that** something is true, it means that – on balance – evidence suggests that the statement corresponds to external reality. If you **believe 'in'** something, it means that you are committed to it, and that you interpret your experience in the light of that commitment.

So, when a person says that they 'believe in' God, they mean far more than simply saying that they believe that God exists. After all, you could believe that God exists as a theoretical possibility, and yet regard such belief as of little importance. On the other hand, to say that a person 'believes in' God implies far more than just facts. You 'believe in' someone when you are committed to them, admire them and so on. It is therefore clear that all language about 'believing in' something, is going to require more than the literal reference to facts, which might have been sufficient for a 'believing that' statement.

d) 'Experiencing As'

John Hick, following the work of Wittgenstein, points out that all experience involves interpretation. We do not just experience things, but experience them 'as' something. Whether the battle ends in victory or defeat depends on which side you are on. From exactly the same evidence, one interprets what has happened 'as' victory, the other 'as' defeat. But this is not limited to descriptions of value; all descriptions are interpretations – indeed, as soon as we start to describe something we are interpreting it, because we are starting to sort out the words and ideas with which to convey what we have experienced.

2 Verification and Falsification

A key feature of arguments about the nature and validity of religious language concerns whether religious claims may be **verified** (shown to be true) or **falsified** (shown to be false). It is argued that statements which cannot be verified or falsified cannot be cognitive – in other words, they cannot convey information.

a) Logical Positivism

In his book *Tractatus Logico-Philosophicus*, published in 1921, Wittgenstein set out a narrow view of what could count as a meaningful proposition. He saw the function of language as being to picture the world. Therefore every statement needed to correspond to some information about the world itself. This idea was developed during the 1920s by the Vienna Circle of philosophers, who – inspired by Wittgenstein and by the success of science – wanted to find a way of showing statements to be meaningful and either true or false.

They produced a theory of meaning known as the **Verification Principle**. They argued that the meaning of a statement was its method of verification. In other words, if I say that something is the case, I mean that – if you go and look – you will see it is the case. A statement is thus only meaningful if it can be proved to be true or false through such evidence. This is termed the '**strong**' form of the Verification Principle.

Of course, it is not always possible to check the evidence for a statement. In which case it was argued that – for a statement to be meaningful – it was enough to be able to say what sort of evidence could count for or against it. This became known as the '**weak**' version of the Verification Principle. It was particularly useful in examining statements about events in the past – you cannot go back in time and see if William invaded England in 1066, but you know what evidence would have shown it to be the case if you *had* been there.

Logical Positivism (and the 'weak' version of the Verification Principle) was popularised by A J Ayer in his book *Language, Truth and Logic,* published in 1936. He argued that the statement 'God exists' could not be either true or false, because there is no empirical evidence that can prove the matter one way or the other, and it was therefore meaningless. On this basis, he rejected the cognitive value of most ethical and religious language.

> **DEBATE**
> Be ready to argue whether or not a 'picturing' function of language, such as is used in science, is adequate for dealing with religious issues.

Note

A popular criticism of the Verification Principle is that it cannot be verified and therefore that, on its own terms, it is meaningless. This apparently clever little criticism is not particularly significant, since the Verification Principle was concerned with statements that are factually significant, whereas the Verification Principle is not a factual statement at all, but only a policy for interpreting such statements.

---

b) Falsification

In 1955 Anthony Flew presented a story (originally told by John Wisdom) to illustrate the way in which people hold on to their beliefs in spite of evidence to the contrary.

In the story, two explorers come across a clearing in the jungle in which they find a mixture of flowers and weeds. One thinks that there is a gardener who comes to tend this clearing, the other disagrees. They wait, but do not see a gardener, and they then set various checks to see if there is an invisible gardener.

No evidence for the gardener is found, but the first explorer still believes there is one. The second cannot see the difference between a gardener who is invisible, intangible and who cannot be detected in any other way, and no gardener at all!

For Flew, the gardener dies 'the death of a thousand qualifications' because every time he fails to be detected, the 'believer' qualifies what he means by his gardener, until nothing is left.

MAKING CONNECTIONS

The idea of using falsification in this way relates to the work of Karl Popper, a philosopher of science, who argued that a theory can only be considered scientific if you can specify what would prove it to be false. He used the principle of falsification to criticise Freudian and Marxist ideas, arguing that people who argued for those theories did not generally allow anything to count against them, but used their theory to explain any challenge.

3 Via Negativa (Apophatic Way)

It may be argued that God is so great, and therefore so beyond the ordinary meaning of the world we use to describe things, that there is nothing we can say about him in a positive or literal way. This is called the *via negativa*.

If that is so, then the most we can say is what he is *not* – in other words, we can deny God the sort of qualities and therefore limitations that might apply to other beings.

This tradition goes back to Pseudo-Dionysius, who lived in the fifth and early sixth century, and whose writings were influential through the mediaeval period. He was a neo-Platonist, in that he was deeply influenced by the thought of Plato, which he linked with Christian doctrine. His reason for taking the *via negativa* was a desire to emphasise the transcendence of God, and therefore to separate him from any literal description which could limit him. He was also a mystic, which means that he thought that one could experience God in a personal way that went beyond the use of language.

MAKING CONNECTIONS

If we can say nothing about God, can we claim that he guides people and gives moral principles? In other words, if we cannot say that God is loving or just or merciful, in any positive sense, how can we use the idea of God to back up moral claims about what is fundamentally right or wrong?

Hence the limitations imposed by the *via negativa* on what can be said about God have implications for all religious ethics.

The obvious advantage of this approach is that it avoids trying to fit a transcendent God into a description that is really suitable only for something that is limited and part of this world.

The disadvantage is that there is therefore very little that you can say about God. Is it possible to worship a God who is described entirely in negative ways: not finite, not visible, not tangible, not limited in any way, not having parts and passions?

On the other hand, most believers do want to say positive things about God, and they therefore have to find appropriate ways to qualify the language they use to do so.

4 Types of Religious Language

Clearly, there are limitations on what can be achieved by using literal language to describe God. Many theologians and philosophers turn to analogical, symbolic or mythological language in order to overcome the limitations imposed by the literal.

a) Analogy

If you use the same word to describe different things, its meaning may be:

1 **Univocal** – if it means exactly the same thing each time (e.g. a black hat and a black night – the meaning of the word 'black' is the same in each case).

2 **Equivocal** – if it means different things when used in the different situations. 'Gay' can refer to someone who is homosexual or someone who is dressed in bright colours. Someone about to be 'stoned' may face the prospect of execution or the recreational use of drugs.

However, when speaking of God, neither type of meaning is of much use. Univocal language will limit God, making him too much like the ordinary things to which the word generally refers. On the other hand, equivocal language will not convey any information.

Thus, for example, if I were to claim that God is loving, in exactly the same way that people are loving, then I run into all sorts of problems, because God does not have a body, or the means of expressing love in an ordinary human way.

On the other hand, if I claim that God is loving in a way that is nothing at all like human love, then I have said absolutely nothing about him, because it empties the word 'love' of any meaning.

Hence the use of analogy. Just as one might refer to a stormy night and a stormy relationship, or a bright day and a bright mood, so it is hoped that the analogical use of words might be able to convey information about God without limiting him to the usual human meaning of the words used.

> **ISSUES:**
> If a mystic says that he or she has had an experience of God, but cannot describe that experience, how can you tell whether it was an experience of God?
>
> What is the difference between seeing God in a dream and dreaming that one has seen God?
>
> What would Flew's second explorer have to say about the *via negativa*?

There are two reasons why people might want to use analogy:

1 In order to make rational statements about their beliefs, they have recognised that literal, univocal language is inadequate, since it does not take into account the transcendence of God.

2 Those who have had religious experiences have sought to express their insights using whatever words are available, but recognise the limitations of those words.

Aquinas argued that language used to describe God's nature should do so analogically. In other words, the meaning of a word when applied to earthly things could be extended to be used of God, once it was recognised that it was being used as an analogy, not in a literal or univocal way.

He set out two different forms of analogy:

1 **The analogy of attribution**. If God is the creator, then human qualities can be expected to be derived from divine qualities. If humans are 'good' they may receive their goodness from God. This would suggest that we can extend the human meaning 'upwards' to apply it to the source of goodness. Equally, of course, we extend human meanings 'downwards' when we say that an animal is 'friendly'. So the analogy of attribution depends upon the idea of God as creator.

2 **The analogy of proportionality**. A human being may be described as 'powerful' and so might God, but we assume that the meaning of 'powerful' in each case is proportional to their respective natures.

The problem with both forms of analogy is that for them to work effectively, you have to have prior knowledge of God. How can you argue that God's love is analogous to human love if you do not even know what is meant by the word 'God'? How can you show a proportional relationship unless you know both things that are to be compared?

Thus, if you believe that God exists as the creator of the world, that he is personal and the source of qualities found in things in the world – in other words, the sort of God that is argued for by using Aquinas' Five Ways – *then* it makes perfect sense to use analogy to explain how one might speak of God. Without those assumptions, analogy is less convincing.

i) Models and Qualifiers

In analogical language, you say something positive but then qualify it. God is described as loving, powerful, merciful and so on – but not in exactly the same way as humans who display those qualities.

This is made clear by the work of I T Ramsey who, in *Religious Language* (1957), used the terms 'model' and 'qualifier'.

A **model** is a word that has a straightforward meaning when applied to ordinary things we experience, but is also used to describe God. So, for example, we know what it means to be a 'creator' – and so, by analogy, we can use the word 'creator' as a model for describing God.

However, it is important that the model should not be misunderstood and used univocally of God. Hence the need for a '**qualifier**'. This is the word that shows how the model is to be applied to God. So, for example, we might speak of an 'infinite' or 'perfect' creator – in which case the words 'infinite' and 'perfect' are qualifiers.

Ramsey went on to explore other aspects of religious language, including the important fact that it expresses discernment (it struggles to make a particular view known) and commitment (it is not simply a detached description).

b) Symbol

Paul Tillich also used ordinary language to point to God, but spoke of the words used as 'symbols'. First of all, he distinguished between a sign and a symbol. A sign is a conventional way of pointing to something – for example, a road sign. We learn the highway code because we need to know what the signs stand for. A symbol points beyond itself, like a sign, but it also shares in the power of that to which it points.

A new car or a set of expensive designer clothes may be a sign that someone is wealthy, but you do not have to look them up in a rule book to understand that they point to wealth. They are a powerful expression of wealth, indeed, they 'symbolise' wealth.

Tillich held that God could only be described by using symbols, never literally. The symbol is self-transcending. In other words, it means something in itself, but also points beyond itself to some higher or greater reality. He saw that as parallel to religious experience, for something becomes religious because it is more than just one being among many, one reality alongside others, rather it is '**being itself**', reality itself. At the same time he insisted that religion was a matter of **ultimate concern**, of what is finally and absolutely of value in life.

So God is known through a collection of symbols, which point beyond themselves towards what is transcendent and ultimate.

MAKING CONNECTIONS

In looking at religious experience, we saw that Otto spoke of the 'schematisation' of an experience – in other words, the gathering together of words and ideas by which that experience could be described. For Tillich the 'schema' for a religious experience comprises the relevant symbols by which we try to describe it.

c) Myth

Myths are stories that are formed out of symbols. There are, for example, a good number of different creation myths. Each of them reflects the insights and values of the people and culture that first composed them – they are stories that tell of something that is beyond literal description.

In common usage, something is described as a 'myth' if it is factually untrue. It implies that the myth is a story which does not have a solid foundation in fact.

In religious and philosophical usage, however, 'myth' takes on a much more positive role. If the divine cannot be described literally, then forming stories that gather together the symbols that express God is the most effective way of expressing religious intuitions about what God is like and what he does.

A creation myth, for example, will try to show the value and purpose in creation, and the place that humankind has within it. It is therefore far more than a scientific hypothesis about how the world started – it is the sort of account that expresses the values and understanding of life of the people who wrote it.

To take an example from philosophy, Plato's 'analogy' of the cave is more than a straightforward analogy, it is a myth – a story about what happens when one of the prisoners breaks free and finds his way up to the daylight. The whole issue of what the escaped prisoner sees, his attempt to return to the cave and explain to his fellows what reality is like, and his failure to take the passing shadows with any degree of seriousness on his return, are parts of a story which – taken together – express Plato's view about how knowledge is gained, what it does to a person's understanding of life, and how such understanding is viewed and valued in society.

DEBATE

Be ready to debate the value for religion of each of the kinds of language described in this chapter and whether each of these forms of language claims to be cognitive, and whether it is so.

MAKING CONNECTIONS

The issue of the nature of religious language can be related to questions of the authority of religion. Most religions depend on the acceptance of their scriptures as authoritative. If they are not literally true, can they still have authority?

▼ ESSAY QUESTIONS

1 a) Explain why someone might claim that religious language is meaningless.
 b) Assess the validity of any such claim.
2 a) What reasons might be given for using analogy in speaking about God?
 b) Do you find such reasons persuasive?

See the 'Further Reading and Websites' section at the back of this book for follow-up work on this chapter.

ISSUES RAISED BY SCIENCE

CHAPTER 5

POINTS TO CONSIDER

Is a modern scientific view of the origin of the universe compatible with religious views of creation?

Is a scientific view of the world necessarily deterministic?

Are miracles, like beauty, always in the eye of the religious beholder?

Science is the systematic examination of the world using experimental methods to determine physical laws and principles in order to explain the way things are. It is used as a basis for prediction and for the development of technologies. Clearly, it has had a powerful impact on people's lives, such that to question the validity of science and the scientific method seems to fly in the face of four centuries of advance in human understanding.

However, religious beliefs also claim to give an overall view of the nature of life, to explain why things happen, and to influence events, through the help of a God or gods, or through the acting out of moral principles.

So it would seem that religion and science offer alternative ways of understanding the world. If that is so, then – given the success of science and technology – religion is likely to lose credibility, or be seen as a pre-scientific or outmoded way of thinking. But is that necessarily so?

It is possible to define the roles of science and religion in a way that prevents them coming into conflict with one another. For example, one could say:

▼ Science is concerned with facts, religion with values
▼ Science examines the world in an impersonal way, religion in a personal.
▼ Science engages the analytic mind, religion addresses feelings and emotions.

However, such divisions will only avoid conflicts provided that religion does not attempt to make factual statements about the way the world is, and science does not have any influence on people's overall values and behaviour patterns.

But neither side will accept that restriction. Religion makes claims about God's action in creating the world, or intervening in response to prayer, or producing miracles – events that go against

TIMELINE	
384–322 BCE	Aristotle
1224–74	Aquinas
1564–1642	Galileo
1632–77	Spinoza
1642–1727	Newton
1711–76	Hume
1724–1804	Kant
1749–1827	Laplace
1804–72	Feuerbach
1919–	Macquarrie
1934–	Swinburne

the scientifically predictable order of things. These things concern the same world that is examined by science and both sides will want to make factual claims.

Equally, as soon as science and technology open up new possibilities – like organ transplants, IVF treatment or space exploration – people will want to make use of them, and they will therefore have an impact on people's fundamental views and values.

Science is not neutral, it does not just deal with facts. The possibilities opened up by science automatically feed into people's expectations and understanding of life.

Knowledge gives control, and control makes a real difference to people's lives.

For example, a disease may once have been thought of as a punishment from God, an inevitable death sentence in the face of which one is powerless. Then along comes medicine and offers the prospect of a cure. It is not just the fact that the person's life may be extended that is changed here, it is the whole relationship between that person and life. What was just a matter of fate is now seen as a challenge.

So there are bound to be areas of overlap between the concerns of religion and science.

1 Historical Perspectives

In modern times there have been at least two important periods of advance in scientific thinking (sometimes called 'paradigm shifts') – when the whole basis upon which science rests is challenged and revised.

The first came with the development of science in the sixteenth and seventeenth centuries. It marked the rise of a systematic scientific method, the rejection of the authority of the Church and of the philosophy of Aristotle, and the development of a view of the universe as an organised, mechanical system, governed by the laws of physics.

As a response to this, some religious people modified their idea of God. Some saw God as an external creator who produced a world that could then continue to function, as if by clockwork. God was not seen as involved with the everyday changes on Earth, since that was all explicable in terms of the laws of nature. God was behind it as its inspiration and prime cause, but was not anticipated in its day-to-day running. This view is known as **deism**. Christianity was therefore to shed its mysterious and (to some) superstitious elements, and was to become a movement for social reform and spiritual uplift.

Some retreated into **pietism**, concerned with spiritual values, but not debating the issues of whether God created the world exactly as in Genesis, or whether miracles were possible.

Others continued the tradition of **natural theology**, thinking about the nature of God in relationship to the world. From time to time (e.g. over the issue of evolution versus the special creation of each species by God), the religious traditionalists and the followers of scientific thinking came into conflict.

The issues at this time were primarily concerned with the authority of scripture and the validity of philosophical speculation – as distinct from the systematic building up of evidence through the sciences.

A key figure here is Sir Isaac Newton, whose laws of physics were hugely influential in all that followed, but who did not see his work as undermining religion. He argued that God had written two books – scripture and nature – both of which could be studied profitably.

The crisis faced by the appearance of ideas that challenged traditional religious authority is best illustrated by Galileo, who was brought before a church court and condemned for suggesting that the Copernican view, that the earth went round the sun, and not vice versa, was the correct one. Galileo appeared to be going against religious authority which held that the sun went round the earth (on the basis of a literal interpretation of scripture). His trial and condemnation illustrated that religious authority was not always going to accept the challenge posed by human reason.

During the period that followed, the regularity of the universe – as described by Newtonian physics – became in itself a form of the Argument from Design (the Teleological Argument). But this position was not without its problems; if regularity showed the rational foreknowledge of God, then what of the imperfections of the world?

Note

Even during times when religion and science appear to clash, there has been no single 'religious' or 'scientific' view. Many scientists were also religious and vice versa.

Another major shift in thinking took place early in the twentieth century, brought about by another fundamental change in the understanding of the universe, through **relativity** and **quantum theory**. The old world of Newtonian physics was suddenly seen as rather parochial, covering the physical laws that operated only within a limited set of conditions here on earth, but incapable of being applied to the extreme situation of the very large (e.g. the origin of the universe) or the very small (e.g. the components of an atom).

This has shown that science needs to be more flexible than in the earlier period, and that scientific theories may not give a fixed or definitive view of a situation. Religion has tended to make the most of the flexibility on the part of the scientific community, in order to present its claims. It has also become more aware of the nature and validity of its own religious language.

At the same time, literalist, fundamentalist religious believers have argued for an older form of biblical interpretation. The debates are (and will be) ongoing.

2 The Origin of the Universe

Science assumes that the universe has a fundamental unity and coherence, and that it is capable of being understood: hence the scientific quest for a TOE (a Theory of Everything), a set of principles that will explain how the universe originated and came to be as it is today.

The scientific quest to do this is not so different from the religious desire for an overall source of creative power and reason (God), which will make sense of everything.

Therefore, once again, we find that science and religion are on parallel tracks, each seeking a goal in terms of understanding the nature and significance of life as we experience it.

a) Dimensions

A paper on the Philosophy of Religion does not require detailed knowledge of cosmology, but some idea of the scale of the universe is valuable, simply in order to put theories of origin and religious views into some overall perspective.

There are estimated to be at least ten billion galaxies in the universe. Our own galaxy is thought to contain 100 billion stars, and to be about 100,000 light years in diameter. The sun, about 32,000 light years from the centre of the galaxy, is a relatively modest star – one of ten billion trillion in the known universe.

It is generally held that the universe is 13.9 billion years old, and that our sun (a second generation star) is around five billion years old.

Note

A light year is the distance that light travels in a year, at a speed of 186,282 miles per second.

If I observe a galaxy at a distance of five billion light years, what I am seeing is the galaxy as it was five billion years ago. An observer on that galaxy today would not be able to observe our sun or planet earth, for they were not yet formed when the light from this part of the universe started its journey towards that observer.

The dimensions of the universe are determined by our ability to observe it. We cannot, for example, observe anything that is moving away from us at a speed greater than the speed of light, simply because the light from it would never reach us. Indeed, we cannot even know whether such a thing is possible.

We are part of the universe, not external observers; we can only see the universe from our own perspective.

b) 'Big Bang' Theory

> ### Note
>
> For the purposes of the Philosophy of Religion, it is necessary to have a grasp of the 'Big Bang' theory to the extent that you can show you appreciate the issues it raises for religious believers, in particular in its relationship to traditional religious ideas of creation and belief in God. The same is true of the dimensions of the universe. In an examination essay, you should avoid the temptation to expound the theory at length, even if you personally find it fascinating. Ask all the time 'How does this relate to religious beliefs?'

As was mentioned above, the further you look out into space, the further you look back in time. Although time and space can be considered separately for terrestrial measurements, when you are dealing with such huge distances, you cannot really consider the one without the other. The change in the dimensions of the universe therefore provides the clue to its age.

The spectrum of light changes and shifts towards the red if a body being observed is moving away at very great speed. In 1929 E P Hubble observed this **red shift** in the light coming from distant galaxies. This indicated that distant galaxies were moving away from us and away from one another. He also noted that those galaxies that are furthest away, are *receding faster* than those nearer to us. Hence, the universe is expanding and from the speed of its expansion it is possible to calculate its age, probably around 13.9 billion years.

Tracing the expansion backwards leads to a 'hot big bang', when all space, time and matter started to expand outwards from an infinitely small point, called a **space–time singularity**.

The 'hot big bang' *creates* space and time, in the sense that space and time as we know them are a feature of what is happening *within* that expansion. It is therefore extremely problematic to try to ask what happened *before* the 'hot big bang' because 'before' is a function of time, and the only time we know is time within our expanding universe. To ask about that 'before' we would have to step outside time and space.

However, it is always possible to imagine earlier states, other universes before this one, and so on. That is because, as Kant explained, the mind imposes ideas of space and time on everything it experiences or even thinks about.

It is, however, difficult to imagine a situation where everything that is now in our universe was compressed into a very small space – and perhaps that is because we think of that tiny space–time singularity as being 'within' a larger framework of space. The theory of a very short 'inflationary' phase, as the start of what is described as the 'big bang', sees the universe moving out from a tiny point to something perhaps the size of an orange. Even if the mathematics and physics suggest that it is so, it is still profoundly counter-intuitive (a term often used for theories that sound crazy) to imagine the universe that size. However, often in modern science it is necessary to step outside the normal way of thinking and visualising things, and to accept that some things can best be described mathematically or theoretically, even if they do not seem to make sense in terms of our everyday way of thinking.

The pure energy of the 'big bang' cooled as the early universe expanded, and became matter, spreading out uniformly in the form of hot gas. This cooled further and condensed, so that matter came together gradually, forming the galaxies.

The unevenness of the present universe, with clumps of galaxies and empty space between them, may have been caused by slight quantum variations during the very earliest 'inflationary' phase of the 'big bang', causing the first 'ripples' in the otherwise uniform universe.

Note

Although the theory was developed from an observation of present expansion, evidence for the 'big bang' comes from two other sources:

1 Background radiation – the final glimmer from that original moment when the universe was very hot and uniform, before matter was formed, has been found uniformly spread in all directions.
2 The balance of hydrogen and other elements in our present universe, corresponds to the quantities predicted by the 'Big Bang' theory.

c) Religious Views

The 'Big Bang' theory is based on observation and reason. It is a working hypothesis, aimed at giving the best possible explanation of the phenomenon of an expanding universe. Aristotle, the Stoics, Aquinas and others believed that the world was a rationally ordered place. Aquinas in particular sought to reconcile Christian faith with the best natural philosophy of his day (Aristotle's).

In principle, therefore, asking how religious views of creation relate to the 'big bang' is not so different from asking how a Christian view of God related to the idea of an 'uncaused cause' or a 'logos' (word) or rational purpose in creation – an idea developed by the Stoics.

i) Creatio Ex Nihilo

Most Christians believe that God created the world 'out of nothing' (*creatio ex nihilo*). In other words, everything comes from God. He is not simply an agent who reshapes existing material, and there is no sense in which the world is independent of him or could have existed in any form before his act of creation.

The idea of creation was expressed in this way in order to distinguish mainstream Christian beliefs from the ideas of those who held the view that matter was evil in itself, and that it could not have been brought about by God. By contrast *creatio ex nihilo* affirms that the world cannot be evil, since it is directly created by God.

However, we need to be aware that, in Genesis, God is described rather more in terms of one who shapes and gives form to previously formless matter. It sees the beginning as without form and void – a watery darkness – before God speaks the word and there is light, and so on, through the whole sequence of creation. Also, there are modern theologians who describe God in terms of his being involved with the ongoing process of creation.

Hence there is no single religious view of creation to contrast with the scientific account of the origin of the universe. As we saw in the previous chapter, religious language is not to be taken in a superficial or literal way, but expresses meaning and significance for believers. Hence it would be naïve to present the 'religious' and 'scientific' views alongside one another as though they were equivalents.

ii) Deism

The full Christian doctrine of God as creator also contrasts with the deist view of God as an *external* agent or designer. For the deist, God is located 'outside' the world, which is like a machine that he has created and left to run on its own.

The theist view, by contrast, is that God is *both* 'immanent' (within the world) *and* 'transcendent' (beyond the world). There is no separate order outside the direct knowledge and control of God.

Note

The Christian doctrine of creation is about **agency** (that God made the world) whereas the 'Big Bang' theory is about the **mechanism** by which the world came into existence.

These are not incompatible. A theist could claim that the 'big bang' was the mechanism by which God created the world.

---

iii) Creationism

Creationists refuse to accept modern, scientific theories about the origins of the universe, since they believe that it was created exactly as described in the Bible. Creationism developed largely as a result of the debates in the nineteenth century about human origins and evolution. Sometimes they offer alternative explanations for the scientific findings, but when they do so, the intention is to bring science into line with the Bible, rather than evaluating different scientific possibilities in an objective way.

Creationism depends on a literal interpretation of the Bible. In other words, it assumes that the Book of Genesis sets out to give a factual account of events that took place at the beginning of the world. Questions about how human beings could know what happened before they were created are dismissed as the Bible is believed to be directly inspired by God, and therefore that God made the facts known to those who wrote the biblical texts.

Creationism sees the authority of the Christian religion as threatened by a non-literal interpretation of the Bible, and that – as inspired by God – the Bible cannot be wrong. Both points can be disputed by Christians who take a different interpretation of the nature of the Bible, and of the authority on which Christianity is based.

iv) Non-literal Interpretations of Creation

Biblical scholars examine the nature of biblical texts, pointing out the way they are put together and the uses that they might have had in earlier times. As a result, it is the generally held view in the academic community that religious stories were told for a religious purpose, not just in order to set down a historical record. This applies particularly to the early 'myths' of creation. By 'myth' is meant a story that is told for a particular religious purpose – its truth is not necessarily to be found in the literal meaning of the words, but in the relationship between God and humankind that it attempts to express.

Theologians (e.g. John Macquarrie, in his *Principles of Christian Theology*) are concerned to examine what doctrines of creation say about human meaning and values. If you do not believe in God as creator, you may think of yourself (and all other creatures) as independent, self-directing and not answerable to any external agency. In other words, the world 'just is' and you are in it – nothing more needs to be said. On the other hand, if you believe yourself to be created by God, you will think of yourself as having been made by him for some purpose. Thus the religious and secular views of creation lead to very different views of the self and of its responsibilities.

This suggests that the actual mechanics of how the world came about are less important for the religious person than the overall view that the world is made by and under the control and authority of God.

> **ISSUE:**
> What kind of 'god' is compatible with what we know of the dimensions and nature of the universe?

d) Implications for 'God'

The relationship between God and the world is expressed by the following terms:

▼ **Deism** – belief in an 'external' God, who created the world but then stood back and let it run itself.

▼ **Pantheism** – belief that the physical world *is* God.

▼ **Panentheism** – belief that God is found within the physical world, although he also transcends it.

▼ **Theism** – belief that God is both immanent in the world and also transcendent (this is also the view of panentheism, which was devised as a way of emphasising that God was not remote, but found within everything).

From a deistic point of view, all that is needed is that the world displays some sense of intelligent design – there is little problem with modern cosmological theories about how it started.

Equally, pantheism presents no problems, since the world is the object of worship, and the more impressive its scale and origins the better.

Theism and panentheism need to emphasise that God continues to operate within the world as the source of creativity. Hence the focus shifts from what might have happened in the first fraction of a second after the 'big bang' to issues about whether the present unfolding of the world shows the action of a creator God.

i) Does our Perception of the World Need a 'God'?

It is tempting to use God to explain only those things for which there is no physical explanation. This has led to the 'God of the gaps' situation, where the 'gaps' in our knowledge, into which God can be slotted as an explanation, are reduced as science progresses.

However, Aquinas used Aristotle's idea of the 'unmoved mover' in order to explain the origin of change. In other words, he identified God with the most general of features of the world – something that was absolutely necessary for the world to make sense. If God is the 'uncaused cause' or 'unmoved mover', then everything depends directly on him – he is not 'tacked on' to an otherwise autonomous universe. By contrast, Newtonian physics argued for a set of fixed laws, with objects continuing at rest or in uniform motion unless acted upon by an external force. Hence, from the perspective of Newtonian physics, only an initial cause or mover was needed – all subsequent movement could be accounted for by the laws of motion.

Clearly, the more comprehensive our understanding of the workings of the universe in terms of physical laws, the less God is able to be introduced 'into' it as one of the factors that cause it to be the way it is. On the other hand, a god who *could* be introduced 'into' the world in that way would not be the God of theism, because that would make him part of the universe – 'a being' rather than 'being itself'.

If the idea of God is to be related to that of a rational and predictable universe capable of being understood by science, then it needs to be as a *source* of order and reason, rather than as an *alternative* to them. This is to reaffirm what Aquinas was arguing for; a God who is not *one* cause among others, but who is *the uncaused cause of everything*.

But the question remains: Is such a God compatible with the personal, intervening God of religion who is involved with human life and responds to prayer?

3 Freedom and Determinism

The issue of human freedom is a topic to be considered under ethics – since, if you are not free to decide what you will do, you cannot be blamed for your action. In this sense, a world where everything is completely determined is one in which morality makes little sense.

But there is another aspect to the issue of freedom and determinism; the aspect that arises out of the scientific approach and the way in which it deals with the idea of causality. This relates to issues such as the nature of God, miracles, prayer and the nature of the self, and it is this sense of freedom and determinism with which we are concerned in this chapter.

Note

The two aspects are closely related to one another, of course. We are here concerned with the fundamental understanding of what freedom and determinism are about and how they colour the way we understand the universe as a whole. The ethical aspect is simply the application of such understanding to the questions of moral choice.

The philosopher Hume said:

> 'tis commonly allowed by philosophers that what the vulgar call chance is nothing but a secret and conceal'd cause.

[From *A Treatise on Human Nature*]

In other words, he is acknowledging what we are not going to examine – the fundamental assumption of science that everything has a sufficient explanation and cause, even if we do not know what that cause is. Randomness and surprise events are held to be a sign that our knowledge is limited, rather than a suggestion that they do not have causes that could, in theory, be known.

Pierre Laplace (1749–1827) argued that an ultimate intelligence that knew everything about the universe in the present and all the laws of nature would therefore also be able to know all future events, simply because all future events arise as a result of causes and conditions that are found in the present. In effect, he was saying that the future only appears undetermined and capable of surprising us because we are ignorant of all the causes working within the world.

Of course, the idea that everything is causally determined may simply reflect the way in which our minds interpret the world. This view was put forward by Kant, who distinguished between:
▼ **phenomena** (the experience we have of things)
▼ **noumena** (things as they are in themselves).
He argued (see page 148) that everything in the world of phenomena is causally conditioned, simply because our minds are organised to impose causality on our experience. Science appears to deal with things in themselves (it is about the 'real' world), but in actual fact, the philosophy of science shows that all science can do is analyse and predict on the basis of what is experienced. In other words, it is still dealing with the 'phenomenal world', and hence, it must always be dominated by the idea of universal causality, because that is the way our minds work.

Complete causal explanations impact upon religious beliefs. What is the place for God in a fully determined world?

Note: Compatibilism

A key question for anyone considering human free will is whether it is compatible with a determinist view of the world. This will be considered in chapter 10.

a) The 'God' Hypothesis?

> ### Note
>
> In presenting his view of the laws by which the universe operated, Laplace was asked by Napoleon where God fitted into his scheme. He famously replied 'I have no need of that hypothesis.'

Although Laplace, in considering the way in which the laws of nature determined every event, thought that there was no need to include God in the scheme, the idea of the world being determined actually helps the idea of an omniscient God:

▼ If everything is determined, a God who knows everything can know the future as well as the past.

▼ If future events are not determined and we are free to shape them, then God cannot know what those events will be, because he will not know what we will freely choose to do.

And it does not really help to argue that God knows what we will freely choose to do, because that implies that our freedom is only illusory – we think we are free, but God actually already knows what we will choose. But does God's knowledge determine what will happen?

The claim that God knows freely chosen choices cannot be proved true or false. For each additional claim to freedom (I changed my mind at the last minute) it can be argued that God knows you are going to change your mind at the last minute, and so on.

Brian Davies, in *An Introduction to the Philosophy of Religion*, suggests that if God is all-knowing, he might well know what I will freely choose to do at some point in the future.

But this seems to create a logical problem:

▼ I am free to make a choice if, and only if, there are at least two possible things to choose between.

▼ If God knows that I can choose freely, he must allow for both the possible outcomes.

▼ Therefore he cannot *know* which of those outcomes I will choose without denying me my freedom to make that decision.

The only alternative to this would be to return to Hume's point – that we only think we are free because we do not understand all the factors at work influencing us. This was also the view of Spinoza, who saw everything in the world as totally determined by physical causes, with no scope for human freedom. We think ourselves free to the extent that we don't understand the universal nature of causality.

Richard Swinburne's approach, in *The Existence of God*, is to argue that to say that God is all-knowing implies that he knows all that it is *logically possible* to know. Hence he cannot logically know the result of an absolutely free decision before it is made.

Hence the experience of human freedom seems to go against the idea of an actually omniscient God, *if God exists in time.* Of course, if you hold that God is timeless (i.e. outside the realm in which it makes sense to speak of past, present and future) then he could know past, present and future *all at once* – for a timeless being would not have a past or a future, just one infinite present.

Such a timeless God is sometimes described as having **acausal knowledge**. In other words, he can know the future without thereby actually determining what will happen in that future. The problem with that, from a religious point of view, is that a God with acausal knowledge is outside time and is therefore impotent. Shaping the future is what action is about, and action takes place within time – a God who does not exist within time, does not act in time, and therefore does not get anything done.

Note

Anselm argued in *Proslogion* that God is not in time, but time is in God. Hence God does not experience past, present and future, but only one continuous present – a permanent 'now'. If that is the case, it makes no sense to say that God is 'free' to decide what will happen in the future, since he is there already. We are free to the extent that we have a past and a future. In a permanent present, we would be absolutely fixed and immovable (because movement is measured in terms of time).

---

b) Hard and Soft Determinism

This distinction is particularly important for ethics (see page 172). The determinism that has been described so far within this section is termed **hard determinism**. This implies that everything, including every action of human beings, is theoretically capable of being explained in terms of its pre-existing causes. If we knew everything that happens in the world now, then we could in theory know everything that will happen in the future – this is the sort of view taken by Spinoza, Laplace and most scientists.

However, in order to maintain a hard determinist position, it is necessary to reduce human beings to the status of machines, programmed to work along certain lines and therefore theoretically predictable. We are part of the global mechanism, determined by cause and effect.

Soft determinists want to hold that we can recognise that there are influences on the way we behave, and that we cannot be entirely free, and yet they are unwilling to say that humans are like machines and therefore 100% predictable. In ethics a soft determinist is termed a **compatibilist** – in other words, human freedom is seen as compatible with the basically scientific view of cause and effect (see page 174).

▼ A hard determinist would say that human personality and choice of action is essentially unreal – an illusion created by our ignorance of all the causes that condition us.

▼ A hard determinist would also have to say that God cannot (without deliberately setting aside the laws of nature, if that is possible) interact with the world. If he does so, then the world is no longer the sort of predictable place where scientists can measure and predict things and formulate theories.

i) God's Action and Prayer

The discussion of freedom and determinism raises a fundamental problem for religious believers. Is the world the sort of place where God can decide to change the normal course of events and human beings act in completely unpredictable ways? If so, it makes sense to pray for things to happen and to anticipate miracles.

Or is the world capable of being understood in a rational way, where events follow a (theoretically) predictable course? If so, it is reasonable to believe that you can examine and predict what will happen, without fear that some spiritual force will decide on a whim to change a law of nature. However, it makes little sense in such a world for God to intervene, nor can prayer be thought to actually make a physical difference to a situation.

MAKING CONNECTIONS

Free will and determinism issues link with:

▼ **The nature of God questions** – Is God omniscient? Can God know the future?

▼ **Cosmological Arguments** – If God is the uncaused cause, and the end term in the causal series, does he not thereby determine everything?

▼ **Ethics** – Morality only becomes a viable experience if we are free to choose.

▼ **Problem of evil** – If God determines all that happens, he is guilty of all that happens.

▼ **Existentialist philosophy** – We can only start to explore what it means to be a human being, choosing between genuine options and shaping our lives, if freedom exists.

▼ **Miracles and prayer** – Both become problematic in a determined world.

DEBATE
Be ready to argue whether God is irrelevant, if the future is determined.

4 Miracles

At the time when the Bible was written, a majority of people believed that events were not determined by fixed laws of nature, but were the result of the action of God or spirits. This was particularly true of unusual events and those that were important religiously, politically or personally. The question people tended to ask was not 'How did that happen?' but 'What does it mean?' or 'Why did God choose to act in this way?'

In the Bible, God is thought of as active within the world, not simply a detached, external creator. He brings about victory or defeat for armies, stops the sun moving across the sky when extra time is needed, heals the sick or strikes people down with illness. Those who disobey him are punished.

Even today, a religious person may ask 'Why should this happen to me?' when something terrible happens. They will not be satisfied by a practical answer in terms of the causes of disease, or the failure of a machine that caused an accident. Rather, they are asking why God should allow this to happen. This is considered as part of the 'problem of suffering'.

The opposite side of the same coin is the idea of 'miracles' – that certain events are interpreted as the direct result of God's action. With the rise of modern science, there developed the general view of the world as an ordered mechanism. Newtonian physics seemed to give an account of the causes of all events in terms of the laws of physics, and therefore miracles came to be regarded as violations of the laws of nature. This is therefore a suitable starting point for considering the idea of miracles, for the philosopher Hume argued that there could never be sufficient evidence to show that a miracle (when defined as a violation of a law of nature) had taken place.

However, after examining Hume's criticism, we also need to look at whether there are other ways of understanding the meaning and significance of miracles – ways that might not come into such direct conflict with modern science.

a) Hume's Criticisms

Note

Hume's argument is not that miracles cannot happen, but that – given the amount of evidence that has established and confirmed a law of nature – there can never be sufficient evidence to prove that a law of nature has been violated.

David Hume was an empiricist, in other words, he believed that all knowledge is based on evidence that we gain through the senses, and which the mind then sorts out to give us the information we need.

He works on the basis of a definition of a miracle as 'a violation of a law of nature', and his argument presents a major challenge to this view.

He argues that laws of nature are based on evidence. The more evidence we have, the more certain we are about them. We proportion our belief to the strength of evidence we have.

However, if a miracle goes against a law of nature, then it represents a single piece of evidence that goes against all the rest. So, for example, if we let go of a heavy object, it falls to the ground. That observation, repeated many times, confirms our understanding of the law of gravity. If I then hear an account of a heavy object floating upwards of its own accord, I ask myself which is the more likely: that the report is mistaken, or that it actually happened.

Hume argues that since we proportion belief to evidence, there can never be enough evidence to prove that a miracle has taken place.

The argument is set out very clearly in the following passages:

> A wise man ... proportions his belief to the evidence. In such conclusions as are founded upon an infallible experience, he expects the event with the last degree of assurance, and regards his past experience as a full *proof* of the future existence of the event. In other cases he proceeds with more caution: He weighs the opposite experiments: He considers which side is supported by the greater number of experiments; to that side he inclines, with doubt and hesitation; and when at last he fixes his judgement, the evidence exceeds not what we properly call *probability*. ...
>
> A miracle is a violation of the laws of nature; and as a firm and unalterable experience has established these laws, the proof against a miracle, from the very nature of the fact, is as entire as any argument from experience can possibly be imagined ... The plain consequence is (and it is a general maxim worthy of our attention), 'That no testimony is ever sufficient to establish a miracle, unless the testimony be of such a kind that its falsehood would be more miraculous than the fact which it endeavours to establish; ...

[From *An Enquiry into Human Understanding*]

Hume also considers the matter of the reliability of the witnesses to a miracle, and whether or not they may be mistaken in their understanding and reporting of what they have seen. It is clear that he sees miracles as belonging to pre-scientific cultures, and is therefore not inclined to believe them. Typical of the scientific and philosophical thinking of his time, he sees the world as a rational and ordered place, and all talk of miracles suggests a return to an earlier way of understanding the world.

i) Inductive Arguments

Note
Remember that scientific laws are **descriptive**, not **prescriptive**. In other words, a 'law of nature' cannot dictate what *must* happen; it summarises what *has been found to happen*.

There are two very different kinds of argument: **inductive** and **deductive**. A deductive argument works on the basis of logic and is based on principles of reason. Because one thing is believed to be true, another is 'deduced' from it.

Inductive arguments are built up more slowly and are based on evidence. Basically, evidence is gathered and a theory to explain the evidence is devised. Based on that theory, it is possible to anticipate what will happen. Observations are made, and if the anticipated thing happens, then it confirms the theory.

Mostly, science is based on inductive arguments – that is why the gathering of evidence is so important for science. What Hume has produced as an argument against miracles is inductive, since it is based on the vast number of occasions when a miracle has *not* happened. However, inductive arguments, being based on experience, always lead to **degrees of probability**, which is why Hume is careful to qualify his argument and explain that there can never be enough evidence to prove a miracle, *not* that a miracle can never occur.

ii) Limitations of Hume's Criticism

As a piece of inductive logic, setting out the likelihood of a miracle taking place, it is difficult to fault Hume's argument. If a miracle is a 'violation of a law of nature' then he has a good case for not believing an account of any such event.

However, from what we have already seen about religious experience and religious language, what makes something 'religious' is often a matter of interpretation, rather than fact. A violation of a law of nature (i.e. an inexplicable event) need not be seen as a miracle, and may have no religious or personal significance whatever. Science only makes progress because it encounters inexplicable events. So, for an understanding of miracles from a religious point of view, something else is needed.

b) Regularity and Particular Events

In the light of Hume's argument, it might be tempting to think that religion is on the side of a world where miracles (in the form of violations of natural laws) can happen, whereas science, with its inductive arguments and gathering of data, leads to a world that is regular, predictable and free from divine influences.

However, matters are not that simple. The Cosmological and Teleological Arguments for the existence of God were based on the idea of a world which displayed regularity and design – a world which, understood as a whole, led to the idea that it was designed and sustained by God.

The problem is that religious believers appear to want to have it both ways:

1 Given the regularity and predictable nature of the world, they argue that this suggests that it is sustained and guided by God.
2 But they may then argue that events are 'miracles' and therefore directly caused by God, simply because they do not fit the regular and predictable nature of the world.

A key issue, therefore, is to decide how the particular is to be related to the general, and which of them is the more important for religion.

Some philosophers of religion look to the rational and regular aspects of the world as evidence of an overall intelligent creator. Others look to miracles and religious experiences – particular moments that go against the general experience of the world – as the basis for belief in a God who is able to disrupt the rational and the regular.

The problem is that belief in miracles suggests that the world is selectively unreliable.

i) Timing is Everything . . .

There are two ways in which some events may be described as 'miracles' but which do not involve the violation of laws of nature. Both involve timing:

A) A natural event that has been either speeded up or slowed down.

Thus, for example, there is the story in the Old Testament of the sun being slowed down in its movement across the sky, in order to give more time for a battle. Equally, a person may recover from a serious disease, but this does not usually happen instantly. Thus it is not *what* happens that counts as a miracle, but the *speed* at which it happens.

This interpretation cannot overcome Hume's criticism, since the speed at which something happens is part of its fundamental nature, and part of what we observe to happen on a regular basis. If plants are said to shoot ready-grown out of the ground, that would be no more credible simply because plants do normally grow in that way, although slowly!

B) A natural event that happens at a particularly opportune moment.

Some might want to argue that an earthquake felled the walls of Jericho, or that a strong wind parted the Red Sea – both perfectly natural events. However, the miracle was that they happened at exactly the right moments for the Children of Israel to take advantage of them.

This does not involve any change in the way things happen, or the speed at which they happen. The event is normal enough – what appears to make it a miracle is its happening at exactly the 'right moment'. But what is a 'right moment'? For the occupants of Jericho, about to be slaughtered now that their defensive walls are down, the earthquake could not have happened at a worse time. Nor would the Egyptian army, bogged down in the mud and about to be drowned, have thought it a good time for the wind to have dropped.

Clearly, then, it is not timing that counts for something to be considered a miracle, but the interpretation of that event – and (as we have seen) that interpretation may be personal and one-sided.

ii) The Unlikelihood of Everything

Every particular event is a unique combination of causes and conditions. You could not be you, with your unique DNA, without a huge number of particular choices made by generations of people. You would not be you without an almost infinite number of sexual acts performed by people who happened to meet, generation after generation, stretching back into pre-history.

On the one hand, given complete knowledge of your entire family history, you are inevitable. On the other, the chances of you happening were millions and millions to one against! If anyone had chosen anyone else as their partner over the many generations, *you* would not be here. Someone would be here, but it would not be exactly you.

So an event cannot be considered a miracle just because it is unique.

POINTS TO CONSIDER

As you are unique, the chances of you existing are so small that it is unreasonable for anyone to believe in your existence.

On the other hand, you were not optional. Given what has happened, you could not but exist.

c) Interpreting Miracles

Unusual, or even unique, events are not automatically to be considered miracles. As we saw above, everyone is unique, every birth is therefore a miracle. The opening of every flower, or the natural recovery from an illness can be seen as a 'miracle' by a religious person. On the other hand, those same events, however wonderful, are not considered miracles by those who do not interpret life as being influenced by a God.

One person's miracle is another person's disaster; it all depends on your point of view. So to call something a miracle is not to describe it, but to give it value. 'Miracle' is an interpretation of an event, not an event in itself. In other words, as found in religion, miracles are those events which express the particular will of God in a situation. However, that leaves open the further issue, which we saw above, about why God, if he exists, should have need of miracles at all. Why, if the world is designed by God, should he need to keep interfering to put right things that do not work according to his intentions?

MAKING CONNECTIONS

Naturally, this consideration of the purpose of miracles leads straight into the 'problem of evil'. If God creates and is in charge of everything, then why should anything bad exist, such that it needs to be fixed by a 'miracle'.

The nineteenth-century philosopher Feuerbach argued that miracles were projections of human desires. They represented the things that people longed for, rather than those that actually happened. Therefore they could be emotionally and religiously important, although he did not believe that they actually took place.

Considering the problems that arise in attempting to show that an event is a miracle, and recognising that miracles are not just unique events, but events which show value and purpose, some people want to redefine miracles in such a way that they do not have to be proved to be impossible on ordinary scientific principles, but are simply ways of showing God's action in the world.

The problem with this is that it effectively makes the concept of a miracle redundant. A religious person may see God acting everywhere, in common events as well as in rare ones. Unless a miracle is *at least* a violation of a law of nature, even if it is many other things as well, then there seems no point in calling it a miracle at all.

i) The Unfairness of Miracles

If God is seen acting in particular situations, using miracles to overcome suffering for some people rather than others, then his action in the world may be seen as unfair. This point is made particularly by Maurice Wiles, a Christian theologian. He wants to consider God's action in the world as a whole – perhaps by inspiring people to help in situations of suffering – rather than intervening to help only the lucky few.

As traditionally understood, miracles – if they are indeed violations of the laws of nature – lead straight to the 'problem of evil'. Not just why God has created a world in which there is evil, but why, if he is capable of producing miracles to help the few, he does not do so for *all*.

d) Miracles and Prayer

There are different forms of prayer. Those that seek to align the believer's mind with God's will, or that simply express thanks, celebration or confession of sins do not present problems – for they do not seek to change what happens, only to understand and evaluate it.

However, petitionary prayer – where the believer asks God to make something happen, or prevent something from happening – directly relates to the issue of miracles.

If God does not 'answer' prayer, in the sense of making something happen, does that mean that he was unable to do so, or that he could have done so but chose not to?

As with the issue of 'unfairness' outlined above, this returns us to the 'problem of evil', since it is assumed that God, if he is both loving and omnipotent, would wish to overcome all evil and suffering.

On the other hand, if the thing prayed for takes place, it might be regarded as a miracle, but how could you tell whether it was a miracle, made possible by God as a direct response to the prayer? Might it have happened anyway?

The significance in calling it a miracle is that it is related to the wishes of the believer. In this sense, it follows what Feuerbach said about miracles in general – namely that they are the projections of people's wishes. There remains no way of demonstrating a direct causal connection between the prayer and the event.

Most religious people get out of the dilemma of petitionary prayer by adding 'nevertheless Thy will be done' to their request. That way, if the event does not take place, they can then seek to understand why it is God's will that it should not happen, rather than simply coming to the conclusion that God does not exist, or that he is unable to respond to prayer.

MAKING CONNECTIONS

There is a link here with the 'problem of evil', since to ask God to do something good that he does not already intend to do, implies that he is not all-loving. So there is no point (if one believes in an all-loving, omnipotent God) in praying for things that are good.

If it is good, God should have done it anyway. On the other hand, the believer might have thought that the thing asked for was good, when in fact it would have turned out to be harmful. In which case, God is wise not to answer the prayer. But, if so, then why pray for things in the first place – since petitionary prayer is either mistaken or redundant.

The implication here is that prayer, like miracles, poses real problems for the idea of an all-loving, omnipotent God. Just as miracles may be reinterpreted to emphasise that they refer to value and purpose, not just the factual occurrence of a rare event, so prayer may be redefined to emphasise its use in shaping the heart and mind of the believer, rather than trying to alter the course of events.

There are many other issues that could be taken up concerning how the idea of miracles relates to the nature of God, prayer, evil and so on. Our discussion here relates specifically to the interface between religion and science. The need to redefine the concept of miracle, moving away from the idea of a 'violation of a law of nature' is an attempt to avoid unnecessary conflict between the religious sense of the special action of God and the scientific understanding of the universe.

▼ ESSAY QUESTIONS

1 a) Explain Hume's argument that there can never be sufficient evidence to prove a miracle.
  b) Do you consider this sufficient reason to reject the idea of miracles?
2 a) Explain why science is often described as deterministic.
  b) Assess the problems that a determinist view poses for religious belief.

See the 'Further Reading and Websites' section at the back of this book for follow-up work on this chapter.

BODY AND SOUL

CHAPTER 6

POINTS TO CONSIDER

How are body and soul related?

If the mind is not in the brain, where is it?

Is it possible to survive the death of the body?

Are you just a body or do you have a body? And if you claim that you 'have' a body, then what is the 'you' that has it?

Just as, when we look at the world, it would be possible to say that it 'just is' and that it does not require any further explanation, so it would be possible to say that human beings 'just are' a certain kind of physical body, and that thought, speech, emotions and so on are all features of their physical systems. Thus it is possible to see a body – along with its brain and nervous system – as a self-contained entity, with no need for a 'soul' or 'self' to make it into a human being. However, people experience themselves as something more than a physical body. They are aware of a subjective 'I' that thinks, wills, decides and so on. But what constitutes that 'I'?

TIMELINE

c.428–374 BCE	Plato
384–322 BCE	Aristotle
1224–74	Aquinas
1596–1650	Descartes
1638–1715	Malebranche
1646–1716	Leibniz
1872–1970	Russell
1900–76	Ryle
1922–	Hick
1941–	Dawkins

1 Greek Ideas of the Soul

a) Plato

Plato was inspired by the life and death of his teacher Socrates who, when condemned to death, accepted it calmly. Socrates clearly thought that he was more than a physical body, and that after death his true self would go to a happier place. The central feature of Plato's view is a clear distinction between soul and body.

His thinking on the subject developed during his life. In the *Timaeus* he saw the soul (or *psyche*) as that which gives life to the body – a self-moving principle without which the body would be a corpse. However, this led him to believe that at some point the soul had to enter the body to give it life, and therefore must have existed prior to entering the body.

Later, in *Phaedo*, he made a further distinction. On the one hand there was the mind, or reasoning part, and on the other there were the emotions and natural responses to life, which he thought of as belonging to the realm of the body.

By the time he wrote *The Republic*, however, he saw the *psyche* as more complex, being responsible for reason, emotion and all other aspects of life. He illustrates the body/soul distinction by means of an analogy he makes between the soul and a city. He suggests that, just as the soul has three parts:

1 the reason
2 the spirited part (from which come emotions and passions)
3 the base appetites

. . . so the city has its philosopher-rulers or guardians, those who defend it and make it work, and the workers, who seek only the satisfaction of their needs.

He is trying to argue that the good working of a city requires the rulers, the defenders and the workers to operate as a unity, with each group playing its appropriate part for the good of the whole.

Clearly, therefore, Plato sees the soul as including, but not limited to, the reasoning part. The ideal life is one in which all three aspects of the self are balanced, with authority coming from the top down.

Hence, the well-balanced person has his or her appetites held in check by a sense of purpose and intention (the controlling or spirited element) and this, in turn, is under the rule of reason.

In *Phaedrus*, Plato describes a person as a chariot. The charioteer is reason, and the two horses that pull the chariot are will and appetite. The task of reason is to keep them in check.

Fundamental to Plato's philosophy (as illustrated by his analogy of 'the cave') is the idea that there is an eternal world of 'Forms', existing over and above the particular things that people can experience on earth. The philosopher, not content with the shadow-play of the things known to the senses, escapes from the cave and discovers the absolute, from which the particular things seen on earth have their source.

By demonstrating the fact that people seem to have an innate knowledge of certain abstract entities – like the principles of mathematics – which cannot be known simply through the senses, Plato argued that they must have a knowledge of these things from a previous existence, before birth into this world. Clearly, by passing through a river of forgetfulness, they cannot remember their previous lives, but nevertheless have this basic form of knowledge. However, Plato was not claiming that people arrive on earth with their knowledge already formed and ready for use. In book 6 of *The Republic* he argued that people were like plants, and that they could only develop if they were planted in good soil, since the soul takes on the characteristics of the environment within which it finds itself.

So it is clear that Plato has a basically dualist view of soul and body.

The body is physical and limited, the soul is essential and belongs to the world of the forms. The body can be destroyed at death, but the soul – not being physical – cannot be destroyed and therefore moves on into another life.

Note

It is important to decide exactly what is meant by self or soul. Is it the mind as a thinking thing? Or mind plus emotions and natural responses to life? Mostly, the general Greek term *psyche* (which we translate as 'soul' or transliterate as psyche) refers to the whole of the animating principle of human life. It is only later with the work of Descartes, that the mind was limited to the thinking aspect. Therefore the Cartesian dualism is rather different from the dualism of Plato.

Note

The Greek term for the thinking mind is *nous,* as opposed to the more general term for the soul, which is *psyche.* For Plato, *nous* or intellect, was given the key function of controlling all other aspects of the person.

---

b) Aristotle

Aristotle thought that all living things had souls, and that a creature's *psyche* was its 'principle of life' – that which distinguished it from a corpse or other inanimate thing. The distinctive thing about humans, however, was that, as well as having a psyche, they were capable of rational thought. He saw the thinking aspect as only part of the whole 'self' or *psyche,* but as that which distinguished humankind from other species.

Aristotle also saw the *psyche* as the 'form' that organised the material body and made it a human being. In this, the soul is not separate from the body, located in one particular place, rather it is what gives the living person their characteristics. The soul actualises the body; the body is organised by the soul. To use his own analogy, you can no more separate soul and body than you could separate the shape given to a lump of wax by a stamp from the wax itself. In other words, wax and shape may be different ideas, but you cannot separate them – where the shape is, there is the wax.

> ## Note
>
> Aquinas, following Aristotle, saw the soul as that which 'animated' the body, giving it life and form. Our word 'animated' comes from the Latin term '*anima*', meaning soul.
>
>> Now the soul is what makes our body live; so the soul is the primary source of all those activities that differentiate levels of life: growth, sensation, movement, understanding. So, whether we call our primary source of understanding mind or soul, it is the form of our body.

[From *Summa Theologiae*, Vol II 76:1]

2 Some Modern Thinkers

The term 'modern philosophy' (as opposed to Ancient or Mediaeval Philosophy) is generally taken to refer to the period starting in the seventeenth century with Descartes. Many of the theories about the relationship between the body and mind that have been argued since that time either follow or react against Descartes' ideas.

In general, there are three possibilities for the mind/body relationship:

▼ That a human being is purely physical; there is no separate soul. (Materialist theories)

▼ That a human being is essentially mind; the body is an illusion. (Idealist theories)

▼ That there exist both bodies and minds, distinct, but joined in some way. (Dualist theories)

Figure 6 There is something uncanny about a 'stone man', who appears to be an inanimate statue until he starts to move. Does that suggest that the soul and body are distinct and separable? Or is 'being alive' simply a way of describing the movement of bodily parts?

Idealist theories have little appeal today; for most thinkers, the fact of the physical body is a basic assumption. Idealism is mainly of interest in terms of epistemology (the theory of knowledge), where it can be argued that all we know directly are ideas in the mind, produced by information fed into the mind by the senses. We cannot know the physical world except through the mind, and it is therefore something that has to be inferred from our mental representations. This, for example, is the view taken by Berkeley.

Materialist theories deny the reality of a separate mind or soul. They either see it as unnecessary to account for the phenomena of human life (e.g. Richard Dawkins) or as a linguistic mistake, such that to describe mental phenomena is simply a way of describing certain aspects of physical behaviour (e.g. Gilbert Ryle).

Mostly we have the various forms of **dualism**, attempting to reconcile the fact that we are seen by others as an animated body, but are aware of ourselves as thinking, feeling and communicating. How are these external and internal worlds to be reconciled?

a) Descartes

Descartes famously found that he could not deny his existence as a thinking being ('I think therefore I am'), he therefore saw a major distinction between the mind (which for him included feelings and sensations) and the body.

The mind was that of which he was aware, and which he could describe, but which he could not locate physically. He therefore made the absolute distinction between the body, which was extended in time and space, and the mind, which was not. Hence there are two very different realms – the mental and the physical.

Descartes therefore saw the mind/body relationship in terms of a conjoining of these two different realms: the mind that was known immediately through introspection, and the body, which was known through the senses and which was controlled by mechanical forces.

His problem was how two such different things as mind and body could influence one another. To appreciate Descartes' difficulty here, we need to remember that his physics required physical contact for one thing to influence another, for he was writing at a time before Newton had developed the idea of forces operating at a distance. Hence, if the mind was to physically make a difference to a body (and clearly it did, otherwise it made no sense to choose to do anything) then there had to be some point in the physical world through which that non-physical mind could operate. He suggested that it was done through the pineal gland – a small part of the brain, located between the right and left hemispheres, for which he could find no other purpose.

Having started on the basis of his awareness of himself as a thinking being, Descartes established this absolute dualism, with the physical on one side and the mental on the other. The problem posed by how the two very different things could come together in order to bring about intelligent activity was to dominate thinking in the philosophy of mind for 300 years.

For Reflection

Did Descartes really solve his puzzle about how the mental could effect change in the physical? Or did he simply tuck the answer away in a conveniently inaccessible place? If the pineal gland is physical, how can it transmit mental commands?

---

i) Later Dualist Theories

Although beyond what is required at AS level, it is worth reflecting on the way in which later philosophers, following Descartes' dualistic view, tried to make sense of the relationship between mind and body.

The two philosophers who pushed Descartes' theory to the limits of credibility are Malebranche and Leibniz. Their theories, which have much in common, are termed **Occasionalism** and **Pre-Established Harmony** respectively. Neither could find a way of getting over the gap between the mental and the physical (later known as 'Leibniz' gap') and so they resorted to arguing that the mental and physical world worked independently of one another, with no causal connection between them. Thus feeling happy may be the 'occasion' of my face puckering up in a smile, but I cannot say that the former actually caused the latter to happen. Leibniz thought that God had established the two separate worlds of mind and matter and that he alone could enable them to work together in harmony.

Neither of these has survived as a popular theory into modern discussions. More relevant today (because of discussions of what is

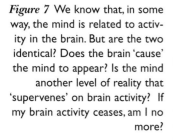

Figure 7 We know that, in some way, the mind is related to activity in the brain. But are the two identical? Does the brain 'cause' the mind to appear? Is the mind another level of reality that 'supervenes' on brain activity? If my brain activity ceases, am I no more?

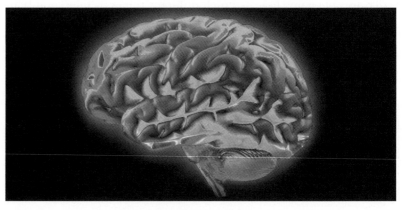

termed supervenience – where one level of reality 'supervenes' over another) is a theory known as **epiphenomenalism**. This argues that the mind is a by-product of the physical body, and in particular of the brain. Although mind and body are distinct, the former can only exist because of the latter. Mental activity is above, 'epi', the 'phenomenon' of brain activity – it is not the same as brain activity, but is caused by the brain.

The difference between epiphenomenalism and materialism is that a materialist might say that mental language is just a way of describing what the brain is doing, whereas an epiphenomenalist says that the mind is real, although brought about by brain activity.

b) Richard Dawkins

The difference between a living person and a dummy is that a living person responds to his or her environment, reproduces and forms a complex ever-changing entity, receiving nourishment and consuming energy. Rational beings also make choices, communicate, set about changing things in order to make life better, and perform a whole range of other physical and mental tasks.

We know that the instructions for putting a human body together are contained in our DNA. We are the product of our genetic instructions. But what about all those other features of life – the mental and personal features? Where do they come from? How are they related to the physical body?

The most radical answer that science can give is to say that behaviour is similarly determined by our genetic make-up. What might seem like a thoughtful act is simply the way we respond to the promptings of our genes. It is this approach, promoted in a range of books by Richard Dawkins including *The Selfish Gene* and *Climbing Mount Improbable*, that suggests that the whole range of living things is the outworking of a process of natural selection.

On the surface, this seems to deny anything corresponding to the 'soul', but in fact it is not quite that simple. Since the rise of modern science, it has been recognised that the physical world forms a closed system of causes. Our behaviour is, at one level, no more than the expression of chemical actions in our muscles and electrical impulses in the brain.

For Reflection

Just because a doctor could explain all the physical processes that are involved in walking, it does not mean that you can no longer claim to be able to walk. So a scientific description does not deny

> mental functions, it simply claims that what is experienced imme-
> diately by the subject self can also be analysed and explained
> physically.

It is also clear that all life, mental as well as physical, can be expressed in terms of bits of digital information. The title of one of Dawkins' books is *Unweaving the Rainbow*, and in it he points out that science is able to take wonderful phenomena, like the rainbow, and express them digitally. But the key point is that this does not make the rainbow any less beautiful, nor does it prevent us looking at nature with a sense of wonder, rather it expresses that wonder in terms of the bedrock of digital facts that make it up.

Dawkins thinks that there is no such thing as a soul. Given his over-all view of life, this is no surprise. The implication of this is that we cannot follow Descartes' attempt to find some pineal gland that will link the physical to a separate mental world. Everything can be described physically, and neuroscience is increasingly able to locate particular sensations and activities with particular areas of electrical activity in the brain.

As Dawkins presents it, everything has developed through a natural process. There is no injection of self or soul from outside; no need (as Plato had thought) to suggest a pre-existence in order to explain our knowledge.

3 Life Beyond Death

Most religions hold that, in some form, what you do in this life has implications for life beyond your own death – whether it is you personally who survive, or whether you await a final resurrection, or whether you take a succession of lives. We shall examine each of these options briefly.

> ### Note
>
> For the purposes of AS level, the key thing here is to be able to relate the issues of life beyond death to the different options in terms of minds and bodies, and to be able to show how some of the mind/body theories lend themselves to particular views about the possible survival of death.

a) Reincarnation

In Hindu philosophy, the self (*atman*) is eternal, and is essentially at one with Brahman, the absolute reality. The ultimate release (*moksha*) is achieved by those who see the separateness of the *atman* as an illusion.

> He who sees all beings in the self, and his self in all beings, he loses all fear.
>
> [From *Isa Upanishad 6*]

However, the *atman* is embodied, and when one body dies, the *atman* moves to take on another. The process that decides the nature of the new body is the law of **karma**, and it is believed that deeds performed in this life will influence the next incarnation.

Reincarnation is therefore dualistic, in that it sees a distinction between the *atman* and the physical body through which it lives. Yet it also claims that the *atman* (unless it has achieved the ultimate *moksha*) is always going to be expressed through a physical body. Hence the soul moves from one life form to another.

Notice, however, that whereas in the West the prospect of living on after death is generally presented as a positive thing, in Hindu thought it is something to be avoided if possible. Hopefully, through good karma, one might get a better incarnation next time, but the ultimate goal is to escape completely from the turning cycle of existence in this world.

MAKING CONNECTIONS

Clearly, the idea of karma and of reincarnation or rebecoming is linked to the traditional 'problem of evil'. If karma is taken literally, then it is possible to see present suffering as in some way linked to actions performed in a previous lifetime. The essential difference between the karmic approach to suffering and that of the western debates is that karma is seen as an impersonal outworking of cause and effect, whereas for theistic religions the problem is made more difficult because of the need to hold that God is both loving, omnipotent and yet allows suffering and evil to continue.

b) Rebecoming

The Buddhist idea of '**rebecoming**' is radically different from Hindu reincarnation and from all other theories of mind/body. This is because Buddhist teaching holds that there is no fixed, eternal *atman*, and therefore nothing that can pass from one life to the next.

But for Buddhists this is simply one aspect of an absolutely fundamental teaching – that there is no fixed self (*anatta*). A person is constantly changing in response to conditions. Not only is the body changing all the time, but so are the emotions, responses, habits and so on. Personal qualities are ways of describing how someone is behaving, they are not descriptions of some secret and permanent feature of the self.

For example

You do not play music because you are a musician; you are a musician because you play music. There is no secret 'quality' locked away called 'being a musician' – that is simply a description of a particular activity and set of skills that you possess. Similarly, it is not that good people do the right thing, but that those who do the right thing are called good. That said, it is also generally held that we can build up dispositions to act in a particular way.

As with Hinduism, the mechanism for change in Buddhism is the law of karma – which is generally understood in terms of actions having consequences. The karma – good or bad – are the natural consequences of your ethically significant actions, in other words, those over which you have exercised a measure of choice.

Rebecoming is a process that is seen throughout life, not simply at the point of death. The reason why it is believed to continue beyond death is that as a person's life comes to its end, some of the karma generated has not yet produced its results. These therefore work themselves out in another life.

But notice that – because there is no fixed self in Buddhism – we cannot really say that the person who experiences the karma that has been left over is the *same* person. Rather the most that can be said is that a future life will be influenced by that karma.

In popular Buddhism, especially in the Tibetan tradition, much is made of those who are spiritually advanced enough to be aware of their former incarnations. Traditionally, Buddhist philosophy has avoided being specific, and the Buddha (probably to avoid being misunderstood) refused to say what happens to an enlightened person after death.

c) Immortality

Clearly, in Hinduism, the soul is immortal. In western thought there is also a tradition of seeing the soul as separate from, and therefore separable from, the physical body. This led some philosophers to argue for the natural immortality of the soul.

Plato argued for the immortality of the soul on two grounds:

1 That all composite things can perish, but absolutely simple things cannot, because there are no constituent parts into which they can be divided. The body is composite and therefore perishable; the mind is simple, and therefore immortal.

2 Some of the things we know – like truths of mathematics, or the 'Forms' that we use to understand what individual things have in common – cannot come from seeing individual things, because they are concepts that come from the eternal realm. Therefore we must have had some knowledge of these things before our present birth, and have therefore 'remembered' them. Hence we must be immortal.

The argument for immortality need not be religious – indeed, Plato's arguments given above make no reference to beliefs, or the agency of God, or any idea of reward or punishment after this life. Indeed, immortality is inevitable if the soul is indeed simple and imperishable.

Similarly, the radical dualism of Descartes would be compatible with this idea of natural immortality, since the 'self' cannot be found in the interlocking series of things that make up the physical world.

i) Disembodied Existence

A problem with the idea of **disembodied existence** is that all that we know of another person – their habits, their likes and dislikes, what they think and what they say – is mediated to us via their bodies. Without a body, it is difficult to see how a person could be known, or could have a personality of any sort. A disembodied existence would need to communicate, but how?

A key problem with disembodied existence is that what we know of a person during his or her life is bound up with the interaction between their physical body and the various circumstances in which they find themselves. Everything about them, from their physical body to their patterns of thought, goes through a process of constant change. The baby will grow to be an adolescent, middle aged and eventually an elderly person – there is continuity, since that same person relates to the world at all stages of life, but it is set within a world in which everything changes. However, at whatever stage of life we meet a person, all that we know about them is given in terms of our relationship with them, which is mediated through the physical. This is not just their physical appearance, but how they speak and act; we know them because of the way they respond to us.

A disembodied existence, as a state that might continue beyond death, is therefore a most curious one. What would it mean to exist without a body? How would a disembodied existence be that of a person in any sense – for a person acts and changes, speaks and thinks, all things that are bound up with the ordinary world of space and time and physical objects?

KEY QUESTIONS

Do you believe in ghosts?

A survey in 2003 showed that 42% of people in Britain did. But how can you show that a ghost is real, has a personality, and is not just a feature of an excited imagination? How can you prove a disembodied existence? Could a ghost appear if it did not take on a body of some sort? Surely, if ghosts exist, you can only know who they are if they have some sort of physical appearance?

Bertrand Russell expressed the problem in this way:

> Our memories and habits are bound up with the brain, in much the same way in which a river is connected with the riverbed. The water in the river is always changing, but it keeps to the same course because previous rains have worked a channel. In like manner, previous events have worn a channel in the brain, and our thoughts flow along this channel. This is the cause of memory and mental habits. But the brain, as a structure, is dissolved at death, and memory therefore may be expected to be also dissolved. There is no more reason to think otherwise than to expect a river to persist in its old course after an earthquake has raised a mountain where a valley used to be.

[From *Why I am not a Christian* ..., Allen & Unwin, 1957]

d) Resurrection

The traditional Christian belief is not that people are immortal, but that they die and are then raised to life. This is important within Christian theology, because the idea of immortality is that you automatically, by your very nature, are able to survive death, whereas the Christian view is that you are completely mortal and have no such eternal element. Rather, what can happen at the resurrection is that you are given a new body, with which your self can live and express itself.

Exactly how the new body relates to the old is described as a mystery – something beyond human knowledge. But at least it recognises that for a person to have any meaningful existence, it is necessary to have a body.

In a modern attempt at restating the case for resurrection, we have seen that Hick believes that it would be possible to create a replica person, who would in effect 'be' the original person. In this way, it is possible to talk about that person 'living' after death, and their 'new' body is simply a replica of their old.

i) Is Resurrection a Logical Possibility?
In *An Introduction to the Philosophy of Religion*, Brian Davies examines the various theories and concludes that death followed by resurrection is at least a logical possibility. This is not the same thing as saying that it is possible. It is logically possible for me to jump 20 feet into the air. I know exactly what such a thing means. However, I also know that it is not *actually* possible.

It is an important first step to show that something is logically possible, because if it isn't then there is no point in discussing it any further. It is not just that square circles are not actual; they are not logically possible either.

In his book *Death and Eternal Life,* John Hick presents a story in order to explore the relationship between our physical body and our identity as a person. In the story, a man dies suddenly in London but then, at that same moment, appears in New York. The person in New York has an identical body, and also seems to have all the memories that belonged to the London man. Does that make him the same person?

The point that Hick seems to be making is not that it is *actually* possible to create some kind of replica person, but that – if it makes sense to think of that replica person as the same as the original – it also makes sense to at least consider the possibility of life after death in the form of a new physical body as a vehicle for expressing personal identity.

A replica might therefore have a body with which to express personality, and also a set of memories to inform the present choices and so on. If the replica 'is' the original person, it implies that life beyond death is at least conceivable. However, it might be argued that to be the same person requires numerical identity as well as physical continuity; and a replica does not have continuity with the original – for if it did, you would never be able to know that it was a replica or the original!

There is a basic question here: Would someone with a body and memory identical to mine actually be me?

If the answer to this is 'Yes', then life after death is theoretically possible. But, it also means that life after death is nonsense – for what we usually mean by death is the cessation of the person or organism. If what is logically possible became actually possible, it would effectively mean that death was a non-event. Whilst immortality assumed that there was a mind or spirit to continue after the death of the physical body, the idea of a reconstituted body effectively means that the changes that happen physically throughout life simply continue after what is called 'death'.

ii) To Conclude

For a materialist, there can be no prospect of a person surviving the death of their body, simply because they are their body. Their body may have changed radically during life – but it was still the same physical body.

For a dualist, the separation of soul and body makes survival at least a possibility. Although disembodied existence is difficult to conceive in another person (since I know others by perceiving them), I can imagine myself existing without a body, simply because I cannot imagine myself other than as existing. (Try it!)

Both materialist and dualist positions might be compatible with the idea of resurrection, but only if some sense of identity and continuity can be shown.

MAKING CONNECTIONS

The discussion of what, if anything, might happen after death has implications for the 'problem of evil', since it was traditionally believed that God might compensate people in an after life for the sufferings endured on earth.

However, this connects with the criticisms of religion from Marx, who saw just such ideas of compensation as a way of keeping people in check, but suggesting that they need not rise up and improve their situation here and now, because God would make it all right after death.

▼ ESSAY QUESTIONS

1 a) Describe the basic features of Cartesian dualism.
   b) Assess its strengths and weaknesses in accounting for what we experience as body and mind.
2 a) Are materialist views of the self compatible with life after death?
   b) Assess whether a materialist can be religious.

See the 'Further Reading and Websites' section at the back of this book for follow-up work on this chapter.

ETHICAL ARGUMENTS

CHAPTER 7

Ethics is the study of how people behave: what they do, the reasons they give for their actions, and the rationale behind their decisions.

There are two approaches to ethics:

1 **Descriptive ethics** – This simply describes the way people in different societies actually behave. It is closely related to sociology and psychology; it examines what we do and the background influences on us. It does not examine issues of right and wrong.

2 **Normative ethics** – This is the examination of issues of right and wrong, and how people justify the decisions they make when faced with situations of moral choice.

Does our behaviour actually follow from reason and principles we hold, or are we socially conditioned? If we had complete freedom to do whatever we liked with no fear of consequences, would we behave differently? This is one area where there is an overlap between descriptive and normative ethics, because descriptive ethics – using insights from psychology – can challenge the reasons people give for what they do. After all, a person may do what seems to be right, but do it for entirely the wrong reasons. It is possible to challenge most theories of normative ethics by arguing that people never act except in their own interest, but that they subsequently fabricate reasons for what they do.

The story of the Ring of Gyges, in Plato's *Republic*, tells of a shepherd who discovers a ring that has the power to make its wearer invisible. Behaving 'like a god among men' he is able to do whatever he likes without fear of being caught. The question posed is this: would there be any difference between what the moral or the immoral person might do, given that ring? Is there value in being moral, quite apart from the fear of being caught doing wrong, or the hope of what we might gain by doing right? If you had absolute freedom to do whatever you wanted without any fear of being caught, would you still obey moral principles?

TIMELINE	
c.428–374 BCE	Plato
384–322 BCE	Aristotle
1711–76	Hume
1873–1958	Moore
1898–1951	Wittgenstein
1905–91	Fletcher
1908–79	Stevenson
1910–89	Ayer
1919–	Hare
1932–	Searle

This is a key theme in the *Republic*, where Plato argues that it is better to be moral than immoral, irrespective of the consequences of one's action. This introduces another major question for all subsequent discussion of ethics: do you judge actions to be right and wrong on the basis of duty or of consequences?

As far as AS level Ethics papers are concerned, we are mainly concerned with normative ethics. Some descriptive ethics may be used, simply in order to set the scene for the moral decisions that are being examined, but descriptive ethics alone is inadequate as a response to examination questions. Later, we shall look at the problem of trying to establish an 'ought' from an 'is', but for now it is enough to be aware that no amount of factual background information, however interesting, is going to be enough to put together an ethical argument.

For a good ethical argument, you need to have facts and examples at your disposal (it would be most unwise to argue about something unless you know at least some basic facts about it). However, those facts are only relevant if they are linked to ethical theories to form part of a reasoned argument.

Hint

Whenever you include a piece of descriptive ethics in your essay, make sure you have a clear idea of the part it will play in your argument. Always imagine your next sentence will start with 'Therefore . . .' or 'So . . .'. If you cannot think of a next sentence that would start with either of those, there is a fair chance that you have not used the facts you know to their best advantage!

For example, you may say . . .

'Statistics show that murder rates are not reduced in states which practise capital punishment.'

But that only becomes part of an ethical argument if you then say . . .

'So . . .' and then argue that such statistics demonstrate that capital punishment cannot be justified on the grounds that it deters people from committing murder.

---

1   Some Key Terms

As we saw above, the term 'ethics' can be used simply in a descriptive sense, to denote the way people behave. Normative ethics, however, may also be called '**moral philosophy**', as it is the rational examination of morality. Generally speaking, the terms 'ethical' and 'moral' mean the same thing, but ethics usually implies a rational and systematic study of moral issues.

It is important to distinguish between the following three ways of describing an action:

▼ **Moral** – An action is moral, for the person performing it, if it conforms to his or her set of ethical norms. These may be personal, religious or established by a group or profession.

▼ **Immoral** – An action is immoral, for the person performing it, if it goes against a professed set of norms. However, that action may be immoral according to one set of norms and moral according to another, so people may not necessarily agree on this.

▼ **Amoral** – An action is amoral if it is done without reference to moral norms, or values that imply a moral perspective. In other words, falling over accidentally may have painful consequences, but it is entirely amoral, because the person did not choose to fall or not to fall. It would only become a moral act if there was some sort of personal responsibility involved.

Note

An action may be seen as moral, immoral or amoral depending on *circumstances*. What may be thought of as moral for one person may be immoral for another, depending on the situation and the cultural and religious norms. Equally, the action of a wild animal is entirely amoral – since animals cannot reason ethically – but for a human being to do the same would be either moral or amoral.

There is another important distinction. Ethical theories that are based on rights and duties are termed **deontological**. In other words, actions are judged good or bad according to rules and principles; if you have a duty to do something, then it is right to do it, irrespective of the consequences.

Alternatively, there are theories that depend on the expected results of an action – for example, the idea that it is right to seek to achieve the greatest good for the greatest number (utilitarianism). All such theories are called **teleological** (from the Greek word 'telos' meaning 'end' or 'purpose').

2 Presenting an Ethical Argument

An argument moves from **premises** to **conclusions**. The premises are the starting point for your consideration of a topic: they include the facts about the particular ethical issue (including its significance, what the law has to say, what society expects, and so on), and also the principles upon which you are going to base your argument. In the next section we will be looking at an outline of the common ethical theories. You need to know these, to decide which of them is relevant to the topic you are going to be arguing about, and to have considered how that particular theory can be applied to the topic about which you are going to argue.

Your essay will be assessed on the premises (did you understand the situation, the law, the theory and so on) and on your ability to argue logically to a conclusion, showing that you can apply the ethical theory appropriately.

Remember:

▼ Facts in themselves do not make an argument. Some of the ethical issues included in examination specifications are complicated. Thus, for example, a medical or genetic issue may be complicated by the number of different approaches and outcomes. Learning these may be useful, but they cannot simply be put down as an alternative to presenting an argument.

▼ If you are using one of the traditional ethical theories as the basis of your argument, make sure you know it and state what it is.

▼ When you state your own conclusions, make sure you also give your reasons for them.

▼ If you are arguing from the standpoint of a particular religion, state that clearly.

▼ Make sure you know at least one alternative point of view from your own. State it and say why you reject it, and why – on balance – you consider your own view to be superior.

3 Meta-Ethics

Meta-ethics is the term used for discussion about the nature and validity of ethical statements. In other words, it is what is generally called a second-order language. Whereas an ethical statement concerns what is right or wrong, a meta-ethical statement is about what it means to claim that something is right or wrong, and the grounds on which it does so.

Hence all questions about whether ethics is meaningless, or about the validity of ethical questions, or how 'good' should be defined, are **meta-ethical questions**.

Before going further with ethics, it is important to get some idea about the meaning of the key term 'good'. After all, if you do not know what counts as 'good' then you have no means of evaluating an action or saying that something is right or wrong. However, there are a variety of ways of defining 'good', and it is easy to get into a circular argument – in other words, you decide what is right and then call that 'good', but in order to decide what is right, you need to have some idea of 'good'.

We may start by asking:

▼ Is 'goodness' a quality that an object or action possesses, quite apart from other people's perceptions of it? Or is it simply that we decide to call something 'good' because we approve of it?

▼ Does 'goodness' depend on each person's view? If so, how do we decide between conflicting views of what counts as 'good'?

▼ Is there anything that all 'good' things have in common?

There are, broadly, three different approaches to defining what we mean by 'good' and therefore the validity of ethical statements. They are:

▼ ethical naturalism

▼ ethical non-naturalism

▼ ethical non-cognitivism.

a) Ethical Naturalism

With this approach, 'goodness' is something that exists and can be described. In other words, there is some point at which you can explain an ethical statement in terms of a non-ethical one. What is good may be found in particular qualities, or in the ability to promote the greatest happiness for the greatest number, or in something that fulfils its intended purpose.

Thus, for example, the philosopher Aristotle argued that everything had a 'final cause', the purpose for which it had been designed, and fulfilling that purpose was what made it 'good'. Thus, a good pen is one that writes well; if you know what a pen is, and what it's meant to do, you have an objective way of deciding whether a particular pen is good or bad. This approach led to the Natural Law theory of ethics, which we shall examine later.

So, if you believe that 'good' can be explained in terms of some feature of the world or of human life, then you can count yourself as an 'ethical naturalist'.

b) Ethical Non-naturalism

With this approach, 'good' is something that cannot be defined in terms of natural phenomena. We cannot point to something and say that it is inherently good because of the way it is made or the function it performs. Goodness is fundamentally something that we use to describe an object or action, not something that we discover within it. In this approach, ethical statements cannot be reduced to non-ethical ones.

For example, in *Principia Ethica* (1903), G E Moore claimed that in many ethical arguments people tended to start with facts and then slip into speaking of moral values, without making clear the basis on which they did so. He called this the '**naturalistic fallacy**', the attempt to derive an 'ought' from an 'is'. In other words, they slipped from saying what 'is' the case to saying what 'ought' or 'ought not' to happen.

He pointed out that you could not define 'good' in terms of some more basic idea or fact, and that values were applied to facts, not discovered among them. This same argument had been presented earlier by David Hume. Ethical non-naturalism does not deny the reality or meaningfulness of ethical statements, but points out that they cannot be proved with reference to facts.

Note

The American philosopher John Searle has argued that there is one sense in which you can derive an 'ought' from an 'is', and that concerns the agreements that people make (e.g. to keep promises). Those agreements can be described, and yet they state that one should keep to them. In other words, 'ought' can make sense in a *social* context. If something is agreed between members of a society, then they 'ought' to do it. Here the facts (the 'is') are about **social institutions**.

This links moral obligation with the philosophy of politics, which gives an account of the agreements made between people. We 'ought' to follow the Universal Declaration of Human Rights, because that is what has been agreed. Moral agreements may be made for mutual benefit.

BUT

Note that such agreements are always 'hypothetical' not 'categorical' (to use Kant's terms, see page 42). *If* you are to obey the law and avoid punishment, *then* you should do this or that. Agreements are not self-justifying.

Hint

Many candidates do not do themselves justice in an examination, simply because they commit the 'naturalistic fallacy'! Having put down all the relevant facts they can remember about a topic – like abortion or genetic engineering or punishment – they think that they have thereby answered the question. But facts need to be put into an argument; they need to be related to ethical theories, and to a candidate's own views. As was pointed out above, facts alone do not constitute a valid ethical argument.

i) Intuitionism

In avoiding the 'naturalist fallacy', Moore came to the conclusion that 'good' was a term that could not be defined or explained in terms of anything more basic; that is why he is described as an ethical non-naturalist.

He believed that 'good' was a quality that things could possess, but it was not one that could be defined – it was something that we naturally recognise and understand. Rather like the attempt to describe a colour, the attempt to define the word 'good' always runs into trouble, although everyone has some idea of its meaning. (Try describing what 'yellow' looks like, without simply indicating things that *are* yellow!)

This leads to an approach which is termed '**intuitionism**' (although Moore himself did not use that term). An intuitionist does not attempt to explain what 'good' is, and cannot do so, but argues that we intuitively know when something or some action is 'good'. Hence, moral judgements are self-evident.

The problem with intuitionism is that it makes ethical discussion very difficult, since there seems to be no reasoned basis upon which to argue. People may have different intuitions about what is right, but if they cannot justify their intuitions in any way, all they can do is continue to state them.

c) Ethical Non-cognitivism

Whether you take a naturalist or non-naturalist view of the meaning of 'good', any attempt to define that word suggests that ethical language is at least meaningful. Through much of the first half of the twentieth century, however, under the impact of an approach to philosophy developed by a group of thinkers known as the Logical Positivists, there was much serious 'meta-ethical' debate that suggested that ethical language was **non-cognitive** – in other words, that it did not give any kind of information, but was merely an expression of the emotions or wishes of the person using it. Hence, they argued that ethical language was *literally* meaningless. This view is termed ethical non-cognitivism.

4 The Meaning of Ethical Language

Clearly, ethical non-cognitivism challenges the basis of what it means to make an ethical statement. If ethics does not give information of any sort, what does it do? In this section we shall look at the challenge of Logical Positivism, and at two responses to it: **emotivism** and **prescriptivism**.

a) Logical Positivism

In *Tractatus* (1921), Wittgenstein argued that the basic function of language was to picture the world, and that it could be verified as true or false by reference to sense experience. This 'picturing' function of language was seen at its clearest in science, where everything depended upon evidence. He argued that the only things that could be said meaningfully were those that could be verified. Anything else might be known by intuition or mysticism, but it could not be described – so there was a definite limit to what language could do.

He started his book with the startlingly simple claim that 'The world is all that is the case', and ended it with the famous 'Whereof we cannot speak, thereof we must remain silent.'

The problem with this rather narrow view of language was that there appeared to be only two kinds of meaningful propositions:

▼ those known to be true by definition (e.g. logic or mathematics)
▼ those known to be true because that truth could be verified by sense experience.

The problem was that neither religious nor ethical claims were simply a matter of definition, nor could they be verified with reference to the sort of facts that science and the senses could provide (remember, you can't get an 'ought' from an 'is'). Hence, the conclusion was that religious and ethical language was literally meaningless – in other words, it did not convey any information; it was 'non-cognitive'.

Note

Wittgenstein's work was taken up by the Vienna Circle of philosophers, who met during the 1920s, and was made popular by A J Ayer's *Language, Truth and Logic*, published in 1936. It is their development of Wittgenstein's ideas that is termed Logical Positivism.

---

i) Threat and Response

The Logical Positivists posed a serious threat to both religious and ethical language, branding both as meaningless because they failed the test of meaningfulness – namely that a statement should either be true by definition, or capable of being proved true by empirical evidence.

Along with this went the argument, put forward by Wittgenstein and others, that we can have no knowledge of another person's mental states. If empirical evidence is all we have to go on, then to say someone is happy amounts to no more than saying that they are smiling and behaving in a manner that we associate with the term 'happy'.

So it is no good trying to justify religious or ethical language with reference to inner states, because they too are hidden and meaningless except in terms of the physical behaviour that is used to indicate them.

How then have philosophers responded to this threat? How – if you can't get an 'ought' from an 'is' – can ethics make sense in a world where everything you say has to have a 'cash value' in terms of evidence that is scientifically testable?

b) Emotivism

A J Ayer argued that you cannot get values – and therefore moral judgements – from descriptions (nothing new in that; it is the familiar 'naturalistic fallacy' from Hume and Moore), but that ethical language is only possible once a set of values is brought to bear on a situation.

> In short, we find that argument is possible on moral questions only if some system of values is presupposed.

[From *Language, Truth and Logic*]

It is these values that lead people to either approve or disapprove of an action, and therefore to make moral judgements about it. These judgements are therefore not factual but **emotive**.

In effect, to say something is right is to say that one approves of it, to say that it is wrong means one disapproves. There can be no factual evidence either way, because it is based on emotions and personal values, not on facts.

The key feature of this approach is that emotivism gives a *subjective* interpretation of the meaning of moral statements. Meaning is related to use, and that use is related to the user's emotions and valuations. Those who criticise emotivism do so because they want to say that there is something inherently good or bad in an action (e.g. in an act of murder) irrespective of what other people may happen to think about it.

A problem

If morality depends on an expression of approval or disapproval, then an act is only 'good' or 'bad' in any meaningful sense if someone comments on it, or at least is aware of it. This point is made clearly by Blanchard (in *Ethics: the Big Questions*, ed. Sturba, page 33f) who uses the example of an animal caught in a trap or an undetected murder to highlight the problem of not being able to say that something is good or bad unless it is known about.

BUT, that objection is not valid, because if one *imagines* an undiscovered murder, one is actually imagining *having discovered it*. Hence the action becomes 'good' or 'bad' in the imagination. If you do not imagine discovering it, then it makes no sense to speak about it at all. Once you imagine the undiscovered murder, you are taking a view about it and expressing your disapproval of it – but that is exactly what emotivism says moral statements are about!

However, emotivism does pose a serious problem for ethical discussions. If moral statements are no more than the expression of emotions, how is it possible to disagree about moral issues? If you say something is 'good' and I say it is 'bad', there is nothing more to be said, and no way of judging between us. To get an argument going, you need to give reasons why you disagree with the other person's point of view. But, from an emotivist point of view, there are no reasons, just expressions of emotion.

Another version of emotivism was presented by C L Stevenson in his *Ethics and Language* (1944). He pointed out that the purpose of a moral statement was to persuade someone of the rightness or wrongness of an action, and said that the word 'good' was a **persuasive definition**. Nevertheless, to say that an ethical claim is 'persuasive' does not suggest that it is something about which there could be factual argument one way or another – it is still essentially a personal expression of value.

Note

Wittgenstein was extremely influential during the middle years of the twentieth century, and his later philosophy, which emphasised the importance of understanding language in terms of its function, influenced the way in which moral statements were viewed. This is reflected in the term '**speech act**', which emphasises that words can actually perform a function. Also termed a 'performative utterance', such expressions as 'With this ring, I thee wed' or 'I promise . . .' do not simply *describe* something, but actually *make it happen*.

The responses to the challenge of Logical Positivism presented here reflect that shift in Wittgenstein's thinking. Ethical language is judged here in terms of what it does. This is termed a '**functionalist**' approach.

c) Prescriptivism

R M Hare (in *The Language of Morals* (1952) and *Freedom and Reason* (1963)) suggested that moral statements were actually doing more than expressing a personal value, they were suggesting that other people, in similar circumstances, should apply that same value and follow that same course of action. In other words, to say that something is right or good is to recommend that other people do it. Hence, his theory is termed **prescriptivism**, because ethical language is essentially 'prescribing' courses of action.

Hare therefore believes that ethical claims are universalisable. In other words, everyone in these same circumstances is advised to take that same course of action – if I say that it is right to do something, then clearly that implies that it is right for everyone. In this, his argument is similar to that of Kant (see page 148).

Notice that Hare is taking a **functionalist approach** – a moral assertion plays a certain role in language, the role of persuading people, on the basis of personal values, of what they should or should not do.

In *Ethics: Inventing Right and Wrong,* John Mackie (1917–81) argued that, even though there are no moral values that can be shown to be objectively true or false, nevertheless ethical language is useful in that it helps people to overcome their own narrow views by helping them to consider and express what is helpful for everyone. In other words, he shows that ethics has a valid function, even if it does not provide us with objective information about the world.

However, Mackie's view can be challenged on the grounds that it does not really explain *why* people take moral views. Why bother to try to overcome narrow views? If ethics is useful, its usefulness is judged by the values people hold. But then we may ask 'Where do those values come from?' Simply saying that we *invent* right and wrong because they are useful does not therefore overcome the basic question about *why* anyone would want to use ethical language in the first place. It simply pushes it one step back, so that we are forced to ask 'Why do we believe that overcoming narrow views is useful?'

Note on Terminology

Notice that the theories associated with Ayer, Flew, Stevenson and Hare are **non-naturalistic**. In other words, they are not based on descriptions of actions or events, but in some way on people's evaluations of them, or their responses to them. They are also **non-cognitive** in that they claim that ethical statements do not convey factual information.

MAKING CONNECTIONS

The issue of how facts are related to values lies behind the non-cognitive approaches to ethics, but is found also in the Philosophy of Religion. For example, in discussions about what we mean by miracles, since it can be argued that a miracle cannot be shown to be such simply by an objective or factual description. Religion, like ethics, gets beyond the narrow confines of factual description.

5 Absolutism and Relativism

Some ethical theories aim to show that there are objective moral principles that hold true for all people in all situations. This approach is generally termed **absolutism** and it is contrasted with **relativism**, which argues that morality should be related to the particular situations in which people find themselves.

A relativist approach would argue that the values upon which moral judgements are made are given to us by the society within which we live, and therefore that the moral judgements we make are always related to a particular society and a particular time. Hence, it would be wrong to assume that ethical views that originate in one part of the world, in one era, or within one religion, can be imposed on others.

In our multi-cultural world, awareness of differences is inescapable, but at the same time, the ethical issues we face may be global – in the areas of environment, warfare, genetic engineering and other issues related to science and business ethics. We are used to the notion that people's ideas on these things will differ, and may be related to their own religious and cultural perspectives.

Why should this be so? Because morality is closely related to fundamental values; and such values are related to and expressed within cultures. Relativism therefore becomes the norm, once we step outside our own religious or cultural group.

Note: Relativism and Descriptive/normative Ethics

Descriptive ethics is naturally linked to the culture and circumstances of the situation or action that is being described. Descriptive statements like 'Muslims do . . .', 'Within traditional Hindu communities, it is expected that . . .' or even 'Most people believe that . . .' present no philosophical problems. They do not imply any critical assessment of the action or attitude involved; they simply describe it.

However, when it comes to normative ethics, actions are assessed according to ethical theories, and we therefore need to consider how this process of assessment should relate to cultural and religious diversity.

a) A Relativist Starting Point

A relativist will generally hold at least one absolute principle, namely that it is wrong to impose absolute moral rules.

It follows from this that a relativist is likely to say that a fundamental feature of all morality is that the autonomy of the individual (or of a society) should be respected. In other words, just as moral rules should not be imposed by one person upon another (because we are all different and situations differ, as in 'Situation Ethics'), so it is wrong to impose one cultural norm of behaviour on those who come from a different culture. 'I may disagree with you, but I uphold your right to disagree with me.'

Such relativism ties in naturally with **consequentialism**, and in particular **Utilitarianism**, an ethical theory we will be examining in the next chapter:

▽ Utilitarianism judges actions to be good or bad according to their anticipated results or consequences.
▽ That action is good which produces the greatest good, benefit or advantage for the greatest number of people.
▽ Act Utilitarianism does this on the basis of individual actions (Bentham).
▽ Rule Utilitarianism takes into account the overall benefit to be gained from following rules or principles (Mill).
▽ Utilitarianism may also differentiate between 'higher' and 'lower' benefits (Mill).
▽ Utilitarianism is therefore essentially **democratic** – it wants to take everyone into account.
▽ 'Interest Utilitarianism' and 'Preference Utilitarianism' continue this democratic trend by taking into account the interests or the preferences of all those concerned in an action and affected by its consequences.

In this way, Preference Utilitarianism promotes the autonomy of the individual, since it avoids imposing particular ideas of benefit or happiness on people, but allows them to express their own values.

Note

Relativism leads to Preference Utilitarianism and vice versa. They belong together since they are both based on the autonomy of the individual and the right of individuals to express their personal and cultural values in the moral choices they make. Together, these theories dominate much modern ethical debate.

Another issue here is the meaningfulness of moral language:

▼ Logical Positivists claimed that religious and moral language was meaningless because it could not be proved true or false by means of evidence.

▼ Such language was then described in terms of expressing approval or disapproval of actions (emotivism) or recommending a course of action (prescriptivism).

▼ Wittgenstein came to believe that moral language was a 'form of life'; that it was one of the 'language games'. In other words, its meaning was found in its use. To know what moral language means, look at how it is used.

▼ Hence, the meaning of morality is shown within the circle of people who use that language – it does not have universal or absolute meaning.

▼ Hence we end up once again with relativism.

b) Alternatives to Relativism and Consequentialism

If morality can be related to some objective feature of the world, then it is possible to apply some basic ethical principles universally.

For example, Aristotle related ethics to the 'final cause', purpose or aim of each individual thing – so that, once you know what something is, you know how it should be treated and how it should behave. This formed the basis of the Natural Law approach to ethics.

Equally, if morality can be related to fundamental features in the way people reason, a case can be made for applying ethical principles universally. Kant believed that there were features of 'pure practical reason' which could be used as a basis for all ethical judgements.

The different formulations of his categorical imperative (that you can will the maxim of your action to become a universal law; that people should be treated as ends and not merely as means; that you should act as though legislating for a kingdom of autonomous individuals) are an attempt to find a **logical bedrock** by which all particular moral judgements can be assessed.

Note

In presenting an ethical argument, particularly where it is related to the ethics of a particular religion, it is important to distinguish between what is claimed as a universal moral principle and what is related to its historical and cultural setting.

The essential difference between relativistic and absolutist approaches is that the former see the setting as determining the validity of moral judgements, whereas the latter claim that there are moral principles that transcend cultural and religious boundaries.

In other words, the absolutist is going to say that some things are right or wrong, quite apart from what society accepts as the norm.

To make a case for an absolutist ethic, going beyond cultural and situational differences you would need to show that:

▼ human life has some inherent value and purpose (irrespective of its situation)

▼ reason can frame principles that are of universal application, and therefore that there is a fundamental form of reasoning that is shared by all

▼ ethical statements can have universal validity, and therefore be shown to be true or false by some means other than pointing to the consequences of putting them into action.

And these imply *either* some form of Natural Law *or* some form of universal principle of reason. Without one or other (or both) of these, you are bound to revert to using relativistic and consequentialist arguments.

Look back later!

In outlining the issues of relativism and absolutism here, it has been necessary to introduce some of the main ethical theories that we will be considering in the next chapter. Once you have studied these, look back at this section and check that you have appreciated the way in which the issue of relativism and absolutism is a good starting point for assessing the validity of those different theories.

▼ ESSAY QUESTIONS

1 a) What is ethical non-cognitivism?
   b) Does a non-cognitive view imply that morality is entirely subjective?
2 a) Describe the fundamental features of moral absolutism.
   b) Assess its strengths and weaknesses.

See the 'Further Reading and Websites' section at the back of this book for follow-up work on this chapter.

ETHICAL THEORIES

POINTS TO CONSIDER

On what logical basis should we decide what is right?

Which should take priority in deciding what to do, moral principles or anticipated results?

Can there be an entirely objective basis for ethics?

TIMELINE

384–322 BCE	Aristotle
121–180	Marcus Aurelius (a Stoic)
1224–74	Aquinas
1694–1746	Hutcheson
1711–76	Hume
1724–1804	Kant
1748–1832	Bentham
1806–73	Mill
1905–91	Fletcher
1919–	Hare
1919–	Anscombe
1932–	Searle

In this chapter we shall examine five ethical theories:

1 Natural Law
2 Utilitarianism
3 The Categorical Imperative
4 Situation Ethics
5 Virtue Ethics

Most rational arguments about ethical matters will be based on one or other of these theories, or may take features from more than one. You should be familiar with the main points of each of them, along with their strengths and weaknesses.

However, there is another factor to be kept in mind. Religious Ethics may often be based on statements from scripture or doctrinal formulae that are considered authoritative for members of the faith community. Moral teachings based on religious authority may be *backed up by* one or more of the rational arguments, but are not actually *based* on them. It would therefore be perfectly valid to come to the conclusion that any one rational theory is *inadequate as a basis* for ethics, but that it offers *useful justification or support* for a moral stance that is part of a person's religious commitment.

For example, Situation Ethics claims that the 'law of love' takes priority in all moral decision making. From a secular and logical standpoint, this may be seen as inadequate as a basis for ethics, but it may be seen as an attempt to explore the implications of Jesus' teachings in the New Testament.

1 Natural Law

The 'Natural Law' theory originated in Aristotle's idea that everything has a purpose, revealed in its design, and that its supreme 'good' is to be sought in fulfilling that purpose.

There are two things you need to know about Natural Law: first, it isn't natural, and second, it isn't law.

▼ Natural Law is NOT simply about what nature does (it is not 'natural' in the sense of being observed in nature). Rather, it is based on nature as interpreted by human reason.

▼ Natural Law does not necessarily give you straightforward and dogmatic answers to every situation. It involves a measure of interpretation and can be applied in a flexible way. It does not simply present a fixed 'law' dictated by nature.

Natural Law and Christianity

Christian morality is based on the Bible and the tradition of the Church, rather than on unaided human reason alone. However, Aquinas and others argued that human reason (given by God) could offer a logical basis for those moral precepts that were also known through revelation, and could be used to apply Christian precepts.

This proved a particularly valuable approach for those moral issues (e.g. genetic engineering) which were unknown in Biblical times and to which there could therefore be no obvious appeal to scriptural revelation. The Natural Law approach dominates Catholic moral thinking, but was opposed by those Protestant thinkers who saw human reason as 'fallen' and therefore unable to provide a sound basis for moral principles.

To understand the key features of Natural Law, we need to be clear about how it originated.

a) Aristotle

Aristotle argued that everything had a purpose or goal to which it aimed. Once you know what something is for, you know how it should behave and what its final 'good' is. A knife is designed for cutting; if it does that well, it is a 'good' knife.

His idea of purpose leads into his idea of what is 'good'. In the opening of his *Nicomachean Ethics*, he says:

> Every craft and every investigation, and likewise every action and decision, seems to aim at some good; hence the good has been well described as that at which everything aims.

The good for humans is *eudaimonia*, which is often translated as 'happiness', but which means rather more than that. It includes the idea of living well and of doing well. Aristotle argued that people might do other things in order to be happy, but that it would make no sense to try to be happy in order to achieve something else!

Thus happiness is the basic good, making everything else worthwhile:

> ...we regard something as self-sufficient when all by itself it makes a life choiceworthy and lacking nothing; and that is what we think happiness does.

[From *Nicomachean Ethics*, Book 1]

Aristotle was also concerned to show that living the good life was not an individual thing, but that it involved living at one with others in society. So a person can enjoy the good life by fulfilling his or her essential nature, and doing it within society.

Happiness is therefore the final goal of humankind and it is to be chosen for itself, and not as a means to some other end. It is what Aristotle sees as making life worthwhile.

Aristotle held that the key feature of humankind was its ability to think. But, for Aristotle, reason was not just the ability to think logical thoughts, but of living the good life, in line with the precepts of reason.

Reasonable thoughts ...

For Plato, Aristotle and other Greek thinkers, reason is not just about understanding, but also about how to act: ethics is reason put into practice. It is very important to keep this in mind, since there are other approaches to ethics (for example in Christian ethics, particularly as presented by Luther) in which human reason is seen as essentially 'fallen' and unable to be trusted.

Morality is concerned with the application of thought and prudence to achieve a chosen end. Aristotle regards intellectual reasoning as the highest of all human activities, for man is essentially a 'thinking animal'. That is why he sees morality as based on reason, not on emotion or in the hope of getting some reward or avoiding punishment.

Aristotle's ideal is the 'great souled' man, who is rational, balanced, good company among equals and independent. In other words he is worldly, but with his appetites and emotions well controlled by reason.

Hence, the starting point for Aristotle's ethics is the working out through reason of one's essential nature and goal, and of acting accordingly.

He also propounded the idea of a 'mean' as a balance between two powerful characteristics. Therefore it is good to be brave and self-assertive rather than too rash and pugnacious on the one hand, or too timid and self-effacing on the other.

b) The Stoics

In Ancient Greece, the **Epicureans** thought that there was no inherent purpose or meaning in life. The world was an impersonal collection of atoms, and we had to set our own goals and ideals, for the natural order offered none. By contrast the **Stoics** believed that there was a fundamental design and purpose to the universe (the *Logos*), and that one's morality ought to be based on aligning oneself with it.

The Stoics – particularly Cicero and Marcus Aurelius – were practical, thoughtful people, determined to bring reason to bear on the political and social issues of their day. They saw reason as the keynote for understanding life and morality.

But since everything, including people's well-being, was under the control of a rational and morally good agent, it made no sense to seek happiness as the goal of life, because things might not work out as we plan, and we would become disillusioned. Rather, the Stoics believed that it was better to try to fit into the overall plan of the universe.

For the Stoics, the natural way to respond to this sense of universal order was to act with integrity, aware of the part we can play within the overall scheme of things. To do what is right is to align oneself with the fundamental reason that guides the whole universe, excluding any thoughts of personal gain, or the promptings of the emotions. This is the Stoic basis of morality.

This approach can be termed 'Natural Law'. It implies that everything has an overall rational purpose within the universe, and that recognition of that purpose is a basis for moral action.

For the Stoics and those who followed them, reason was at the heart of the universe. The cosmos was an interconnected whole, with everything ordered and having its place, function and true nature.

Genetic Programming?

Following Aristotle, the Stoics saw the nature of a thing as its internal principle of change – in other words, an acorn will grow into an oak tree, given the right circumstances, because it has an inner principle which directs its growth. Today we might well term such an 'inner principle' its 'genetic make-up', since the blueprint for change that is being used is determined by the genetic code.

---

c) Aquinas

The ideas of Aristotle and the Stoics were taken up in the thirteenth century by Thomas Aquinas, who saw that the principles of Natural Law could give a sound underpinning for Christian morality.

Aquinas (in *Summa Theologiae*) argued that what was good was what was reasonable, and that a rule should be 'an ordinance of reason for the common good'.

If the world has meaning and purpose, and if we can know the part we play within it, then we know our own 'final cause'. Once we know that, we can use our human reason to understand how we should act.

▼ As presented by Aquinas, the Natural Law is based on the conviction that God created the world, establishing within it a sense of order and purpose that reflects his Will.

▼ If everything is created for a purpose, human reason, in examining that purpose, should be able to judge how to act in order to fulfil itself and therefore find its own goal and ultimate happiness.

▼ Since Natural Law is based on reason, it is in principle discoverable by anyone, whether religious or not. For the same reason, it is universal, rather than limited to any one religion or culture.

Note

Aquinas believed that the whole universe was ordered rationally by God (in the logos, or principle of creation), and that virtue would consist in following one's nature, ordered towards the final goal of knowledge and love of God. Based on reason, he thought that Christian revelation would complement this and clarify it.

Aristotle had distinguished between efficient causes and final causes and it is the final cause or purpose of a thing or an action which determines what is morally right. Natural Law is therefore based on a rational interpretation of purpose and design within the world; it is not simply an objective account of what is in fact the case.

Being subject to divine rule is therefore, for Aquinas, the means of achieving one's own final purpose or end:

> ... some things are so produced by God that, being intelligent, they bear a resemblance to Him and reflect His image: wherefore not only are they directed, but they direct themselves to their appointed end by their own actions. And if in thus directing themselves they be

subject to the divine ruling, they are admitted by that divine ruling to the attainment of their last end; but are excluded therefrom if they direct themselves otherwise.

[From *Summa Contra Gentiles*, Book 3, section 1]

Human beings, since they are intelligent, are therefore able to direct themselves and take responsibility for doing God's will. If they fail to do that, they are also acting against their own fundamental nature.

d) Rules and Situations

Let us be clear that Natural Law is not a matter of accepting authoritative statements and laws, nor is it a matter of trying to act in a way that *mimics* nature (i.e. it is *not* biology acted out as morality). It is generally seen as backing up traditional Christian morality, but may not necessarily do so.

However, Natural Law does claim that we should use our reason to examine the place and purpose that everything has within the universe, and act in a way that reflects that understanding. It is not a utilitarian assessing of results or pleasing a majority, it is not based on intuitions or emotions, but on reason.

It is important to recognise, however, that Natural Law does make allowances for the differences between particular situations. In other words, human reason can take the general principles offered by Natural Law, and can seek to apply them in particular instances. This approach is sometimes termed '**casuistry**', which is often a rather pejorative term used to describe a situation where someone uses clever arguments to show why they can get out of obeying a universal moral principle in their particular circumstances.

The other issue to be considered is the principle of '**double effect**'. Actions often have more than one effect, and we have to decide which of these is the real motive for choosing to perform the action. For example, I may understand that taking a little red wine is good for my physical health; it may also happen to taste good and make one drunk. Now the fundamental question is whether the purpose in drinking the wine is to get drunk, and the health benefits are a secondary effect, or whether the intention is to promote one's health, and becoming drunk is a secondary effect. (This is not a very good example, of course, because if taken in sufficient quantity to induce drunkenness, the health benefits of the wine are eroded.)

The key question is this: What was my intention in taking this course of action? If my primary intention was good, I should not be blamed for any secondary effects that result.

> ### The purpose of sex?
>
> In terms of its biological function, the purpose of sex is procreation; but it may have a secondary purpose in giving pleasure and strengthening the relationship between sexual partners. A traditional Natural Law approach would argue that sex always needs to be open to the possibility of procreation, since that is its primary purpose. This implies that sex which denies the primary purpose (e.g. masturbation or homosexual intercourse) is wrong, even if it is actually undertaken for the sake of a secondary effect, such as pleasure. (See page 203 for a further discussion of this.)

e) A Key Problem

▽ *If* the world makes sense and everything has a 'final cause' or purpose *then* we can decide what is right or wrong

▽ *but* if we do not believe there is a 'final cause' or purpose, then the Natural Law argument makes no sense.

Hence, the Natural Law approach to ethics depends for its validity on metaphysics – on seeing the world as a rationally ordered creation. If you don't believe that the world is ordered according to reason (e.g that it is entirely impersonal and that everything happens by chance), then Natural Law makes little sense.

f) Advantages of the Natural Law Approach

Natural Law opposes two common approaches to ethics – **scepticism** and **relativism**. (Scepticism effectively says that moral rules have no overall validity, you can't decide rationally what is right or wrong. Relativism argues that everything depends on circumstances, and that there are no universal moral rules.)

It can claim an advantage over those ethical theories (like Utilitarianism) that are based on the expected results of an action, because results are often unknown or uncertain. By contrast, Natural Law declares an act to be right or wrong quite apart from its consequences.

Natural Law may also claim the advantage of being rationally based; it does not depend on the feelings of the person concerned. Feelings can change, but the issue of right and wrong remains fixed. Something cannot be made right just because I happen to want to do it.

Natural Law may also claim an advantage in that it does not depend upon any particular culture or society. Just because everyone else does something, it doesn't make it right.

2 Utilitarianism

In its simplest form, Utilitarianism is based on the 'Principle of Utility' which is that, in any situation where there is a moral choice, one should do that which results in 'the greatest happiness for the greatest number of people'.

Utilitarianism is probably the most widely used ethical theory today. Seeking to achieve the greatest good or benefit for the greatest number, and evaluating actions by their intended results, is seen as a common sense principle by a majority of people.

a) Origins and Development

Utilitarianism as an ethical theory developed in the eighteenth century. Hutcheson used the phrase 'the greatest good for the greatest number' to describe his way of assessing political systems. It was an argument in favour of democracy.

Seeking the happiness, advantage or benefit of people comes from what is generally called the 'moral sense' approach to ethics which argues that everyone has a natural sense of compassion when encountering someone who is suffering, and that we have a moral sense that wants to help them restore their happiness.

Equally, being aware of and promoting the happiness of others is found in Aristotle, in the Bible, in the teachings of the Buddha, in Confucius and elsewhere. Utilitarianism seeks to find a rational means of assessing how best to put that into practice.

▼ The earliest form of this is **Act Utilitarianism**, where what is right is based on assessing the results of particular actions.

▼ This is supplemented by **Rule Utilitarianism**, which allows the general benefit to society in people following general rules to be taken into account.

▼ More modern developments seek to examine the 'interest' of 'preferences' of everyone concerned, and are very much based on the rights and autonomy of individuals.

b) Bentham: Act Utilitarianism

Bentham argued for the 'Principle of Utility', by which an action is judged good or bad according to the results that it achieved:

> By utility is meant that property of any object, whereby it tends to produce benefit, advantage, pleasure, good, or happiness (all this in the present case comes to the same thing) or (what comes again to the same thing) to prevent the happening of mischief, pain, evil, or

[From *An Introduction to the Principles of Morals and Legislation*, Chapter 1, section 3]

unhappiness to the party whose interest is considered: if that party be the community in general, the happiness of the community: if a particular individual, then the happiness of that individual.

Since he believed that everyone had an equal right to happiness, irrespective of their situation or status in life, he argued that everyone counted equally in this assessment of the benefits of an action.

He also argued that the benefit should be measured in terms of:

▼ its duration (clearly a very short-term benefit should not have the same weight in the calculation as something more permanent)
▼ its intensity
▼ how near, immediate and certain it is (a 'possible' benefit is less valuable than one that is certain)
▼ how free from pain the benefit is, and whether or not it is likely to lead on to further pleasure or happiness.

In an age when science was gaining ground, Bentham offered a way of calculating the happiness afforded by a course of action, and made that the basis of deciding whether that action should be considered right or wrong. Bentham also took the view that, overall, following this principle of seeking the happiness of the majority would also benefit the individual who did so, and would itself lead to that individual's greatest happiness.

c) Mill: Rule Utilitarianism

Mill argued that not all forms of happiness or pleasure were of equal value – which is what Bentham had seemed to imply. He also recognised that, in life, it is easy to settle for the more immediate and sensual pleasures, rather than the nobler and more refined ones.

Capacity for the nobler feelings is in most natures a very tender plant, easily killed, not only by hostile influences, but by mere want of sustenance; and in the majority of young persons it speedily dies away in the occupations to which their position in life has devoted them, and the society into which it has thrown them, are not favourable to keeping that higher capacity in exercise. Men lose their high aspirations as they lose their intellectual tastes, because they have not time or opportunity for indulging them; and they addict themselves to inferior pleasures, not because they deliberately prefer them, but because they are either the only ones to which they have access or the only ones which they are any longer capable of enjoying. It may be questioned whether anyone who has remained equally susceptible to both classes of pleasures ever knowingly and calmly preferred the lower, though many, in all ages, have broken down in an ineffectual attempt to combine both.

[From *Utilitarianism*, chapter 2]

Thus Mill goes beyond the simple calculation of happiness, by recognising that there are many different ways of assessing its value.

Mill was concerned to link his utilitarian theory with Jesus' teachings, by claiming that to love your neighbour as yourself constitutes 'the ideal perfection of utilitarian morality'. He also gave a positive role for self-sacrifice:

> The utilitarian morality does recognise in human beings the power of sacrificing their own greatest good for the good of others. It only refuses to admit that the sacrifice is itself a good. A sacrifice which does not increase or tend to increase the sum total of happiness, it considers as wasted.

[From *Utilitarianism*, chapter 2]

Example

If a person rushes into a burning building to save someone trapped inside, but dies in the attempt, Mill's argument suggests that they were morally right to attempt the rescue, but that their death was not good in itself, if it did not achieve its goal, and was therefore wasted. This reflects a common sense approach, for what is applauded in the person who gives their own life for others is not their death, but the strength of their desire to help others, a desire which took precedence over their own sense of self-preservation.

Mill also suggested a positive place for rules within an overall utilitarian approach. To use his own example, he argues that society needs the principle of truthfulness, without which nobody would ever be able to trust anybody to be telling the truth. Therefore, the rule that one should tell the truth is a means of securing the greatest happiness for the greatest number within society as a whole. To tell a lie might therefore offer immediate advantages to those concerned, but that should be weighed against the more general threat to society if telling lies became the norm.

Thus Mill promotes 'Rule Utilitarianism'; general rules should be obeyed, since they give overall benefit to society, but they may be broken in exceptional circumstances. Mill's examples of this are that one should generally tell the truth, but not if that involved giving information to someone who is likely to use it to further an evil purpose, or giving bad news to someone who is dangerously ill, and who might be harmed by hearing the truth.

i) 'Strong' and 'Weak'

Strong Rule Utilitarianism holds that one should never break a rule that is established on utilitarian principles.

Weak Rule Utilitarianism holds that there may be situations when the assessment of the results of a particular act may take precedence over the general rule (e.g. in Mill's examples – given above – of when it might be right to tell a lie), although the general rule still needs to be taken into account in assessing what is right.

d) Preference and Interest Utilitarianism

A key problem with utilitarian arguments is that Utilitarianism itself does not define the nature of 'good'. Just as Mill argued that there were higher and lower pleasures, so people might have very different ideas about what constitutes their benefit, advantage or happiness.

Hence it is important to consider what is in people's interest, recognising that what is in the interest of one person may go against the interest of another. But there is a further problem. How do I determine what is in the interest of another person? Since utilitarian arguments originated at a time when democracy was developing, and sought to reflect a political situation where everyone counted, it is only reasonable to allow everyone concerned to express their own preferences, rather than have someone else's idea of a benefit imposed on them.

In *The Language of Morals*, R M Hare argued for his 'prescriptivist' approach to moral language (see page 131). Saying that something is right is a way of 'prescribing' it as a policy for other people. If that makes it sound as though Hare sees morality as seeking to prescribe or impose values, another aspect of his ethics can act as a counterbalance to this, for he introduced what is generally termed '**Preference Utilitarianism**'. In this form of Utilitarianism, it is important to take into account the preferences of the individuals involved, except where those preferences come into direct conflict with the preferences of others. The right thing to do, therefore, is to maximise the chances that everyone's preferences will be satisfied.

e) Limitations of Utilitarian Arguments:

▼ Utilitarian arguments depend on predicting the results of an action, but you can never know *all* the consequences of your actions.

▼ You cannot derive an 'ought' from an 'is' (that is the 'naturalistic fallacy', see page 126); but Utilitarianism appears to derive an 'ought' from the expected results.

▼ The values upon which utilitarian arguments depend (e.g. the desirability of doing good to others; basic equality of persons) cannot themselves be validated by a utilitarian argument, for that would result in a circular argument. In other words: 'You should seek the greatest happiness for the greatest number, because that is the way to achieve the greatest happiness for the greatest number' does not get us anywhere. You can always ask 'Why?'

▼ If morality is determined by results alone, wrong motives can still lead to right results (e.g. selfishness may motivate a system that yields positive results for a majority, is it therefore morally right?). Critics argue that results alone should not determine morality.

▼ The fundamental question 'What should I do?' is seldom presented in a utilitarian way. If it were, there would be no problem — one would automatically go for that which obviously brought about the maximum good. Moral dilemmas only come about because either the quality or quantity of that 'good' are in doubt.

Therefore we could argue that Utilitarianism is inadequate, taken on its own, as a moral theory. It is a way of allocating and applying moral values, but that is not the same thing as a self-contained theory that can account for and resolve moral dilemmas.

f) Advantages of a Utilitarian Approach

▼ It is straightforward and based on clear principles.

▼ Given a common desire to benefit the majority of people, and a common sense of what is to their benefit, it yields results that are in line with common sense.

▼ It is easy to demonstrate that Utilitarianism is fair, since its basic principles are widely accepted.

▼ It does not appear to require the acceptance of any prior beliefs about the nature of the world or of religion, and its moral discussions can therefore be appreciated across different religions and cultures.

▼ Utilitarianism is the moral side of democracy. If giving everyone an equal say is (in your view) the most fundamental reality for determining how we should live, then you will have no problem with accepting the results of utilitarian arguments. (If, on the other hand, there are occasions when you might want to claim that something is absolutely right, no matter what the consequences, then you will need to supplement your Utilitarianism with values from other sources, such as Natural Law or religious authority.)

Moral dilemmas arise because there are genuine disagreements about what is the right course of action. They may involve the individual or social values of the people concerned, or the religious views they hold. Examining the predicted results of an action is therefore part, but only part, of that process of moral debate. Utilitarian arguments depend upon established values and principles; they cannot adequately generate them.

3 Kant's Ethical Theory

> ## Note
>
> Immanuel Kant (1724–1804) is best known for his 'Copernican Revolution' in the theory of knowledge. He argued that space, time and causality were features of the way our minds organise experience, rather than features of the external world.
>
> We can only know the world as it appears to us, not as it is in itself.
>
> To understand the world as we experience it, we need to understand the way our minds work. Similarly, to understand morality we need to start with the experience of an unconditional sense of the moral 'ought' – something which cannot simply depend on external facts about what the world is like, or what results we can expect from our actions.

Kant's moral theory was based on principles of pure practical reason, rather than on a utilitarian assessment of the expected results of an action. He started within the awareness of a moral 'ought', and aimed: 'To seek out and establish the supreme principle of morality.' [From the Preface to his *Groundwork* . . .]

From reading Hume, and from his awareness of the emerging sciences, Kant was very aware of the ambiguity of evidence, and the failure of factual arguments to prove either the existence of God or an adequate starting point for morality. Rather than accepting the traditional arguments for the existence of God, he made way for faith by making God one of the postulates of moral experience (see page 41). For morality, he found his new starting point in the idea of a 'good will':

> There is no possibility of thinking of anything at all in the world, or even out of it, which can be regarded as good without qualification, except a *good will* . . . The sight of a being who is not graced by any touch of a pure and good will but who yet enjoys an uninterrupted prosperity can never delight a rational and impartial spectator. Thus a good will seems to constitute the indispensable condition of being even worthy of happiness.

[From the opening of Kant's *Groundwork for the Metaphysics of Morals*]

So Kant, by starting with the 'good will' is making a radical shift in ethics – he is not starting with anything that can be demonstrated 'out there' in the world (either by way of anticipated results, or of a final cause or purpose) but only with the internal experience of morality, the fact that a person wants to make a moral choice, expressing their 'good will'.

a) Duty

Kant considers that the important thing for morality is to do one's **duty**. That is a matter of conscious moral choice, and mixed motives will not do. It is not enough to do what is right because you enjoy it or benefit from it – morality is about consciously deciding to do what is right, irrespective of consequences.

He considers that an action would not be called good unless it came as a result of the 'good will' of the person who performed it. And that, however beneficial the action might be, what counted was the 'good will' of the person performing it. Thus even a failed attempt to do something can be considered a good and right act, on the other hand, to achieve accidentally a useful result with evil intent would not be considered morally right.

Our aim in acting morally is not necessarily to be happy, but to be *worthy* of being happy. The **highest good** (*summum bonum*) for Kant is this joining of virtue and happiness, but for him, virtue has to be the starting point, because it is the virtuous person who possesses the 'good will' which is necessary for morality. Happiness is an optional bonus, but is certainly not guaranteed.

> ### Note
>
> Kant's theory of ethics was developed in *Groundwork for the Metaphysics of Morals* (1785) and in the *Critique of Practical Reason* (1788).

ISSUE:
Are our motives ever completely pure? In the real world people act for all sorts of mixed and confused reasons. Should we say that they are not doing what is right unless their motives are pure?

MAKING CONNECTIONS

Kant's 'Postulates of the Practical Reason' are included in the Moral Argument for the existence of God (page 41). He believed that the joining of virtue and happiness in the *summum bonum* would only be possible if there were a God to bring it about.

Kant thought that to be moral, you should seek to do your duty, no matter what your inclinations or the consequences involved. Whether you or others benefit from what you do is irrelevant to whether that action is morally right or wrong.

Hence Kant would argue that your actions are irrelevant for morality if:

▼ You do something from which you yourself expect to benefit. In other words, enlightened self-interest does not count as morality, even if you are doing things that benefit others as well.

▼ You are motivated by natural interest. Your actions would not be moral, even if others benefit, since your motives were essentially selfish. Your action may not be called 'wrong', but it is irrelevant in terms of making moral choices.

▼ You act because ordered to do so by someone in authority. Obedience may be a virtue, but your choice to obey is not the same as making a decision about whether your action is right or wrong.

Hence, all that counts for morality is the rational choice of actions, based on a disinterested sense of duty.

b) The Categorical Imperative

Kant therefore sought an *objective* criterion for morality, some logical way of determining right and wrong. Morality is a positive act we take in order to shape our world as we think right. It is an act of the will – our pure practical reason – and Kant therefore wanted to understand the principles upon which the pure practical reason operated.

Note

The term **categorical imperative** refers to an absolute moral obligation, an 'ought' that does not depend on results, an 'ought' determined entirely by the practical reason – in other words 'You should do X.'

By contrast, a **hypothetical imperative** is one that says 'If you want Y, then you must do X.' In other words, it depends on results.

Most references to Kant's 'Categorical Imperative' are to the criteria by which 'categorical imperatives', in the more general sense, should be assessed. The three main forms of this are outlined in this section.

Kant's moral theory is therefore a way of judging whether an action is in accordance with the pure practical reason. The test he used is called the **Categorical Imperative**.

There are several different forms of this, but they are variations on three basic ones:

1 *So act that the maxim of your will could always hold at the same time as a principle establishing universal law.*

> ### *Note*
>
> A **maxim** is a subjective principle of action. In other words, it is a kind of mental guideline in the form 'Whenever X happens, I consider it right to do Y.' The maxim is important, because that is what constitutes the 'good will', or the intention to do one's duty. For Kant, it is the maxim that counts, not the actual or anticipated results, because it indicates that you acted from a good will.

This implies that something is right if, and only if, I can will that the maxim (or principle) that I use to decide what I should do in this particular situation should become a universal law.

Kant illustrated this with the following example:

If I decide to make a promise, with no intention of keeping it, that decision can only be right if I can, at the same time, will that everyone should act on the maxim 'Whenever I am given the opportunity, I may make a promise with no intention of keeping it.'

But if that were to be so, then the whole idea of making promises would become nonsense, and therefore against reason. Hence Kant would see it as wrong, according to the first form of the Categorical Imperative, ever to make a promise with no intention of keeping it.

Notice what this does *not* claim. It does not claim that everyone should be able to do exactly the same thing that I now choose to do in order for it to be moral. That would be a practical impossibility. It simply claims that everyone should be prepared to act on the same maxim – the same 'principle of action'.

Kant always seeks to universalise rules, because he wants each person to be free and rational, and if rules are not universalisable, then other people will not enjoy the same benefit that the person putting forward the rule is able to claim. The principle here is not whether universalising makes life difficult, but whether holding a rule that cannot be universalised, while claiming that all human beings are free autonomous agents, is self-contradictory.

In other words, I should be prepared to give everyone else the freedom to act on the same moral principles that I use. If I can't do that in any particular case, then what I propose to do is wrong.

2 *Act in such a way that you always treat humanity, whether in your own person or in the person of any other, never simply as a means, but always at the same time as an end.*

The second form of the Categorical Imperative follows from the first. If I am prepared that everyone else should be free to make that same moral choice that I now make, I have to allow that all others are free, autonomous moral agents. So they must be 'ends' rather than simply 'means'.

To treat another person simply as a means to an end that I have chosen, is to deny them the very thing that I am claiming for myself.

3 *Act as if a legislating member in the universal kingdom of ends.*

The third form is less often used in outlines of Kant's work, but it follows from the first two. It proposes that one should only act in a way that is compatible with being a legislator in a kingdom where everyone is treated as an end and not as a means – in other words, your moral choices should be compatible with a society of free and autonomous moral agents.

Kant sought the autonomy of the individual, but that did not mean that each individual was free to determine his or her own morality, rather that the free individual had the capacity to understand the principles of pure practical reason, and to follow them. Reason must be absolutely impartial, but that means that it must will its principles to be applied equally to all.

The principle upon which I act should be one that I can, without contradiction, set down as a law in such a society.

Note

The third formulation of the Categorical Imperative is included here because it clarifies what many people take to be the main thrust of Kant's argument. For practical and examination purposes, however, students need understand and apply only the first two.

---

c) Kant and the Real World

An interesting challenge to Kant's ethics is presented by Christine Korsgaard (reproduced from a 1986 journal article in the Sterba anthology). She points out that obeying the moral law puts a person at a disadvantage when dealing with people who are wicked. If I treat people as free moral agents, rather than trying to restrain them when they are doing something wrong, then I am effectively colluding with them in their behaviour, and that behaviour is going to lead to a rational contradiction. The same thing happens with the third formulation – legislating for a kingdom of ends. That represents an ideal situation, and not a practical one. In the real world people do not always choose to follow what pure practical reason requires.

However, the first formulation – that one should act in such a way that the maxim of one's actions could become a universal law – it is possible to justify, for example restraining someone from doing harm to another. This is because it is perfectly reasonable to work universally with the maxim 'Whenever I see someone about to harm another, I will restrain him or her' without contradiction.

Working with an ideal situation, rather than with the messy contradictions of ordinary human beings, is not confined to Kant. A more recent example is John Rawl's political philosophy, where he considers a group of people who meet without knowing who they are or their circumstances. He uses this fiction in order to work out basic rules of justice as fairness. In practice, people do know their situation, and may be inclined towards self-interest, rather than the overall benefit of society. The problem of the 'kingdom of ends' is always that there will be some people who see everyone else as simply a means to their own personal end – with chaotic results if they are not in some way restrained.

d) Evaluating Kant's Theory

Notice the contrast with Utilitarianism:

▽ For Utilitarianism, you start with 'the good' (e.g. happiness or benefit), and something is judged 'right' if it brings about and maximises that good (e.g. 'the greatest good for the greatest number').

▽ For Kant, you decide – on grounds of pure practical reason – what is right and your duty; and you should follow this irrespective of your inclinations or the results that your action may have.

▽ For Utilitarians, the starting point is the welfare and happiness of all; for Kant, it is the recognition of everyone as a free, autonomous moral agent, to be treated as an end and never simply as a means.

MAKING CONNECTIONS

In looking at the Moral Argument for the existence of God (see page 41), we saw that for Kant, God was one of the postulates of the practical reason. In other words, it is one of the things that makes sense of the experience of acknowledging a moral obligation and responding to it.

However, Kant's 'Categorical Imperative' can stand on its own as an ethical theory, and does not depend upon God as a postulate.

It is therefore quite important to keep these two aspects of Kant's philosophy separate for the purposes of your AS level examination, but recognise that the experience of morality (in the form of a 'Categorical Imperative') lies at the heart of both the argument for the existence of God and his moral theory.

> ### Note
>
> Alasdair Macintyre (in *After Virtue*, Duckworth, 1981) has argued that Kant's ethical system only works if there is a prior agreement in what the final end and purpose of humankind is. The problem, of course, is that there is no such agreement.

Kant's is a morality concerned with self-realisation, with applying pure practical reason to one's actions, and therefore fulfilling oneself at the same time as allowing everyone else to do so as well.

For Kant, morality, like religion, does not come from outside to be imposed on humankind, but grows from within, through the exercise of reason. But his is not a secular morality, for it still depends on some notion of God in order to justify the view he takes of a rationally ordered world, in which – morally – we can seek both to do our duty and anticipate that it will lead to our highest good.

Kant's theory has some clear advantages over others:

▼ It is very straightforward and based on reason.
▼ It gives criteria by which to assess universal principles of morality.
▼ It makes clear that morality is a matter of doing one's duty, not following one's inclinations.

However:

▼ Its abstract and general principles may seem far removed from the immediacy of moral situations.
▼ General principles do not always help where there are choices to be made between options, each of which could be justified.
▼ Motives are seldom pure; people seldom act from the pure practical reason.

4 Situation Ethics

Much ethical debate is a matter of applying rules to situations. Sometimes those rules are regarded as absolute; sometimes they are flexible enough to take particular circumstances into account. Very seldom are there rules that never allow for exceptional circumstances. Nevertheless, in the main, ethical arguments have been **deductive**, in that they have started with fixed rules, and then applied them to particular situations. This process is sometimes termed '**casuistry**'.

A key issue, therefore, is whether it is valid to start with rules and then apply them to circumstances, or whether it is better to start with circumstances and apply only general principles to them, working out what is right in each particular situation.

Joseph Fletcher's *Situation Ethics* was an influential book in the 1960s, because it reflected a demand for a more liberal approach to moral issues. It opposed the deductive method of ethical reasoning, replacing it with what he saw as the fundamental feature of Christian morality: love. He argued that in any situation, it was right to do whatever was most loving, whether or not that required the breaking of a traditional moral rule. He pointed out that the rule of love had always been central to Christian ethics.

A note on love

In Christian moral argument, the Greek term used for love is *agape,* which denotes a love which is disinterested, rather than selfish, seeking only the benefit of the one who is loved. This is in contrast to *eros* (erotic love) and *philia* (friendship). An ethical theory that seeks to apply *agape* to situations is termed **agapeism**.

Erotic unreason

Eros, or erotic love, was traditionally seen as belonging to the realm of emotions and the animal instincts. One who is dominated by *eros* is seen as dangerously out of control. *Eros* does not necessarily follow reason, as anyone who has been in its grip knows.

Agape is different. As used by Fletcher and others, the application of *agape* is reasonable; the love that is required is expected to be based on a reasonable concern for the one who is loved. As a theory, agapeism can therefore be presented and defended rationally.

Advantages of Situation Ethics:
▼ It is easy to understand.
▼ It is based on concern for others (the '*agape*' form of love) which lies at the heart of all ethical systems.
▼ It allows individuals to make up their own minds about what is right or wrong in any particular situation. In other words, it can be flexible, whilst being based on a widely accepted key concept: love.

However, it also creates problems:
▼ It does not answer the person who says 'Why do what is most loving?' In other words, *if* you accept that *agape* is central to morality, then it works well. If you do not, it does not offer a rational basis for morality.
▼ It is difficult to see how there can be any meaningful discussion between

people who take different views about what is most loving in any one situation. Everyone's interpretation of love appears to equal everyone else's.

5 Virtue Ethics

Virtue Ethics stands in contrast to the two major ethical theories that have dominated western philosophy in the modern period: Kantian absolutist ethics and Utilitarianism.

It is also very different from the earlier Natural Law approach to Christian ethics.

All three of these take as their starting point the moment of moral choice. They require you to assess whether a chosen action is:

▼ in line with a rational interpretation of nature (Natural Law)
▼ able to be universalised (Kant)
▼ likely to give the greatest happiness to the greatest number (Utilitarianism).

But when we describe someone as 'good' or 'moral' we do not generally refer to particular decisions they have made (a good person may sometimes make a mistake; a rogue may sometimes behave honourably), but to a **disposition** – a quality that they have as a person. It is not so much concerned with what we should *do*, but what sort of person we should hope to *be*.

Virtue Ethics is about the virtues that make for the good life. Alasdair Macintyre (in *After Virtue*, Duckworth, 1981) defined 'virtue' in this way:

> A virtue is an acquired human quality the possession and exercise of which tends to enable us to achieve those goods which are internal to practices and the lack of which effectively prevents us from achieving any such goods.

This approach, which became popular once more from the middle of the twentieth century, developed an approach that had already been explored by Aristotle. Because it originated in Greece, it is sometimes known by the Greek term **Aretaic Ethics**, which comes from the Greek word for virtue, *arete*.

Note

The other approaches acknowledge virtues, but make them secondary to formulating general principles and rules of moral action. The virtues are seen as dispositions to follow certain principles or rules. Virtue Ethics, by contrast, makes them central.

a) Aristotle's View of the Virtues

Let's start by taking a look at what Aristotle said (in his *Nicomachaean Ethics*):

> ... lovers of beauty find pleasure in things that are pleasant by nature, and virtuous actions are of this kind, so that they are pleasant not only to this type of person but also in themselves. So their life does not need to have pleasure attached to it as a sort of accessory, but contains its own pleasure in itself. Indeed we may go further and assert that anyone who does not delight in fine actions is not even a good man; **for nobody would say that a man is just unless he enjoys acting justly, nor liberal unless he enjoys liberal actions, and similarly in all the other cases. If this is so, virtuous actions must be pleasurable in themselves**.

Aristotle saw 'happiness' (*eudaimonia*) as the goal in life. But that was about living a good life, as much as enjoying the good things of life. He considered qualities that enabled people to live together; only when those qualities were displayed could one enjoy happiness, because they were necessary for one's development as a social being. Developing qualities is not antisocial, or unrelated to the needs of others.

So developing the virtues is a necessary feature of living alongside others – it is therefore a social, political and moral feature of life, not just a personal one.

Aristotle also considered it important to strike a balance (or mean) between extremes, and it is recognising that balance that leads to virtue. Here are some of his examples:

Meanness – deficiency
Extravagance – excess
Liberality – the mean

Cowardice – deficiency
Rashness – excess
Courage – the mean

But note that 'the mean' is here applied to qualities or virtues. It *cannot* be applied in the same way to actions. For example, it would be a misuse of Aristotle's theory to try to apply it to theft: that never stealing is deficiency, always stealing is excess, and sometimes stealing is the mean.

The mean is *not* about being some kind of 'average person', but of having a balanced personality, able to display virtues that express a view of life that is based on reason. It is reason that gives balance and objectivity to the virtues – and for Aristotle, humankind's chief characteristic is the ability to reason.

Notice that while virtues may help us to achieve happiness, they are not judged according to whether or not they achieve a particular result. For example, there may actually be a time when being mean or cowardly produces the best consequences for the person concerned, but that does not make them good qualities in themselves. Once you evaluate virtues in terms of results, you are actually reverting to a utilitarian ethic. On the other hand, the exercise of the virtues would result in the optimal working of society, for Aristotle sees a life ruled by reason as one that leads to good social consequences.

For Aristotle, you can't explain right or wrong simply in terms of rules, but rather you can show how a virtuous person can be trusted to do the right thing in a variety of situations, each of which may be unique and cannot therefore be covered by way of a rule.

Four **cardinal virtues** (the word 'cardinal' comes from *cardo*, meaning a hinge) are found in Plato, Aristotle, the Stoics (who considered them to be the basis of the moral life) and Aquinas. They are: temperance (moderation), justice, courage and wisdom. They represent the human qualities that reason suggests are required in order to live a moral life and to achieve the 'final cause' or overall purpose in life.

The opposite of these cardinal virtues are the seven **capital vices**: pride, avarice, lust, envy, gluttony, anger and sloth – often referred to as the 'seven deadly sins'.

Notice, therefore, that these virtues and vices, as they appear in Aquinas, are based on reason and on the sense of purpose in life. They stand independent of any specifically Christian revelation. Thus, for example, the cardinal virtues might be contrasted with the theological virtues – faith, hope and love – which appear in the New Testament.

For Virtue Ethics, morality is about the person, not so much the action. What is it like to be a good or moral person? What qualities should I develop?

Virtue is a disposition, a habitual way of acting. You can only gain virtues by practice, and you are only described as virtuous once you are seen to act in a particular way, apparently of your own free will and with honesty of intention (i.e. pretending to be kind in order to gain something is not the same thing as actually being kind).

Note

Virtue Ethics may be compatible with a 'Natural Law' approach, since a virtue can be seen as a potentiality – a quality that is likely to be displayed in action. Acting out and therefore realising one's potential is what Natural Law uses as a guide for moral action, since the final purpose of everything is that for which it is designed, its potential, within a rational universe.

b) Modern Approaches

Virtue Ethics was revived by an article written by Elizabeth Anscombe in 1958, entitled 'Modern Moral Philosophy'. In it she developed an approach to ethics based on the qualities or virtues that are associated with someone who lives a 'good' life.

This was in contrast to the prevailing ethics of the day because it moved moral debate away from general rules and principles of behaviour, and towards more general questions about value and meaning in life, and qualities that were worth developing and encouraging. It was thought that the other main theories – particularly Utilitarianism and Kantian ethics – were inadequate and lacked a sound foundation, since many people no longer believed in God as an external lawgiver or guarantor of rewards. And without a sense of ultimate reward or punishment, Anscombe felt that the older systems could not be effective as guides for the moral life. The only answer, she felt, was to return to some Aristotelian idea of what it was to live well (*eudaimonia*) – a goal which would be good in itself, as well as producing good for society as a whole.

Kant had argued that you should do your duty even if (and especially if) it goes against your natural disposition, and that doing something you enjoy takes away any sense of moral obligation. By contrast, Virtue Ethics sees the virtuous person as one who has a natural disposition to do what is good. In other words, doing what is right is about being good, or kind, or generous. It is not simply a matter of obeying an external command, nor being able to add up expected results. In a world where a majority do not believe in an external lawgiver, and all results are ambiguous, there needs to be some other criterion for moral action.

Virtue Ethics involves personal responsibility and is entirely secular – it is about developing qualities that will promote *eudaimonia*. It is therefore compatible with religion, but independent of it.

The revived Virtue Ethics appealed to **feminist thinkers**, who felt that the other ethical theories, based on rights and duties, were a particularly male way of approaching life, whereas Virtue Ethics included a recognition of the value of relationships and intimacy.

Virtue Ethics is **naturalistic**: it moves away from the idea of obeying rules, to an appreciation of how one might express one's own fundamental nature, and thus fulfil one's potential as a human being.

But we need to remember one other key feature of human behaviour. Most people do not simply do what is most rational. They act from all sorts of motives, and (especially if the philosopher Hume is to be believed) people act on the promptings of their emotions, and find reasons for their actions afterwards, to explain or justify them.

Now we need to remember that Kant said that you are only behaving in a moral way if you act according to the pure practical reason,

ISSUE:
What do you do when you are faced with two different possible courses of action, neither of which seems to be any more an expression of virtue than the other? Moral dilemmas occur because people want to be good, but do not know what they should do to be good.

and that you are only doing your duty if you do it because you know it is your duty, not because you enjoy doing it anyway. In other words, the better you are naturally, the less your behaviour is moral. Now that seems crazy – being naturally kind, compassionate and so on, should be a sign of the moral life, not an *alternative* to it.

With Virtue Ethics, there is no moral difference between doing something because you believe it is your duty and doing it because you have developed a quality such that it is the natural thing for you to do. If you act virtuously, then you are doing what is right.

Virtue Ethics has shown that morality goes beyond rules and regulations, and should be concerned with questions about the value and purpose of human life:

▼ What is the good life?

▼ How might being virtuous help to promote the good life?

▼ Is it more important to frame sets of rules in order to understand morality, or would it be better to give attention to how a virtuous person might behave?

▼ Is morality universal, or does it depend on the abilities and circumstances of the individual?

A great plus for Virtue Ethics is that it does take into account the needs and desires of the individual and also those of society – and basically (following Aristotle) sees the two being held in balance, each helping the other, because people are basically political animals. Aristotle, of course, was very much the political animal – he always thinks of people in terms of their role within society as a whole. Hence the virtues he wants to see promoted are those that are good both for the individual and for society. Hence his fear of extremes, his concentration on the 'mean' or norm, and the ideal he puts forward of living in comfortable moderation. Ethics, for Aristotle, is very much a matter of training for the good life. And like all training, he did not consider that it could come naturally, but by constant thought and practice. A virtuous person does not become virtuous by accident, but by behaving well, following the example of those who are generally considered to be virtuous. And, in doing this, Aristotle sees society as benefiting generally, and as flourishing.

Virtue Ethics strives for personal autonomy for the individual, but does so within the context of the needs of society.

MAKING CONNECTIONS

Virtue Ethics raises questions that impact upon other areas of Philosophy and Ethics. For example:

Do we have a fixed 'essence', with qualities that we choose to exhibit, or are we mostly shaped by our environment and upbringing?

If we have little control over the way our personalities are shaped, are we truly responsible for our actions? Can I be praised or blamed for virtues that I happen to have or lack?

These questions relate to the issues of freedom and determinism (Am I ever free to choose what to do, and therefore accountable morally?), and also to the Moral Argument for the existence of God (If morality simply expresses virtues which I happen to possess, can that be the basis for an argument for God? It may be the environment and upbringing, rather than God, which determines what I do.). They are also key to questions about the nature of the self (Am I a fixed 'self' or 'soul' that might exist apart from my body, or is my character assembled from virtues that I inherit? Do I have what Aristotle would have seen as a purpose, related to the 'real me'?).

▼ ESSAY QUESTIONS

1 a) Describe the basis of a Natural Law approach to ethics.
   b) To what extent do you consider this to offer a genuinely objective approach to moral arguments?
2 a) Compare Act and Rule Utilitarianism.
   b) Assess the strengths and weaknesses of each.

See the 'Further Reading and Websites' section at the back of this book for follow-up work on this chapter.

9

RELIGIOUS ETHICS

All ethical systems have to be based on something – whether it is a sense of purpose for each thing or action, or an assessment of results, or the pure practical reason. That foundation provides the starting point, and its basic ideas and values inform every ethical decision that is taken.

Clearly, some people come to ethics simply from the point of view of human reason, or an attitude of concern for all other human beings, or for life in general. Others, however, come from a background in one of the world's great religions, and the ultimate beliefs and values of that religion will colour their ethical thinking.

As we shall see in this chapter, each religion sets out moral principles by which its members are expected to live, and those principles are backed by the authority of the religion, whether it is through its scriptures, its tradition of teaching, or through the culture or caste within which the religion operates.

But how are religious moral principles related to those that are given through the rational arguments and theories that we have considered so far?

In general there are three ways in which religion and ethics may be connected:

▼ **Autonomy**. Ethics is said to be autonomous if it is independent of any external religious influence or values. What is more, an ethical argument may be autonomous, even if the person putting it forward is a member of a religion. Autonomy simply relates to the way in which that theory or principle can be validated. If it is based on human reason alone, then it is autonomous.

▼ **Heteronomy**. Ethics is said to be heteronomous if it is informed by the values and general principles given by a religion. Most religious ethics are heteronomous, since – whatever arguments are subsequently used to justify them – the basic reason for following that particular set of ethical principles is that they are backed by the authority of religion.

▼ **Theonomy**. It may be argued that there are some basic principles and intuitions that inspire and inform both secular ethical theories and religious beliefs. To use a religious term, both are 'theonomous', since both come ultimately from God. Of course, this is the way a religious person might describe an ethical theory that is not based directly on religious rules or regulations, but is in line with the general values expressed by that religion. A secular thinker would have no reason to call the ethics 'theonomous'.

Note

Religious and non-religious people may come to the same judgement about what is right or wrong, but the arguments they use, and the foundations upon which those arguments are based, are likely to be different. Secular and religious moral systems can often agree on fundamental values, for example 'love' or 'respect for persons'. It is not the moral conclusions that distinguish the secular from the religious, but the methods at which they arrive at those conclusions and the ways in which they justify them.

For the purposes of an AS-level paper in Religious Ethics, students should know the basic ethical stance of the religions studied on major issues, although a detailed knowledge of all religious rules and regulations is not necessary. However, it is important to be able to relate religious ethics to the ethical systems studied on the course. Hence, it is important to think about whether, or to what extent, the ethics of each religion are related to a Natural Law view, Utilitarian or Situationist view, for example.

The range of moral issues addressed by the world religions is huge, and cannot be adequately covered here. The aim of the sections that follow is to set out the principles and sources of authority that characterise the ethics of each of the six major world religions, and then to look briefly at how they relate to the main ethical theories.

1 Judaism

Jewish morality is based on the *Torah* (Law). It is based on the first five books of the Hebrew Bible, and includes rules for dealing with religious, ethical and social concerns. The best-known core statement of these rules is the Ten Commandments (Exodus 20:1–17), and the moral principles of the *Torah* were summed up by Rabbi Hillel in the first century BCE with the single principle: 'What is hateful to you do not do to another.'

The application of *Torah* to new situations grew into an encyclopae-dia of rules and traditions – the *Talmud*. It contains the *Mishna* (a col-lection of oral traditions, believed to have been originally given to Moses by God), along with the written *Torah*, and a further commen-tary on the *Mishna*, called the *Gemara*.

Jews are required to follow these in the correct way, and this is called the *halakah*, or 'path'. Within Judaism there is variation in the strictness with which different groups put these rules into effect. Some take them literally in every detail, others follow rather more general principles, adapting where necessary to some perceived requirements of modern life.

Reason and conscience both have a part to play in Jewish ethics, but Judaism is mainly concerned with the interpretation and applica-tion of the rules of the *Torah*.

The *Torah* is seen as having the authority of God, given to human-kind for its benefit. By keeping the rules of his or her religion, a fol-lower of the Jewish faith is not simply obeying authority or voluntarily adopting a particular style of life, but is also entering into a commu-nity and a tradition with a very long history.

▼ Clearly, the ethical principles within the *Torah* are believed to have the authority of God. The role of human reason is limited to interpreting those rules and applying them to particular situations.

▼ Hence Jewish morality is **deontological** (having to do with duties) rather than teleological (based on achieving an end result).

▼ There are some parallels with Natural Law, since the Torah is seen as bound up with the rational principle behind the whole created universe, but (unlike the Natural Law tradition) Jewish ethics predates, and is therefore independent of, the philosophy of Aristotle.

▼ Although rules need to be interpreted to fit new situations, there is little in common with Situation Ethics.

▼ Some Jewish principles are in line with Kantian ethics, but they are cer-tainly not seen as derived from the pure practical reason, as in Kant.

2 Christianity

Since Judaism and Christianity have common roots in the religion of the Scriptures that Christianity calls the 'Old Testament', Christianity shares with Judaism the moral basis of the Ten Commandments, and the Jewish *Torah* is part of its own scriptures.

However, Christianity interprets the rules of the *Torah* in the light of the life and teaching of Jesus Christ, a significant feature of which was that Jesus was prepared to set aside the detailed requirements of the Law in the interests of an expression of love or compassion in par-ticular situations. (However, in doing so, the scriptures suggest that he was not setting the Law aside, but rather fulfilling and completing it.)

With the admission of Gentiles into the Christian community, and its emergence as a separate religion, the social customs and many of the rules given in the *Torah* were no longer taken as the base for a Christian life. Nevertheless, Christians and Jews hold a common core of moral tradition. Christianity makes a point of emphasising that it is based on faith in God and in Jesus Christ, rather than obedience to religious rules as the basis of life. It is therefore less rule-based than Judaism, even where it shares the same values.

Sources of authority for Christian morality vary in terms of emphasis from one Christian denomination to another. But they include:

▼ the authority of the Scriptures (regarded as inspired by God)

▼ human reason (particularly as used in applying a 'natural law' basis for morality and in the application of traditional moral rules to new situations)

▼ conscience (as given by God)

▼ the direct inspiration of the Holy Spirit (particularly within charismatic and other groups, feeling inspired)

▼ the authority of the Church (believed to be inspired by the Holy Spirit), particularly, for Catholics, the pronouncements of the Pope, the Bishop of Rome.

Differences of emphasis between different groups of Christians may generally be traced back to which of these sources of religious and moral authority take precedence. In general, for example, the Catholic Church has emphasised the authority of the Church teachings and the Pope, and gives human reason a supporting role. By contrast, some Protestant groups place far greater emphasis on the divine inspiration of Scripture. There is also wide variation in the appreciation of the role of human reason. Some see it as God-given and able to aid with the interpretation of Scripture or of Natural Law, others see reason as 'fallen' and therefore of limited value.

▼ Clearly Christian moral positions are directly linked to Natural Law (which – under Aquinas – was a deliberate attempt to match Aristotelian ideas with the Christian ethical tradition).

▼ They are also directly reflected in Situation Ethics, which grew out of a radical interpretation of the Christian perspective on morality.

▼ Utilitarian arguments are less clearly related to Christian ethics, although it needs to be said that many who developed Utilitarianism thought that they were expressing Christian sentiments in the attempt to see that all alike had their interests taken into account.

▼ Immanuel Kant was a Protestant Christian, and the postulates of the pure practical reason are seen as underlying the experience and implications of the Categorical Imperative.

3 Islam

Fundamental to Islam, and the root of the terms Islam and Muslim, is the principle of 'submission'. Muslims believe that everything should submit to Allah, living in a natural way. Most creatures do this automatically, and every child is born with a natural ability to submit to Allah. But human beings have reason, and can therefore choose whether or not to submit to God. Since Allah is seen as the fundamental reality and creator of everything, submission to him involves living in a natural way, in tune with the creator.

So a first principle of Muslim ethics is to live in harmony with the creator. Beyond this, however, Muslims have two written sources of authority:

▼ **The Qur'an.** This is believed to be the revelation of the will of God, given to Muhammad in a series of visionary experiences. Moral principles embedded in it are therefore seen as coming direct from Allah.

▼ **The Hadith.** This is a collection of the sayings and deeds of the Prophet Muhammad, used as an example for Muslims to follow.

The *Shariah* (or 'path') refers to a natural law, created by God, to guide everything in the universe, including human behaviour. The term *Shariah* is used for the strict code of Muslim law.

Muslims use the principle of analogy in applying moral decisions found in the Hadith or Qur'an to present-day issues. In matters of dispute over a point of law, a ruling is given by a gathering of Muslim scholars (called the *ulama*).

▼ As with Judaism and Christianity, Islam offers a communal basis for its ethics, building upon a tradition of interpretations, but with an absolute authority in the Qur'an and Hadith.

▼ There are parallels with the Natural Law approach to ethics, since fulfilling its natural function in the universe is exactly what 'submission' to Allah is all about.

▼ Clearly Muslim ethics are deontological rather than teleological, since they are based on the duties of Muslims in following the *Shariah*.

▼ There seems little scope within Islam for a utilitarian or situationist approach to ethics. Human reason is valuable in interpreting the *Shariah* and for understanding the natural state of submission, but is not in itself a sufficient basis for ethics.

▼ Issues in Kantian ethics may find parallels in Islamic law, but the basis of the two is quite different. Kant is based on pure practical reason, Islamic law is based on submission, obedience and interpretation of the *Shariah*.

▼ The process of adapting and interpreting laws to suit particular situations is accepted, and may reflect two of the names for Allah – 'the merciful' and 'the compassionate'.

4 Hinduism

Unlike the three monotheistic religions, in which there appear to be agreed sources of authority, Hinduism represents a broad tradition of spiritual beliefs and practices originating in India. It is, therefore, more difficult to specify the sources of authority and ways of justifying moral positions. Much of what is included under Hindu ethics represents the cumulative social traditions of that particular culture, rather than an ethic deduced from particular scriptures or teachings. Nevertheless, there are some key features that apply generally across Hindu society.

The term for 'duty' in the Vedas is *Dharma*, which can be translated as right or appropriate action or duty. *Dharma* sustains society and ensures that it conforms to the natural order of things. This may be expressed through *Svadharma*, which is '*Dharma* for oneself' – in other words, each person will have a particular duty to perform, and one's *svadharma* is the *Dharma* as it applies to you as an individual. However, one's particular *Dharma* is determined by the caste group into which one is born (*varna*), and also one's own status in life (*ashrama*). The term for *Dharma* made specific by these two things is *Varnashramadharma*.

The four main *varnas* are: *Brahmin*, *Kshatriya*, *Vaishya* and *Shudra*. Beneath these come those who are outside the caste system, and who therefore hold the lowest place in society. There is flexibility between and within each of the four main *varnas*, but a sense of moral duty is closely related to the traditional obligations of one's *varna*.

The four *Ashramas*, or 'stages in life', are: Student, Householder, Retired, Ascetic. Not all Hindus go through all four of these stages, but the fact that one's *dharma* is related to them indicates the flexibility of the Hindu social and moral system.

Hindu ethics is flexible in recognising that different people, at different stages of life, will have different norms of behaviour. It has the advantage of not having to constantly adapt generalised laws to the needs of particular groups of people. On the other hand it is difficult within such a system to distinguish between what is right or wrong in any absolute sense, since it is difficult to distinguish between moral principles and social custom.

The *Manudharma Sastra* (or *Manusmrti*) sets out four aims of life:
1 *Dharma* (virtue/right conduct)
2 *Artha* (wealth)
3 *Kama* (pleasure)
4 *Moksha* (liberation)

In the 'path of action' as a method of liberation, one is advised to follow five principles:

1 *ahimsa* (not killing)
2 *satya* (speaking the truth)
3 *asteya* (not stealing)
4 *brahmacarya* (continence in matters sensual)
5 *aparigraha* (avoiding avarice)

Ahimsa (not killing) is a key feature of Hindu ethics. This is particularly emphasised with the ascetic tradition, and was also a main feature of the moral campaigns of Gandhi. However, the needs of society, and the dilemmas of living in a world where military force was needed, led to a modification of this and other ascetic principles. Hence there are really two levels of morality – the ascetic and the social. At the latter level (as shown in the Gita, where there is a discussion about whether it is right to kill enemies in battle) there is a compromise position, in which one can do one's duty, and yet remain detached from the results of doing it.

Hence the sources of authority within Hinduism can be derived from the scriptures, but in practical terms they are mediated to people via the social customs and traditions in which different people in different situations find themselves.

▼ Unlike Utilitarianism, with its emphasis on individual autonomy and equality, most Hindu ethics are social and accept social differences.

▼ Unlike Kantian ethics, Hinduism does not attempt to frame universal rational principles in ethics – since even *ahimsa* may need to be set aside if society requires it.

▼ Unlike Situation Ethics, which tends to come from a very western perspective of free individuals in situations where they are free to choose what to do, Hinduism tends to view people and their dilemmas in a social context, as a concern about how to follow one's duty when it conflicts with one's natural desire.

▼ Overall, there is a sense of *Dharma* which can be fulfilled through the path of ethical action (the *karma marga*), which comes fairly close to a Natural Law approach.

5 Buddhism

Unlike the other religious traditions, Buddhist ethics do not generally speak of good or bad, right or wrong, but of thoughts and actions being either *kushala* (skilful) – if based on compassion, generosity and wisdom – or *akushala* (unskilful) – if based on hatred, craving and delusion.

The reason for this is that Buddhism recognises that an action may have very different moral implications depending on the circumstances within which it is performed. In general, skilful actions are those that are able to bring about an increase in happiness. The Buddhist aim in life is to overcome the suffering caused by greed, hatred and illusion, and to develop happiness through peace, joy and insight. Buddhists believe that all ethically significant actions (*karma*) have their consequences, and therefore skilful actions will lead to good consequences.

Setting aside the issue of whether or not Buddhism should be considered a religion at all, there is a fundamental difference between Buddhist beliefs and ethics and those of the other traditions. That is, Buddhists are required to accept teachings only if they are personally convinced of their truth and applicability to their lives. Hence the question of authority, which in other traditions tends to focus on the interpretation of scriptures, is within the Buddhist traditions divided up between respect for traditional teachings and the scriptures that contain them, respect for individual spiritual teachers, and the requirement of respect for one's own personal integrity in accepting the teachings.

Buddhist moral guidelines are summed up in the five precepts:

1 Not to destroy life (of all sorts, not just human).
2 Not to take what is not given (extending beyond simple theft to include any situation where money or goods are appropriated from those who do not choose to give them).
3 Not to indulge in harmful sexual activity (generally extended to include indulgence of the senses generally).
4 Not to speak falsely (to include self-deception and giving the wrong impression).
5 Not to take those things which cloud the mind (generally extended beyond alcohol and drugs to include all mind-numbing activities).

Buddhist ethics are also informed by the desire to cultivate four mental states:

▽ Love: towards all living things and also towards oneself.
▽ Pity: compassion for all who suffer.
▽ Joy: a conscious sharing in the happiness of others.
▽ Serenity: freedom from anxieties about success or failure, and equanimity in dealing with others.

▽ Buddhist ethics come closer than those of other religions to taking a utilitarian view. That is because the promotion of happiness is key to the Buddhist view of life.
▽ Since Buddhist teachings see all things as interconnected and lacking inherent selfhood, it is difficult to see parallels with a Natural Law approach to ethics – which requires individual things to have specific final goals or ends.
▽ Whereas Buddhism would accept the second formulation of Kant's

Categorical Imperative (to treat people as ends rather than means), in general it rejects the idea that maxims can be universalised as a basis for accepting moral principles.

▼ It is largely situationist, in that it accepts that individual circumstances generally determine what is skilful.

6 Sikhism

Sikhs believe that people are naturally prone to live in a state of illusion, in which they are dominated by the five evil impulses:

1 lust
2 anger
3 greed
4 attachment to worldly things
5 pride.

Sikhs therefore seek to be inspired by God to overcome these and to cultivate their opposites:

▼ self-control
▼ forgiveness
▼ contentment
▼ love of God
▼ humility.

A major feature of life in the Sikh community is the emphasis on equality. This stems from the origins of the religion, as embracing both Hindu and Muslim traditions. As a symbol of this, every Gurdwara (Sikh temple) has a *langar*, a communal kitchen and dining area where worshippers sit and eat together.

A second feature is the concern for justice. Sikhs who belong to the Khalsa (having committed themselves in a ceremony to follow the Sikh way of life) are required to carry a sword (*kirpan*), to be used in self-defence. It should be used only when all peaceful means of resolving a dispute have failed, and only to re-establish justice where there has been a wrong (for example, to defend the Sikh community), or in a direct act of self-defence.

In terms of authority, Sikhs accept the teachings of the ten Gurus and of the Guru Granth Sahib, the holy book. In practical terms, Sikh ethics are included in a book called the *Rehat Maryada: A Guide to the Sikh Way of Life*, which is a translation of a book produced by a group of Sikh scholars in 1945 and accepted as authoritative.

▼ The Sikh emphasis on the universal requirement of justice and equality as fundamental principles of the ethical life are similar to Kant's attempt to find universal moral principles. However, whereas Kant is based on pure practical reason, Sikh ethics are based on the traditions of the Gurus.

▼ Sikh ethics are deontological – based on duties towards others, both within and beyond the Sikh community.

▼ The Sikh emphasis on developing qualities through devotion and service to the community may find its closest secular equivalent in Virtue Ethics, since the issue is one of becoming habitually attuned to a way of life, rather than simply responding to individual situations.

▼ Whereas the equality of the *langar* and other features of Sikh life may suggest a utilitarian approach, Sikhs would not see issues of good or evil as being defined through a utilitarian assessment of results, but as given by God and through the inspiration of the Gurus.

▼ ESSAY QUESTIONS

1 a) Describe ways in which religion might influence ethical debate.
  b) Assess the relative value of religious and secular ethics.
2 a) Describe the sources of authority for moral statements in one religion you have studied.
  b) To what extent does that authority detract from the inherent value of ethical debate?

See the 'Further Reading and Websites' section at the back of this book for follow-up work on this chapter.

10

FREE WILL AND CONSCIENCE

1 Freedom, Will and Moral Responsibility

'Should implies can.'

'Morality implies freedom.'

If you are not free to choose to act in a way that reflects your wishes and intentions, then you cannot be blamed for what happens, since praise and blame – and the whole array of moral arguments that stem from them – are based on the assumption that individuals are free to choose how they act, and to take responsibility for what they do.

Hence, the distinction is generally made in law between an action committed by someone who is of sound mind and someone who is certified insane. Being insane is regarded in law as a mitigating circumstance – the person is judged ill, rather than good or bad. In this case, being insane renders moral considerations inappropriate, because the person is unable to make a rational decision about how to behave.

In considering the issues of science and religion (see page 94) we examined the problems raised for religious belief by the idea of determinism – that everything that happens is explicable in terms of the laws of nature, and could not be other than it is. In terms of ethics, 'determinism' is the view that, whether we realise it or not, we are actually determined in all that we do by factors that are outside our control. This creates particular problems both for the meaning of moral statements – and hence the validity of ethics as a whole – and also for the sense of moral obligation.

If, following Kant, we know what it is to experience a moral demand (a 'Categorical Imperative', see page 150) and to judge that something is done with a 'good will', that implies that we also believe that people have a measure of freedom to choose how to act. Without freedom, moral obligation makes no sense.

a) How Free?

It is clear that nobody is totally free:

1   Physical limitations. There are some things that I am physically incapable of doing. I cannot be blamed for this, and such limitations have little ethical significance.
2   Psychological limitations. This is more complicated. If the science of psychology can predict choices, then – even if I sense that I am free – I am in fact determined by my background and psychological make-up. Am I therefore responsible for what I do?
3   Social limitations. We may be limited by the financial, social and political structures under which we live. Does conforming to the norms of a society in which I have grown up justify the way I see moral choices?

In considering the moral significance of an action, we need to assess the degree of freedom available to the agent.

MAKING CONNECTIONS

A strong form of determinism is very relevant for any study of the mind/soul and its relationship with the body (see chapter 6 on Body and Soul).

What is the mind? Can it make a difference? If it is revealed only in the electrical impulses within my brain, and if those impulses are predictable, does that mean that – whatever my experience of freedom – I am in reality no more than an automaton?

Figure 8 Am I free to choose what to do, or is my every action determined by causes outside myself, like a piece being moved on a chessboard? Determinism is an important issue for Ethics, for if I am not free, then I cannot be held responsible for what I do. Nobody blames a chess piece for having lost the game!

> ## Note
>
> If human beings are genuinely free to make moral choices, then
> – like God – they are outside the realm of cause and effect. But
> how is that possible? How can we not look at the choice someone
> makes and see the things that have caused it to be made that
> way?

b) Compatibilism

Compatibilism is the view that you can be both free and determined
at the same time. In other words, you do not experience any external
constraints on your free choice, but at the same time, looking at all
the factors at work, you can be seen as determined by them.

This is rather like Kant's two ways of looking at things: as **phenom-
enally determined** (since all things obey the laws of cause and effect,
because we impose such laws on all our experience), but at the same
time as **noumenally free** (in other words, free in terms of our own
experience, but determined in terms of other people's observation
of us).

The alternative to compatibilism is '**incompatibilism**', which is the
view that you can be either free or determined, but not both.
Therefore there are two alternative views that an incompatibilist can
hold:

▼ Libertarianism – if freedom exists.
▼ Determinism – if it doesn't.

Observe also that the mind influences, but does not determine, physical action. I may, for example, choose to fly, or to jump thirty feet
into the air, but choosing to do so is as far as I am able to get with
either aspiration. There are always going to be physical constraints.
Whatever is done is in line with the normal actions of physical bodies.
The effect of the mind is to select between the almost infinite number
of possible physical actions that can take place.

Thus, I choose which word to utter. My tongue is equally physically
capable of articulating 'Yes' or 'No'. In terms of physical causation,
there is nothing to choose between them.

The defence of the libertarian position is generally made on the
grounds of:

▼ The experience we have of personal freedom.
▼ The sense of moral responsibility, which implies freedom.

And these things are often linked to a person's religious views, and
their experience of conscience.

c) Freedom and God

Note

If God exists, all depends on him and we can do nothing against his will. If he does not exist, everything depends on us.

[Camus, from *The Myth of Sisyphus* (1942)]

Note

Aristotle argued that statements about the past and the present can be either true or false, but those about the future cannot be either true or false.

In the broad sense, this follows most criteria of truth – namely correspondence to objective facts. If truth depends on evidence, there can be no evidence for the future, because the source of evidence does not yet exist. Hence it makes no sense to say of a statement about the future that it is either true or false.

Can God know the future? What could such knowledge mean? We cannot know *now* that the statement that I will do something next week is either true or false, because the only way of confirming its truth is to wait for that future event to become present.

Clearly, the issue of free will and determinism creates problems for religious belief. Traditional theistic belief (as held by Jews, Christians and Muslims) involves a God who is **omnipotent** and **omniscient**. In other words, God has created everything out of nothing; he is able to do anything and is totally in charge of his creation, active within everything that happens. He also knows what has happened, what is happening at this moment, and what will happen in the future. But *can* he know the future? What does it mean to 'know' something that has not yet happened?

For a religious person, the 'problem' in regard to God is similar to the 'problem' that the secular person has with science – for just as science seems to offer a closed system of forces which can totally explain and determine what happens, so God too (if he knows the future) must thereby determine what will happen. But how can either scientific determinism or an omniscient God fit in with our experience as individuals who can choose what we will do and take responsibility for our actions? In other words, the idea of an omniscient God appears to support determinism, for, if he knows that it is true that I will do X tomorrow, then I am going to do X, whether I want to or not!

KEY QUESTION
Is God's foreknowledge compatible with free will?

Now there is a terrible catch for believers here. Theists generally argue that if you experience yourself as acting morally, that implies that you believe in God, freedom and immortality. This was the basis of Kant's 'moral argument' for the existence of God (see page 41).

The problem is this:

If you believe in an omniscient and omnipotent God, then human freedom appears to vanish (we cannot do anything freely if God already knows what we will do, and effectively does it himself) – freedom and creativity on the part of humans are little more than an illusion. God does it, but we are fooled into thinking that we do it. If so, what does that do to morality and human responsibility, the very things that religion requires?

But if we are genuinely free to choose and to act, to create and to shape the future, what does that do to the traditional concept of an omniscient creator God?

Just as it appeared that you cannot be totally committed to a scientific view of the world and still accept human freedom . . . so it seems that you cannot be totally committed to a theistic view of the world (if the traditional concepts of God are taken literally) and still believe in your own freedom of choice.

One way round this problem is to argue that God 'knows' the future, but in a way that is not causal. In other words, he knows it will happen, but does not thereby cause it to happen.

This appears to get around the immediate problem, but only raises another: If God knows what will happen, even if he does not cause it himself, should he not intervene and stop something evil happening? Once again we are returned to the old 'problem of evil' where God is either impotent or uncaring.

MAKING CONNECTIONS

Ideas about 'the freedom of the will' relate to:

▼ The nature of God – since he may be claimed as omniscient and as a creator '*ex nihilo*', both of which seem at odds with the genuine ability of human beings to make free choices and act on them.

▼ The problem of evil – since if God knows that evil happens in the future but does nothing to prevent it, he is co-responsible for it. Why does God allow people the freedom to be wicked?

▼ Existential Philosophy – Heidegger, Sartre, Camus etc. point to the ability of human beings to assert their own authenticity by the free choices they make.

2 Conscience

Conscience is the inner conviction that something is right or wrong. It is found in both secular and religious ethical discussions.

In a religious discussion, it may be thought of as the 'voice of God', speaking within the individual, and even as a direct revelation from God. In the New Testament (Romans 2:15), conscience is described as the witness to the 'requirements of the law' being written on the heart. The implication of this would seem to be that, through following their conscience, everyone can follow the requirements of the divine law.

In a secular discussion, it is more likely to be seen as the natural way in which people are able to apply their general moral principles to the particular situations in which they find themselves.

In order to be able to operate, conscience seems to need two things:
▽ freedom
▽ knowledge of the good.

Unless you are free to do something, it makes no sense for your conscience to tell you to do it or not to do it. Equally, conscience implies some innate knowledge of what is 'good', for without that, it is difficult to see how conscience could suggest what one should do.

So conscience plays a part in relating a general sense of what is good (often in the form of moral rules) to the situations in which we are free to choose what to do. But if it is a natural and universal human phenomenon (without which you might be branded a psychopath), what part does it play in moral decision making?

a) Aquinas

Aquinas saw the conscience as the natural ability of a rational human being to understand the difference between right and wrong, and to apply the most basic moral principles to particular situations. He did recognise, however, that there were problems with simply leaving everyone to follow their own moral sense – for example, a person might have their judgement clouded by their passions, or by ignorance, or by long-established habits. He also saw that different societies had different views of what constituted right and wrong.

Hence, although he is able to say that it is always right to follow one's conscience, he does recognise that people may still get things wrong, through ignorance or through making a mistake. There were, therefore, two possible ways in which that process could go wrong:

1 A person might not be aware of the relevant moral principle. In other words, for conscience to work, a person needs to have some background information about what is considered right and wrong.

ISSUES:

Is it always right to follow one's conscience?

Why do people who follow their conscience sometimes differ in what they believe to be right?

Which comes first, your principles or your conscience? (If you did not have any principles, could you have a conscience?)

2   A person might know and agree to a general moral principle, but be unaware that it applied in a particular situation.

It is therefore quite possible for a person to do what – by any objective standard – might be considered wrong, and yet to be right in following his or her conscience. In other words, his idea of conscience is very much as a tool for applying already accepted moral principles.

Notice carefully what is implied by this. Aquinas considers conscience to be the means by which individuals apply the general moral principles that they hold. When Aquinas says it is always right to follow your conscience, what he means is that it is always right to apply your moral principles to each individual situation, to the best of your ability. It does not mean that by following conscience, one is always in the right – for if your principles are wrong, then your conscience is going to lead you astray.

Notice the way in which Aquinas' thinking about conscience reflects his general position on ethics. He believes that people need to accept general principles, and they apply them (with the help of conscience) to particular situations.

But is that actually how morality works? Do we always use reason, guided by conscience, to determine what we do? In commenting on Aquinas, Copleston makes the important point that for most people the emotions rather than reason provide the starting point for moral choices.

b) Butler

Whereas Aquinas saw the conscience as the means of applying moral principles, Joseph Butler gave conscience a rather different role, as a guarding or controlling influence over the different aspects of human nature. He wanted to avoid an approach to human nature that was based on egoism, and provide a place for conscience, recognising that people sometimes restrain their appetites for the sake of doing what is right.

He considered that there were two very different parts or aspects to human beings. On the one hand there were the passions and appetites, including the affections that people have. On the other, there were the more thoughtful aspects of benevolence towards others and conscience, as well as self-love.

Butler argued that these various parts of the self were ordered in a hierarchy. Thus there are situations when conscience, being superior in the hierarchy, is able to over-rule the promptings of the appetites or the affections. For Butler, the moral life was a matter of getting that hierarchy ordered in the right way. But within that hierarchy, conscience comes at the top, because it has the additional role of sorting out the conflicting claims of self-love and benevolence – and that balance is crucial for making moral decisions.

In some ways, Butler's account of the role of conscience is rather like Plato's view that reason should control appetite. When a person acts in a morally appropriate way, according to Butler's theory, it means that the conscience sorts out the balance between self-love and benevolence towards others, and controls the appetites and affections accordingly.

In a sense, you might sum up Butler's view by saying that a good person is someone who has his or her priorities well sorted, with the promptings of conscience ranking highest among them.

Note

Clearly, Butler's view has the advantage of accounting for moral dilemmas. We have to balance which part of our nature should take priority in any situation, and that is why we may sometimes feel uncertain about what we should do.

---

c) Freud

Conscience is closely associated with a sense of guilt, in that we feel guilty if we go against our conscience. This was of particular interest to Freud, who sought to give a psychological explanation for it.

He argued that, through our early upbringing, we learn values that continue to influence our moral awareness and our conscience later in life. He distinguished between three elements in the mind – the **ego**, the **id** and the **super-ego**. At its simplest level, the ego is the rational self, the id is the self at the level of its physical and emotional needs, and the super-ego is the controlling, restraining self. Clearly, conscience is an aspect of the operation of the super-ego.

For our purposes, the importance of this view is that it challenges the role of the conscience, and also raises questions about our freedom.

If conscience is simply an expression of the unconscious application of rules that we have been given in our early childhood, then it does not qualify to be taken seriously in an ethical discussion, since it is no more than an expression of the wishes of one's parents or other significant adults. It cannot be the voice of God, or the highest element in the hierarchy of the self, but simply an unconscious return to our ethical potty training!

But equally, if our conscience shapes our moral decision making, and if it comes from the unconscious promptings of our early years, then are we really free to make a moral choice at all? It could be argued that our external rules are given by society and our internal conscience is given by our parents – and we are trapped in the middle!

d) Innate or Acquired?

Freud's challenge to the traditional idea of conscience raises a key question: is conscience innate or acquired? If it is innate, then we may expect everyone to have a conscience, and for that conscience to operate in much the same way in every individual. Why then are there differences in what people think they ought to do? Clearly because the moral principles they hold are different. But where did they get those principles? Well, they could come from religion, or upbringing, or society in general. In other words, they could have been acquired.

Notice, however, that it is the moral principles that are acquired, not the conscience itself. The conscience appears more like a *skill* than a set of rules. It is the ability to apply rules to practical situations of moral choice. Like other skills, listening to conscience can be developed (i.e. someone who is sensitive to moral issues might be described as having a well-developed conscience).

As a skill, it may well be innate. This is suggested by the fact that those who appear to have absolutely no conscience at all are regarded as psychopaths – there is something 'wrong' with them, they are not normal. It is normal to have a conscience of some sort. However, its operation will depend on the moral principles or parental rules that it applies – and these are almost certainly acquired.

▼ ESSAY QUESTIONS

1 a) Describe what is meant by 'compatibilism' in ethics.
   b) To what extent does compatibilism require a compromise between the demands of science and the experience of morality?
2 a) Describe Freud's view of the conscience.
   b) Assess the strengths and weaknesses of his view.

See the 'Further Reading and Websites' section at the back of this book for follow-up work on this chapter.

PRACTICAL ETHICS I

1 Abortion and Euthanasia: The Right to Life

TIMELINE

354–430	Augustine
1224–74	Aquinas
1724–1804	Kant
1946–	Singer

In all probability, you will have already considered the moral issues concerning abortion and euthanasia at GCSE level, and will therefore be familiar with the basic arguments for and against each of them. At AS level, the same information will be relevant, but it is also important that you relate the arguments to the various ethical theories that you have studied, and are able to present your own views in the light of them. The book *Issues of Life and Death* in the *Access to Philosophy* series gives further details of the issues and arguments, and is suitable also for A2 level.

In this chapter we shall simply look at some features of the issues, the way these relate to ethical theories, and some religious responses to them.

Abortion

The abortion debate has centred on the apparent conflict between the right to life of the foetus and the right of a woman to choose whether or not she will have a child, for whatever reason. Hence the opposing camps have generally been labelled 'pro-life' and 'pro-choice'.

Central to this debate is the issue about when human life begins. At what point in the process that goes from the tiny bundle of cells that forms the early embryo, through the developing foetus, to the moment of birth, should what is growing be regarded as a new human individual?

Clearly, once you have a human individual, he or she should be given rights and be protected by the law – just as a new-born baby is given protection under the law, even though it is still quite helpless and dependent upon the care of his or her mother. But when does a developing embryo or foetus become independent?

Note

The term 'embryo' is used for the developing bundle of cells in the first 8 weeks after fertilisation; the term 'foetus' is used from that point through until birth.

In the UK, The Abortion Act of 1967 allowed abortion up to 28 weeks' gestation, provided that the approval of two doctors was given, and if continuing the pregnancy threatened the life or physical or mental health of the mother or the physical or mental health of existing children, or if there was substantial risk that the child would be born with serious physical or mental handicap.

There are two separate elements in this legislation: the upper limit beyond which the foetus is considered to be 'viable' if born, and the reasons that justify an abortion below that limit. Prior to 1967, abortion was illegal.

The Human Fertilisation and Embryology Act, which came into force in 1991, reduced the upper limit to 24 weeks, except if a mother's life or health was in danger, or if there was a serious risk of foetal handicap. This change came about because developments in medical technology made it possible for babies to be born and to survive from 24 weeks' gestation.

The principle behind this legislation, therefore, is that, whatever the validity of reasons for an abortion, a foetus should be given legal protection if it is possible for it to survive outside the womb. If that principle is adhered to, then with the advance of technology and the

KEY QUESTION

At what point does the life of an autonomous human being, with rights as an individual, begin? Is a foetus an individual? Do we become individuals with rights only at birth?

resulting viability outside the womb at an earlier stage, the legality of abortion will be progressively reduced.

One idea put forward by Peter Singer and Deane Wells in *The Reproductive Revolution* (1990) was an **ectogenetic** solution to this problem. Ectogenesis is the keeping alive of a young foetus in an artificial womb. If that became possible, they argued, then the issue of whether a woman should continue with her pregnancy could be separated from the issue of killing the foetus, since it could simply be transferred out into an artificial womb.

At the moment, that solution to the problem is not technically viable, and it also tends to follow the traditional line of weighing the rights of the mother over those of the foetus. But what would be the moral situation of those in charge of such an artificial womb? Would they not take on exactly the responsibility and moral dilemmas of the mother? What if the foetus was shown to have abnormalities at a later stage? Should it then be 'aborted' from its artificial womb? The problems remain.

A rather crude but vivid analogy in favour of the right of a woman to choose abortion was presented in a controversial article by Judith Jarvis-Thomson entitled 'A Defence of Abortion' (1971). She asked the reader to imagine the situation of a woman who is kidnapped and wakes up in a hospital, finding that she has her circulatory system plugged into that of a famous violinist, whose supporters have kidnapped her for that very purpose. The hospital staff explain that she has exactly the right blood for the violinist and must remain attached to him. On the other hand, she should not complain, because she could be unplugged in nine months' time.

Jarvis-Thomson argued that, in those circumstances, it would not be unjust for the woman to request to be unplugged from the violinist, even if he were to die as a result. On the other hand, if the violinist did in fact survive, the woman would not have the right to kill him.

Notice how crucial this is. Some people argue that the foetus has a right to life if it can be shown to be an individual person (in other words, that its rights can be separated from those of the mother). Jarvis-Thomson argued, however, that even in the case of a separate adult human being, there was no absolute right to make such a claim on the body of a woman.

However, there are several problems with this argument:

First of all, the violinist is a separate individual, who is imposed upon the kidnapped woman, whereas the developing foetus may be considered to be part of her body. Whatever the moral justification for doing so, the act of unplugging the violinist is therefore very different from that of terminating a pregnancy.

Secondly, the woman is effectively being used as a machine for supplying blood. Let us suppose that a philanthropist had loaned to the hospital a life-support machine. A desperately ill person is hooked up to it and is being kept alive. Then the philanthropist returns and demands his machine back, unplugging the patient. Would that be morally acceptable? Is there not an implied contract, if the arrangement is freely entered into? Jarvis-Thomson's argument could then only support abortion in the case of rape (which would effectively be the situation she describes, since the woman is kidnapped, and finds herself 'pregnant' with the violinist against her will).

By saying that unplugging the violinist is not the same as taking active steps to kill him once he has recovered, she implies that abortion is not acceptable once the foetus has reached the point of viability.

Some books, for example *The Abortion Myth* by Leslie Cannold (Allen and Unwin, 1998), have argued that one should take into account the whole experience of pregnancy and motherhood, and that women should be trusted to make their own decisions over abortion. It also takes into account the social and gender issues surrounding abortion.

If it is argued that a new life exists and should be protected from the moment of conception, there is a further problem: twins.

There are possible stages at which the embryo may divide and produce two or more individuals:

▼ It can happen on about the fourth or fifth day after the egg is fertilised. In this case, each twin will go on to develop its own placenta.

▼ It can happen at about the time when the embryo becomes implanted in the womb. In this case, the twins will have the same placenta.

▼ It may happen at about the twelfth or fourteenth day, by which time the resulting twins will have to share the same amniotic sac, and may be joined ('Siamese twins').

Until about the fourteenth day, it is therefore not possible to say whether there will be a single or multiple birth. Is it, therefore, sensible to think of the embryo as a unique human person before the time when it is possible that it will become twins?

Sometimes twins are formed, but then re-combine to result in a single birth. If each is an individual with rights from the moment of conception, is the surviving foetus guilty of murder? This extreme situation highlights the problem of taking the single genetic identity established at conception as the unquestioned basis of human individuality.

Euthanasia

In the case of euthanasia, the fundamental issues are similar to those of abortion. First of all there is the question of when life should be considered to have ended, and secondly, the right of any individual to take active steps to end his or her life, or the life of another person.

The intentional killing of another person is considered to be murder (unintentional killing is manslaughter). In the case of the intentional killing of someone on compassionate grounds, the penalty may be reduced to manslaughter, on what is generally termed 'diminished responsibility' (a term which is used in a variety of situations, where there are exceptional circumstances leading up to the killing).

Hence, while suicide was made legal in the UK in 1961, helping someone to kill themselves (**assisted suicide**), killing them at their own request (**voluntary euthanasia**) and killing someone in order to save them further suffering even though they have not requested it (**involuntary euthanasia**) all remain illegal in the UK.

Note

In some countries (e.g. Holland, Australia) euthanasia has been allowed under strictly controlled circumstances. Ethical debate here concerns whether or not there are *any* circumstances in which it should be permitted, and – if so – what controls should be put in place to ensure that it always operates in a way that is directly and obviously in the best interests of the person concerned.

Further issues to be considered in the euthanasia debate concern the difference between actively taking steps to end the life of someone who is seriously ill (**active euthanasia**) and simply discontinuing treatment that keeps them alive (**passive euthanasia**). This distinction arises mainly in the context of medical ethics and the legal and professional obligations of doctors to save or maintain life.

A second set of questions concerns the status of someone seriously ill. Should a person whose life is maintained on a machine and who is in a '**permanent vegetative state**', unable to communicate or participate in the normal activities and relationships that constitute human living, be considered to have a life that is worth prolonging? Should a person who is conscious of being in such a state have the right to ask for that life to be ended?

Beyond that are questions about when life can be considered to have ended anyway. So, for example, a person on a life-support machine may appear to be 'alive' in the sense of having a heart beat and respiration maintained artificially. Normally, a person is considered to be dead if brain activity ceases, either across the entire brain, or in the brain stem, which is the part of the brain that controls the functioning of the body.

ISSUE:
For both abortion and euthanasia, the key question is 'What constitutes a human life?' Only once that is answered can we sensibly decide when human life should be considered to have started or stopped, and when it should have the protection of the law and receive moral consideration.

a) Applying Ethical Theories

Utilitarianism – especially in the form of 'Preference Utilitarianism' – is particularly important in the areas of medical and nursing ethics.

Autonomy of the individual is a key consideration here. Doctors should not be allowed to follow their own wishes, or research interests, in determining treatment. Patients come first: that is basic to framing professional ethics of all sorts.

But can 'the wishes of a patient' necessarily always be followed? What if the patient seeks his or her own harm? The difficulty is in establishing criteria which all can accept for what constitutes benefit or harm. Utilitarianism only works if one can assess the results of an action, and decide whether or not, on balance, they are to the advantage of all concerned.

Hence, a utilitarian will consider the preferences of the mother, in the case of abortion, along with the potential harm to other children in the family, for example. In the case of euthanasia, the utilitarian balance is between the advantages of life rather than death, both for the person concerned but also for their relatives, friends and carers.

The limitation of this process is that it requires careful and impartial judgement. But can we be detached and objective enough to assess what should be done, without acknowledging that our judgement is clouded by our own history and experiences?

I may know, for example, that it is in the best interests of an old or sick pet that it should be put down. That might also correspond to my own interests at a practical level. But that does not make the decision any easier; and in the end it is generally taken because there is a prior and overwhelming desire to see an end to the animal's suffering.

In other words, the utilitarian judgement may be used as justification for an action that is taken primarily on the basis of a strong emotional reaction to an intolerable situation.

Pro-life groups and others cannot accept a simple utilitarian judgement on such matters, since they hold that human life has an absolute value, a value that must be upheld, even if the result is additional suffering for those concerned. In other words, that it is better for a natural course of events to take place, whatever the consequences, rather than to take life.

Natural Law claims that we should use our reason to examine the place and purpose that everything has within the universe, and act in a way that reflects that understanding.

Hence it is very different from a utilitarian argument in terms of what it takes into account. That does not discount the benefit of those concerned, since Aquinas argued that Natural Law should provide 'an ordinance of reason for the common good', but it makes the ben-

COMMENT

All human life will eventually come to an end; so the sum total of all advantages and disadvantages is zero. What counts is not an end point, but the value of the process that leads to that point – the quality of life, or enjoyment etc., along the way.

Thus, the fact that we cannot achieve a final or definitive assessment of happiness should not, in itself, deflect us from using a utilitarian argument.

efits to those concerned a secondary matter, compared with the fundamental nature of the act of euthanasia or abortion in itself.

So, in the case of abortion or contraception, for example, Natural Law looks at the place procreation has within our understanding of what it is to be human. What does it mean to have conceived a child?

From this perception, the act of abortion appears to go against Natural Law, since it frustrates the natural outcome and purpose of conception.

Kant's second formulation of the Categorical Imperative states that people should be treated as ends, never only as means. If the unborn child is considered to be an individual, then its life should not be assessed on the basis of the benefit or otherwise that it offers to the mother and others concerned, but should be treated as an end in itself. Similarly with those who are seriously ill; their lives should be viewed as ends in themselves, and the needs of other people should not be used to justify ending them. Hence, abortion or euthanasia could only be justified if it were seen as being directly of benefit to the person concerned – i.e. that continuing to live would, on balance, be against their own interests on the grounds that it would involve more suffering than that person (if able to make a rational decision) would find acceptable.

A situationist view would be that it is unrealistic to try to legislate on such matters, and that what counts is to do the most loving thing in each situation. This would be very much in line with those who support 'mercy killing' on the grounds that love demands that they no longer allow a situation of intolerable suffering to continue.

b) Religious Responses

A religious response to any of these issues might argue that all life is created by God and is therefore sacred. God alone has the right to decide what should happen, and intervention using artificial techniques – whether for contraception, fertilisation or the ending of the life of a foetus – goes against the belief that a person should trust in God and his purposes.

Christianity opposed the Greek and Roman practice of killing weak or deformed infants by exposing them to the elements. It did so on the grounds that each person had an eternal soul and was made in the image of God.

However, this left open the issue of *when* a foetus received its soul. St Augustine thought that this happened at a point about seven weeks after conception, and argued against abortion after this time. A similar point was made by Aquinas. (English law originally followed that principle, and distinguished between abortions before and after 'quickening' – the time when a mother might feel the movement of the child within her.)

ISSUE:
A key issue for the Natural Law approach concerns when an individual human life can be said to begin. At conception? At birth? At some point in-between?

Science gives only a general guide on this:

Something is generally defined as being alive if it is a complex system that is self-replicating and self-determining.

It is then said to be conscious if it responds to the environment and appears to do so in a way that implies choice.

For example, a wooden block responds to being pushed by toppling over. An animal similarly pushed will turn, look at the person pushing it, and will decide how to respond. Hence the animal is conscious and the wood is not.

A specifically Catholic response, based on Natural Law as well as the traditional teachings of the Church, would add that artificial intervention frustrates the natural usage of these things. Hence, action should be taken only in very extreme circumstances (e.g. abortion when the life of the mother is directly threatened).

Equally, the Catholic encyclical *Evangelium Vitae* sees life as an extraordinary gift from God, and therefore regards euthanasia and abortion as fundamentally wrong.

Earlier, two encyclicals *Casti Connubi* and *Humanae Vitae* argued for the rights of the unborn (the latter also being important because of its opposition to contraception).

All the theistic religions are against the taking of innocent human life, and all express the value of human life for its own sake as a gift of God. From an Eastern perspective, both Jainism and Buddhism – following the ascetic tradition of Hinduism – see *ahimsa* (the refraining from taking life) as central to their ethics.

Note

Eastern religions see all such taking of life as leading to bad **karma**, and therefore to be avoided both for the sake of the life under threat, but also for the spiritual benefit of the person contemplating either abortion or euthanasia.

MAKING CONNECTIONS

The situations in which euthanasia or abortion are contemplated could have implications for the 'problem of evil' and hence for belief in a loving God.

2 The Right to a Child

The first question to consider here is this: 'Is there any absolute "right" to have a child?' If so, are there to be any limits set on the technology employed?

Clearly, the issue is whether someone has the right to have a child who carries their own unique genetic identity. So, for example, it would be possible to adopt a child and bring it up as one's own – caring for it as a surrogate parent – but that would not be the same as producing one's own child.

The issue has come about since the development of *in vitro* fertilisation (IVF) as a technology to help those who could not conceive naturally. IVF enables an embryo to be fertilised artificially, using sperm from the husband or from a donor, and then implanted in the womb. A key ethical question arising from this practice is that there are more embryos produced than are able to be implanted, and therefore whether it is right to destroy them or use them for research purposes. The issue here is that a fertilised embryo is already a potential individual with a fixed genetic identity. Do the donors of sperm and egg have a right to what they have donated? Whose property is genetic material?

Leaving aside for a moment the issues of genetic engineering and embryo research (which will be considered in the next section), we need to look at the basic ethical responses to the question of whether potential parents have the right to use technology in order to assist the birth of a child.

An extension to this issue is whether parents should have the right to choose the sex of their children. This in turn raises all sorts of issues about sexual discrimination and social expectations. To decide not just when children are born, but also their sex, seems to introduce a whole new level of control over the idea of the family – a level of control that some might see as leading to 'designer families'.

a) Applying Ethical Theories

From a utilitarian standpoint, what counts are the wishes and benefits anticipated for all concerned. If it is *possible* to conceive a child with the help of artificial means, then a utilitarian is likely to argue that it should be done, since those concerned have much to gain by doing so.

From a Natural Law standpoint, however, the matter is more complex, since *in vitro* fertilisation is not a 'natural' process. One might argue that nature sets limits to fertility, so that not every member of a species is going to be equally able to produce offspring. If so, then to try to get round such a natural method of population control could be seen as going against 'natural law'.

It is difficult to see how a Kantian argument can sensibly be used for these situations, since the example is so specific that any attempt to universalise it would be unrealistic. However, one could hold the maxim that 'everyone who wishes to have children but is unable to do so naturally, should be able to employ artificial methods to assist conception'. One could argue, however, that the desire for a child implies that the child is being treated as a means (i.e. to satisfy the desires of the parents) rather than an end in itself. Thus it could be argued that the artificial conception of a child automatically implies going against the second formulation of the Categorical Imperative. However, once born, there is no reason why the child should not be loved for itself and not simply as a means to gratify its parents.

Situation ethics would suggest that it is an issue for the potential parents and the doctor to decide, and that it would be unrealistic to legislate on the matter.

b) Religious Responses

In general a theistic and religious response to this issue is to say that a child is a gift from God and therefore not something that should be expected as a right. At the same time, a religious view of prayer and of miracles might suggest that there are occasions when children are born to couples who had previously believed themselves to be infertile, or born in response to prayer. If that is the case, one might ask whether – for a religious believer – resorting to technology if prayer fails to bring the desired result might be seen as an action of lack of faith, and lack of appreciation for the providence of God.

3 Genetic Engineering and Embryo Research

There are a huge number of ethical issues that arise because of genetic engineering, including the impact that genetically modified crops can have on the environment, and the use that can be made of genetic information on individuals to predict their future health. In this section we are concerned primarily with those issues that arise from the impact of genetics on our ability to understand and control our fertility.

Choosing Your Children

The consultation paper on 'pre-implantation genetic diagnosis', produced in 1999 by the Human Fertilisation and Embryology Authority, recommended that, where an embryo is produced by means of artificial fertilisation, it can be checked and should only be implanted in the womb if it has no genetic abnormalities.

This seems eminently sensible, for it would be irresponsible to implant an embryo that was known to be defective, and it enables those involved in the process to screen out serious conditions, such as cystic fibrosis and muscular dystrophy, which result from genetic abnormalities. But this same process of checking could equally be used to select embryos by other criteria – by sex, or intelligence, or susceptibility to illnesses. In effect, the ability to examine the genetic code has given science the ability to predict and therefore manipulate the future – a child can be selected at this stage to fit the requirements of parents. The other side of the same coin is that defective embryos could be destroyed.

Clearly, this raises many issues. Is it right to choose children by colour of hair or other characteristics? These seem trivial, and might easily be dismissed, but should you choose a child whose genetic make-up means that it can be a suitable donor of bone marrow for a sibling who is seriously ill, and for whom a compatible donor cannot be found?

This situation arose in the United Kingdom in the early months of 2003, and was debated in the courts. At the time a 'pro-life' group opposed permission to select the embryo, on the grounds that there should be no selection of some to be implanted and others possibly to be destroyed. Against this was weighed the potential benefit of giving birth to a child who could be a compatible donor. Permission for the selection to take place was finally upheld.

However, the debate reflected a general concern about the selection of embryos. The Oxford Amnesty Lectures for 1998 (published in *The Genetic Revolution and Human Rights*, OUP, 1999) set out the various issues here, including cloning, access to genetic information and eugenics. In that book, Hilary Putnam argued that people should be treated as ends and not used as means, and that children should be valued for what they are, not produced to fit in with some pre-conceived notion.

He argued that it is essential that offspring should be diverse, rather than designed to the specification of their parents. He feared that children who are cloned, or otherwise selectively bred, are actually being treated like consumer objects.

Cloning

Sexual reproduction produces variety in the species, since each child is born as a result of the joining of two different DNA strands. Variety in itself is fundamental to the process of evolution, since it is through the tiny genetic variations that species develop. Variety is also fundamental to any understanding of individuality, since it is differentiation from others that constitutes a recognition of a person.

Hence the process of creating variety in offspring – children being in some ways like one or other or both parents, and in other ways different from them – is fundamental to the way nature works, and to the ethical principles concerning individuals and their rights and relationships.

Cloning is different, because it simply reproduces an existing individual by implanting existing DNA to artificially fertilise an egg. It therefore effectively brings to a halt the natural process of variety and selection. The person cloned is 'designed', created deliberately in order to be like something else, not essentially unique and individual.

Reproductive and Therapeutic Cloning

When cloning is discussed, the thing that most immediately comes to mind is the 'reproductive' purpose – to produce a particular individual, where for some reason that cannot happen by natural means. However, we need to be clear about what that entails. In the case of identical twins, a single fertilised egg results in two or more genetically identical foetuses. Two things are clear when we consider identical twins:

1 Later in life, the twins might still look alike, but would not be identical in terms of personality, since their experiences will have been different. So cloning cannot guarantee that the resulting individual will be exactly like the person cloned, except in genetic, physical characteristics.

2 In the case of identical twins, they are exactly like one another, but *not* like any other living individual. In the case of cloning, however, where a nucleus from an existing individual is used to replace the nucleus of a fertilised egg, the resulting child has the same DNA as an existing human being. And that is something that cannot happen naturally.

Reproductive cloning therefore raises questions about human identity, the purpose of a human life and whether children should be treated as means or ends.

However, there is another aspect of cloning, and that is the potential, through using genetic material, of artificially 'growing' spare parts to be used in place of the present situation where organs are donated and introduced into the body. This is termed 'therapeutic cloning', and it involves the production of adult stem cells which can adapt and grow into any organ of the body. At the moment, the main problem with organ transplants is that the body will reject the transplant, recognising that it is 'foreign', and drugs must be given to suppress this rejection process. The advantage that therapeutic cloning might one day be able to offer is that the organ that is grown and implanted is effectively recognised as part of the host body – it simply replaces the diseased organ with a new one that is genetically identical.

The problem with ethical discussion of cloning is that the therapeutic use is based on technology that would also allow the reproductive use, hence criticism of the latter tends to colour discussion of the former.

Criteria for Medical Research

Nevertheless, the key feature in discussing this is to set out the criteria by which medical research into these issues can be justified. In general (and as set out in 1964 by the World Medical Association) the criteria for doing medical research are:

▽ That the objectives of the research should be in proportion to the inherent risk to the subject. (In other words, the likely results of the research should outweigh any potential harmful effects experienced by the subject of the research.)

▽ Before starting any clinical trial, the risks involved should be assessed in terms of the foreseeable benefits to the subject. (In other words, the person taking part in the medical trial should be expected to benefit personally. It would not be acceptable to expect a person to accept a risk just for the sake of some future unspecified gain in medical knowledge, however important that might be held to be.)

In the case of cloning, the subjects affected are the embryos that are created. Some of them will be destined to be implanted, others will be frozen pending future use, and still others will be used for medical research and then destroyed. Unlike medical experiments on human beings – which is all that the World Medical Association could contemplate 40 years ago – we need to consider the benefit or otherwise to fertilised but not yet implanted cells.

Those who take a strictly 'pro-life' stance on all these issues might argue that no action that results in the destruction of embryos can be justified, no matter what is promised by way of long-term gain.

Failure Rates

In the cloning of a sheep called 'Dolly' in 1997, the failure rate involved in that process was considerable. Dolly was created by cell fusion, in which the nucleus of an already differentiated adult cell was fused with an unfertilised egg from a donor animal. Of the 430 attempts to do this, 277 reconstructed embryos were produced, 23 of which developed sufficiently to be introduced into 13 foster mothers, and only one (Dolly) was successfully taken through to term. There were many severe genetic abnormalities leading to miscarriage.

Figure 9 The cloning of 'Dolly' was a remarkable event, but she was the only survivor out of 277 reconstructed embryos. It may be argued that the failure rate in reproductive cloning causes unacceptable amounts of suffering and therefore should not be applied to humans. But what if the techniques were perfected? Would it still be wrong?

Imagine the scale of physical and emotional suffering involved if this process, in its present form, were used on humans. In a discussion of human cloning in March 2003, it was argued that a success rate of up to 30% might be possible. This still raised the issue of the suffering caused by the remaining 70% of failures.

Even given a successful human clone brought to term, there remain doubts about the overall health of a clone, and about whether the illnesses that led to the death of Dolly were due to the circumstances of her life, or to the fact that she was a clone.

Who Decides?

Manipulating genes may be able to eradicate genetically transmitted diseases, promote particular physical qualities and detect and eliminate features we don't like, but the question is: Who decides what is a good gene and what a bad one? Which is preferable for humanity, variety or perfection? Do we shape human life to fit a preconceived ideal? If so, whose ideal should it be?

a) Applying Ethical Theories

Note

Many issues in ethics depend on the idea of autonomy. We ask, for example, when an embryo becomes a separate human being with rights of its own. But when is a human being autonomous? Clearly an embryo depends on the life of its mother, but so does a newly-born child. Are you autonomous at the age of 16, or 18, or 21 or 85? At what point can you live independently of others? At what point do you stop being influenced by your past and sustained by others around you in the present?

It can be argued that human autonomy is a compromise put together for legal and other purposes, for we are all free to some extent, and yet also dependent upon others. Autonomy is always a matter of degree, never an absolute.

In all issues of medical ethics, including genetics, there are advantages and disadvantages in trying to use Natural Law arguments. There are always two things to keep in mind in this:

1 Natural Law is not about what happens in nature.
2 Natural Law is not a 'law' in the sense that it is not an externally imposed set of rules.

Let us take each of these in turn:

Natural Law, as we saw above, is nature as interpreted by human reason. In other words, it looks at nature and from it deduces the final aim and purpose of everything. This in turn assumes that there *is* a purpose in everything, and that the world is a rationally ordered place.

Natural Law seeks to identify those things for which a creature or an action has a natural and rational propensity. In other words, if it acts in accordance with its essential nature, then it will do well, and benefit all concerned. If it goes against its essential nature, then it is unnatural and therefore wrong.

Now, this need not involve externally imposed rewards or punishments; if life has an essential nature and it will only flourish if it follows it. On the other hand, if you believe that the world is created by God for a purpose, then deliberately frustrating that purpose is putting oneself against the will of God, and that would seem to bring about its own hazards in terms of punishment, or at the very least failing to live up to one's designed and essential nature.

With any medical or genetic issue, Natural Law is going to suggest that human beings have an essential nature, and manipulating nature (e.g. through genetic engineering) may be seen as frustrating a natural ordering of things, and therefore wrong.

In the case of embryo experimentation, for example, a Natural Law approach would emphasise the absolute unique value of a human life, and would then seek to protect that life. It would not be right, on this basis, to sacrifice the life of an unborn child, for example, even if its birth and life might bring about further suffering.

As with most Natural Law approaches to these issues, there are bound to be exceptions to the rule because circumstances throw up exceptional cases. However, it gives a clear guideline and sense of what human life is, and what it is for.

Note

Remember, a key feature is that if you go against your essential nature, then your action is likely to be self-destructive; follow it and the likely result is self-fulfilment.

For utilitarian approaches the basic issue to be faced is the complexity of expected and actual results of any action. Whether in medical or embryology issues, there are a range of short- and long-term consequences, not all of which can be known and quantified. This is a general limitation of utilitarian approaches, but is particularly true of medical matters.

In other words, we might genuinely want the preferences of everyone concerned to be taken into account. But what do we do when those preferences cannot be expressed? We cannot discuss with a fertilised embryo what his or her potential as a human being might be, and try to compare it with the benefit of selecting another embryo to be implanted? It is the fact that we do not know the sum total of the potential benefits of a course of action that makes a strictly utilitarian assessment so difficult.

As with earlier issues, the key feature of Kantian ethics that can be applied here is the second formulation of the Categorical Imperative – namely that people should be treated as ends and not simply as means. In principle, the act of deciding what sort of children are to be born suggests that they are seen as 'means' to an overall end of creating a certain kind of society. The uniqueness of human beings – even if that involves suffering – does suggest that each is an individual in its own right, and should be treated as such.

b) Religious Responses

The religious responses here are the same as for the previous section. Traditionally, those who have argued for the absolute sanctity of life have opposed cloning and the selection of fertilised embryos based on genetic criteria. As before, the basic argument is that life is given by God, and any attempt to select who is to be born and who is not goes against that fundamental belief.

MAKING CONNECTIONS

Issues connected with genetics inevitably raise questions about the relationship between religion and science. The selection of embryos could also relate to the question as to whether God can know the future, and – if so – whether he knows which embryos are to be selected for implantation.

As with the 'problem of evil' issues, the question arises of God's fore-knowledge and omnipotence. If God's knowledge is acausal (i.e. he knows what will happen, but his knowledge does not actually cause it to happen) can we also say that he is both omnipotent and loving if he does nothing to stop harm being done?

A postscript for discussion

All the debates connected with human life and death assume that we can say when a human life starts and when it finishes. Based on this, individuals are given rights.

But, if you examine the natural process, there is no point at which life starts or stops.

At some point sperm and eggs are generated within the body (a continuous process in the male; pre-birth in the female). Those sperm and eggs are the product of nourishment and genetic information – they simply take and reorganise material that already exists. Eventually they meet, and life continues – this time in forming a baby, which grows into an adult, which produces sperm, or whose eggs are used to produce a baby in whom there is a further supply of eggs.

By the time the adult dies, there is a good chance that his or her genetic material is already living elsewhere, and so on, and so on.

The atoms of which we are made pre-date the earth. We are merely a temporary arrangement of them, and long after we, as individuals, are no more, those same atoms which now form our most intimate bits of flesh will have reformed and will exist elsewhere.

It is a matter of convenience that we separate the stream of life into manageable chunks, which we call humans, animals, plants and so on. At another level, they are simply temporary aspects of an ongoing flow of life. Cells continue to divide, and will do so in an unbroken chain from one generation to the next.

▼ ESSAY QUESTIONS

1 a) Explain the basis of a 'Natural Law' opposition to abortion.
   b) Examine the strengths and weaknesses of this position.
2 a) On what ethical basis might cloning a human being be justified?
   b) 'Cloning a human being is an inherently evil act.' Discuss.

See the 'Further Reading and Websites' section at the back of this book for follow-up work on this chapter.

PRACTICAL ETHICS II

POINTS TO CONSIDER

As with the previous chapter, you need to be aware of sufficient facts about each of the features of life included here to be able to appreciate the ethical issues they raise. You should also consider how the various ethical theories contribute to understanding these issues, and also the contribution of religion to the debates.

1 Environmental Ethics

At AS level, you need to be aware of the general issues relating to humankind and the natural environment. This will include exploitation of natural resources, pollution and the destruction of habitats. Religious ethics will be based on the perception of the natural world in relation to God's creativity and the responsibility that humankind should therefore show towards it. A wide range of issues and examples are relevant here, some of which are set out in *Environmental Ethics* in the *Access to Philosophy* series.

A key topic for examining Environmental Ethics is the issue of animal rights, since the ethical issues involved go beyond any basic anthropocentric arguments. We shall therefore look at approaches to this, before looking at the application of ethical theories more generally.

Peter Singer argues that animals are capable of experiencing pleasure and pain, and that they therefore have interests. In other words, they want to avoid suffering, and their desire to do so can be taken into account in any utilitarian assessment of the pain or pleasure that an action is likely to cause.

Against those who would argue that animals simply do not count, whether or not they experience pleasure and pain, Singer would refer back to arguments that limited consideration to members of a particular gender or race. In other words, there was a time when women and ethnic minorities were discounted, or were given less consideration than white males. This is now generally viewed as wrong – race and gender should not count in any moral assessment. People may be different, but they are all equally entitled to have their preferences taken into account.

In the same way, Singer argues that – just as we have realised that sexism and racism are wrong – so we should recognise that 'speciesism' is wrong. In other words, we should not limit consideration to members of our own species.

However, it is clear that you cannot simply equate the feelings of a very simple animal form with that of a human being. Singer therefore qualifies his position by saying that we should give the same respect to animals that we would give to human beings at the same mental level.

He also points out that both the physical characteristics of animals and their mental abilities affect the degree to which they can experience pleasure and pain. The balance of interest to be taken into account must allow for this.

For example, a gentle prod to a horse or an elephant would totally destroy a butterfly. You could not claim to have given the horse and the butterfly equal consideration if you prodded each of them with equal force!

However, there are many questions to be asked of this approach. Clearly, a higher primate (say, a chimpanzee) is similar to a human being in terms of its signs of pleasure and pain, and in terms of its social interactions. We can recognise in a chimpanzee actions that are parallel to those of a human. It therefore makes sense to take the welfare of that chimpanzee into account. But what of the worm? This has a very much lower level of physical and mental activity. Therefore we do not need to take its welfare into account to the same degree.

But just as it is argued that you should not allow sexism and racism to intrude on moral considerations between humans, and should not allow speciesism to stop animals from receiving due consideration, so it could be argued that creatures should not be judged simply on account of their mental ability. To do so is to judge everything by human standards. In other words, it is to say that the more like humans a species is, the more its members should be taken into account morally. But that is no different in principle from saying that the more like a white male a person is, the more they should be taken into consideration – and we are back in the realm of racism and sexism.

It is therefore very difficult, in practice, to allocate due consideration to life forms of different levels of physical and mental complexity. Almost any attempt to differentiate between species displays an anthropocentric bias – we like those creatures that are like ourselves, or are cuddly! Those that are very different, ugly, disgusting and so on, are given very little consideration.

ISSUES:
The key issue in any ethical argument concerning the relationship between humans and other species, or humans and the environment in general, is whether other species have inherent worth, or whether their value is bound up with their usefulness to the human species. Thus, for example, the saving of rainforests and the variety of the flora found in them is often argued on the basis of medicines that may in the future be derived from such plants. Any such argument is utilitarian and human-centred. To say that they should be preserved for themselves, even if humankind derives no benefit from them, is to acknowledge their inherent worth.

Figure 10 These fish died because 5 million cubic metres of toxic water were accidentally dumped into the Guadalquivir River near Seville in 1998. To what extent, if all life is interconnected, are humans responsible for the environment? Is nature to be protected only for its benefit to humankind, or – as 'deep ecology claims – for its own sake?

Interconnectedness

It may be argued that moral arguments of a utilitarian nature cannot finally be divided into human-centred and life-centred, simply because humankind shares the same biosystems as other species. The fate of one species is therefore bound up with all the other species, and it is difficult to say exactly what the long-term effect on humankind might be as a result of a general change in the biosphere. Hence it can be argued that a human-centred utilitarian argument is rather short-sighted, since in the long term the human species cannot flourish except within a viable biosphere.

Hence, an overall view that is concerned with the welfare of the biosphere as a whole may eventually prove to be also in the best interests of the human species, since it is impossible to know in advance whether the dominance of the human species on the planet is going to be a good or bad thing for the species itself (e.g. it may come to suffer from the effects that its rise in power and control has had on the planet as a whole), as much as for other species.

The distinction is often made between **shallow ecology** (in which the environment is cared for simply in order to make conditions better for humankind) and **deep ecology** (in which the environment is preserved for its own sake).

This distinction gives rise to another pair of terms. The environment is said to have **extrinsic value** if its value is based on what it can do to benefit humankind, and **intrinsic value** if it is of value in itself, quite apart from any relationship it has with humankind.

MAKING CONNECTIONS

Environmental ethics relates to the discussion of what it means to claim that God is the creator of everything, and particularly to the Teleological Argument for the existence of God.

a) Applying Ethical Theories

Clearly, most ethical arguments about the environment are based to some extent on Utilitarianism. Since it is clear that destruction of the environment can bring long-term harm to all species (humankind included), a utilitarian argument will balance that harm against any short-term gain that may be found in exploiting natural resources.

The crucial question here (and the reason why the issue of animal rights is so central) is the criterion by which any such utilitarian judgement is made. Do you assess the value of the environment solely on the basis of what is good for human beings? Do you include the welfare of other species? Does your concern for their welfare reflect a potential benefit for humankind in preserving them, or are they to be given consideration on their own terms?

All utilitarian arguments need to be based on some consideration of what is to be to the benefit or happiness of those concerned. Hence, if other species are to be taken into account, there needs to be a prior assessment of what it means to seek their benefit or happiness.

The other crucial factor here, and one that has come up elsewhere in considering utilitarian arguments, is that we never know the *final* result of our actions. What may seem to be to the advantage of the environment now may, in the longer run, be found to be to its harm.

Example

Protecting one species may be at the expense of another further down the food chain. If hedgehogs eat the eggs of sea birds, do you allow the hedgehogs to flourish at the expense of the birds, or do you cull them in order to save the more rare bird life? Similarly, if red squirrels are being driven out by grey squirrels, do you accept that as a feature of natural selection, or do you take positive steps to protect the reds?

Utilitarian arguments in themselves may not be able to decide between the options here.

Situation Ethics may run into exactly the problems given in the example here. It may be far from clear what the most loving thing would be in any situation, since choices have to be made, none of which can avoid suffering of some sort.

In considering Virtue Ethics, there might be a case for examining the implications of Aristotle's 'mean' – in that either a rash or a timid approach to dealing with the environment may do more harm than good. A prudent approach may be able to strike a balance between allowing nature to flourish unchecked, and satisfying the needs of humankind.

In assessing actions that might do harm to the environment, Kantian Ethics may be relevant, in that the first formulation of the Categorical Imperative requires a person to take into consideration the effect of making the maxim of an action into a universal law. In other words, if it's all right for me to do this, then I must allow that everyone else can follow the same principle. This, of course, would prohibit many forms of exploitation or pollution of the environment, where it would clearly be illogical to want everyone to be able to do it.

b) Religious Responses

The key feature of religious responses to environmental ethics springs from the concept of God as creator and sustainer of the world. Humankind may then be seen to hold a stewardship of the created order, responsible before God for their treatment of it. According to Genesis, however, humankind is given dominion over other species (see Genesis 1:26) and this has been seen as justification for the use of animals for food and other purposes. In other words, whatever rights an animal may have, they are seen as inferior to those of humankind, and may therefore be overruled by human need.

The Teleological Argument for the existence of God (see page 33) sees God as the overall designer of the universe, giving purpose to everything. Belief in such a God therefore implies a respect for his creative design.

2 Sex and Relationships

Relevant issues for consideration under the ethics of sex and relationships include homosexuality, marriage and divorce, cohabitation, fertility and feminist critiques of sexual roles. There is a long history of moral debate concerning each of these, and further details can be found in *Sex and Relationships* in the *Access to Philosophy* series.

For AS level, you should be aware of the main issues and of the contribution to discussion of them made by the various ethical theories. You should also be aware of particular religious perspectives on the issues.

When looking at sexual issues in an historical context it may be valuable to keep a feminist perspective in mind, in that sexuality is an interesting touchstone for changes in society, and many earlier arguments about sexual ethics may be based on an unquestioned assumption that one sex is superior to the other.

In some societies a wife may still be regarded as the property of her husband, and in Britain, before 1882, married women were legally required to surrender all control over their own property or money to their husbands.

This in turn influences the view of marriage and fertility, especially in situations where marriage is arranged for reasons that are based on social or economic advantage rather than mutual attraction between partners.

Part of the skill in discussing the ethics of sex and relationships is being aware of such unexpressed assumptions, and taking them into account in coming to a balanced judgement. Most ethical thinkers have been male, and their values and arguments may therefore have been influenced by their gender.

Prior to the eighteenth century, men and women frequently worked alongside one another, often in agriculture or local businesses. With the coming of the industrial revolution, however, more men took paid employment away from home, while women took the domestic role in bringing up the children, and were therefore dependent on male earnings. Hence the development of inequality between the sexes and the adoption of different roles. Mary Wollstonecraft's *A Vindication of the Rights of Women* (1792) campaigned for education, for equality in work, and for a place in civil and political life. The economic system and socially acceptable ways of behaving were challenged on the grounds that they were devised for the benefit of men.

In considering issues connected with faithfulness in marriage, homosexuality, divorce, sex outside marriage, contraception and so on, you should therefore take care to be aware of the potentially different perspectives of men and women, especially in historical documents.

a) Applying Ethical Theories

In many ethical discussions of matters of sexuality there is a fundamental division between those who take a Natural Law approach (particularly from a Catholic perspective) and those who base their arguments on utilitarian considerations.

The Natural Law approach tends to separate off the sexual act itself from general issues of sexuality, sexual orientation, and the social context of sexual activity. Since the natural and biological purpose of sex is procreation, it tends to regard a sexual act as objectively either right or wrong, depending on whether or not it includes the possibility of fulfilling its natural function – the procreation of children.

On this basis, anything that cannot lead to procreation is deemed to be wrong. This would include masturbation, homosexual acts and heterosexual intercourse using contraception.

The limitations of this approach

The natural end and purpose of an action is not 'given' in nature, it is the result of a rational assessment, and it may be far from clear what that nature is.

Is sex a means of conceiving children? Or is conceiving children a by-product of sex, whose basic purpose is forging relationships for mutual support?

(You could argue, for example, that – if sex were only there for the purposes of conception – sexual attraction would be limited to those occasions and partners with whom conception is a likely prospect. This is, after all, the situation with many animals, where sexual attraction is mainly found only at the time when the female is able to conceive. On the other hand, if sexual feelings arise naturally without any desire or ability to conceive, it might suggest that those feelings are designed with some other end in mind. It is, therefore, by no means absolutely clear that sex has a single purpose.)

Sexual orientation itself, however, if it does not lead to specific sexual acts, does not come under the same criticism. Thus, for example, a Catholic 'Natural Law' approach to homosexuality may see homosexual orientation as a disorder, but not as something inherently wrong, whereas any resulting homosexual acts would be seen as wrong.

By contrast, a utilitarian approach to any of these issues simply considers the preferences or happiness of those involved. Sexual acts between consenting adults would therefore be assessed simply in terms of any harm those acts might cause other people, or even the persons involved, compared with the happiness generated.

Thus, for example, contraception would be approved as it would avoid unwanted pregnancy, where this would lead to hardship or a social situation that caused unhappiness, perhaps through abortion or through motherhood for someone not ready or able to take on that commitment.

Situation Ethics thrived in a period when more liberal sexual attitudes were making traditional moral rules and regulations unacceptable. The situationist approach of taking the single principle of doing the most loving thing in each situation would seem to be particularly appropriate to these issues. However, there is one major problem with this: the influence of strong emotions in connection with sexuality. The assessment of what is most loving is inevitably going to be coloured by the emotional and physical drives encountered, and the intimate relationships involved. As an overall attitude to relationships it may sound fine, but it is difficult to see how intellectual rigour can be maintained in situations where there is a genuine moral choice.

> ### *For example*
>
> If the situation is one of doing what most expresses love, or of obeying a traditional moral rule, the situationist is in no doubt that love should be given the priority. However, if there is a choice between two courses of action, both of which offer happiness, but both of which also involve pain to one or more people involved, the situation is no longer clear. In such situations, Utilitarianism is easier to apply and justify than Situation Ethics.

Kantian ethics can be used for discussing sexual issues. In Kant's first Categorical Imperative, it is not simply required that you should wish for everyone to do what you yourself think it right to do (sexually that might result in chaos!). Rather, it is the maxim of your action that should be willed to be a universal law. In other words, the principle or maxim (which takes the form: whenever I am in this situation, I consider it right to . . .) should be universally valid for something to be considered to be right. It is, therefore, quite feasible that one could use that principle in assessing the morality of sexual acts.

More immediately applicable, however, is the second form of Kant's Categorical Imperative – namely that people should be treated as ends, and not simply as means. This is in line with most broadly based ethical approaches to sexuality. It is of key importance for taking mature sexual decisions, since within the realm of sexuality it is all too easy to regard the object of sexual desire as simply the means by which to satisfy one's own sexual appetites.

It is also possible to stand back from the conventional arguments of Natural Law, Kant and Utilitarianism and examine moral choices primarily from the standpoint of the individual with his or her personal qualities, virtues and ideals. This is an important approach, promoted by, for example, Mary Warnock in *An Intelligent Person's Guide to Ethics* (1998). In contrast to approaches based largely on Utilitarianism, or questions of rights and obligations, the key issue here is 'What does it mean to be moral?' 'What does moral choice require of me?'

Virtue Ethics can consider such questions to be primarily about the personal ideals by which a person chooses to live, and which will influence his or her choices in such situations of moral choice.

b) Religious Responses

Each of the major world religions sets out general principles by which its members can decide what is right or wrong in matters of sexuality. In Christianity there is something of a division between the Catholic approach, which has generally been based on Natural Law, and the

Protestant, which has been more utilitarian in its application. Both, of course, look to the New Testament for basic teachings to back up their views. Situation Ethics, likewise, goes back to the New Testament, and claims to be following the example of Jesus, who was prepared to break rules where love demanded it.

Both Judaism and Islam have specific rules to regulate and promote the status of marriage and that therefore impacts on their view of sexuality.

In both Christianity and eastern traditions of Hinduism, Buddhism and Jainism, there is a long history of **asceticism**. Sexuality and family life are then sometimes presented as being spiritually inferior to the celibacy and simplicity of the ascetic life. By contrast, in Islam and Judaism, marriage is considered the norm.

A significant aspect of the traditional Christian approach to sexual ethics is the interpretation of the story of Adam and Eve, and their 'fall' in the Garden of Eden. Through their disobedience, sin was said to have come into the world, and the transmitting of this 'original sin' through successive generations is by means of sexual activity. Hence, even if (as with St Paul) sexuality is seen as being validly expressed through marriage, nevertheless it is a constant reminder of humankind's 'fallen' state.

MAKING CONNECTIONS

Issues of 'fallen' human nature relate to Augustine's view of the 'problem of evil' (see page 63).

As with all consideration of religious ethics, it is important to be clear about the nature and authority of ethical positions. Some are justified on the basis of the authority of scriptures or the traditional teachings of that religion. Of these, many will remain relevant over long periods of time, whereas in other cases (perhaps because of new situations, like the danger of HIV infection with unprotected intercourse) it is necessary to consider the present situation only by analogy with earlier ones, applying principles established earlier to new situations. This, in any case, is what happens in case law, whether religious or secular – fundamental principles are applied to particular cases.

However, it can be argued that other 'religious' moral principles cannot be related to the fundamental beliefs of that religion, but have arisen within the society within which the religion has been practised. The treatment of women is a particularly appropriate example of that, with societies sometimes treating women in a way that cannot be justified by their scriptures or tradition, but which reflects social custom.

3 War, Peace and Justice

What is justice? Plato's *Republic* is a dialogue about the nature of justice, and the way that it functions in society. In it, one of the characters – Thrasymachus – argues that 'justice' is whatever is in the interest of the strongest, and that self-interest is therefore its only basis. In reply, Glaucon points out that if everyone acts from selfish motives, then everyone will end up being exploited by everyone else. The rules imposed by society in the name of justice are therefore a way of protecting everyone from suffering at the hands of everyone else.

Plato wants to take the debate further and presents the idea that all elements in society (like parts of a human body) need to work together for the general health of the whole, with the physical and assertive aspects (taken to represent the workers and defenders of society) controlled by reason (the philosophers/rulers who alone could judge what was best for society as a whole). Justice, like health, is a matter of achieving harmony between the different parts of society, determined and imposed by reason.

Of course, both Plato and Aristotle claimed to base their ethics upon reason, but were certainly not free from the prejudices of their day. For example, Aristotle (in *Politics*, Book 1, chapter 5) is quite prepared to say that the proper function of slaves is to obey their masters, and that women should naturally obey men. All philosophy and ethics reflects the values of society within which it is expressed. We cannot get value-free ethics, nor a value-free definition of justice, for in a value-free situation, most ethical debate and the desire for justice would be meaningless.

Many thinkers have contributed to the idea of 'justice':

Hobbes (in *Leviathan*) argued that there should be a contract between people and their ruler, with the ruler agreeing to protect the natural rights of the people, to act as an arbiter in disputes, and to establish just laws. In return, the people agree to accept the authority of that ruler and of such governments and laws as are established.

Locke (in *The Second Treatise on Civil Government*) argued that people should surrender some of their individual rights to the community, but that nobody (not even the ruler) should be above the law. Authority should reside in the institutions of state, as chosen by the majority of the people. Individuals are given rights – free speech, freedom to worship, freedom to hold property – and it is the duty of government to uphold these rights. Locke's basic principles underlie the ideas of justice in modern democratic systems.

Hume argued that it was impossible to achieve a justice based on what people deserve, simply because people will never agree about what each of them deserves. He also felt that it was impracticable to try to impose equal shares on everybody, since people are unequal in their abilities, and some will therefore prosper more than others.

Rousseau argued for a social contract to form the basis of individual liberty, and that in a democracy, people and rulers should have the same interests and work together for mutual benefit. He argued that primitive people have natural instincts of self-preservation and sympathy shown towards other people who suffer. By contrast, civilisation tends to corrupt people (e.g. by imposing ideas of private property, thereby creating inequality and consequent resentment) which destroyed the simplicity and co-operative possibilities of the primitive society.

He argued that under a social contract, imposed by 'the general will', people would agree to give up some of their natural liberty in order to establish 'civil liberty'. In this way, an individual subsumes his or her will to that of the community as a whole.

Thomas Paine further developed the idea of a social contract. He argued that an individual should be given liberty, and allowed to do anything (including the right to pursue his or her own happiness) as long as no harm is done to others in the process. His views influenced the American Declaration of Independence, which allows to each person life, liberty and the pursuit of happiness as a fundamental right.

In his book *On Liberty*, **J S Mill** expressed the concern that, under a social contract, individuals and minority groups might suffer by being made to conform to the wishes of the majority. His answer to this was that a majority should only interfere with a minority if that minority is doing something that is directly harmful to the interests of the majority. Hence, free speech should be allowed, even if the person speaking is thought to be clearly wrong or misguided. He considered that this was less dangerous than allowing an authority to decide what could or could not be said, which would result in a loss of liberty for all.

A modern version of social contract theory is found in *A Theory of Justice* (1972) by **John Rawls**. He imagines a situation in which a number of people gather together to decide the rules under which they are to live. But they are made to forget who they are, so that they establish principles of justice that cannot reflect personal bias. He argued that, in such a situation, people would agree to two principles:

1 Each person has an equal right to the maximum amount of liberty compatible with allowing liberty for all.
2 Inequalities are only to be allowed if there is reason to think that such inequalities will benefit the least well-off in society.

These, he believes, represent the principles upon which a just society could agree, if any sense of personal advantage was removed from the process.

The Ethics of War

Note

Authority is central to issues of war and peace. What is the appropriate authority to declare war? Should this be an individual nation or the United Nations or another international organisation?

In the case of the Iraq war of 2003, the USA and Britain went to war on the basis of existing United Nations resolutions, but without a formal second resolution that would have made explicit the threat that war would follow if Saddam Hussein did not give up the weapons of mass destruction he was believed to have.

Within the Security Council of the United Nations, it was uncertain whether or not a majority of members would approve a second resolution and France declared that it would veto any such resolution.

Within a nation, war is declared if approved by the democratic process. At the time of declaring war on Iraq, a majority of votes in the House of Commons approved the decision, but this was not thought to reflect the nation as a whole, where a majority were believed to approve war only after a second United Nations resolution on the matter.

All these levels of authority are relevant to the issue of whether or not a war is legal. Within the army, individual servicemen and servicewomen may perform actions (such as killing) which would be illegal if performed in a private capacity, but may be done under authority.

What happens if there is no law, no overall sense of justice? What would life be like if we lived in a natural state, without any agreements or political structures, and if each person was responsible for his or her own security? Here is one view:

> In such condition, there is no place for industry, because the fruit thereof is uncertain; and consequently no culture of the earth; no navigation, nor use of the commodities that may be imported by sea; no commodious building, no instruments of moving or removing such things as require much force; no knowledge of the face of the earth; no account of time; no arts; no letters; no society; and, which is worst of all, continual fear and danger of violent death; and the life of man solitary, poor, nasty, brutish and short.
>
> [From *Leviathan* by Thomas Hobbes (1588–1679)]

Hobbes wrote at a time when he was all too well aware of social chaos caused by civil war, and he recognised that civilisation depended on security and peace. Hence warfare threatens not just the lives of those who fight, but the whole fabric of society. The key question is whether it is right to use (or threaten to use) lethal force in order to attempt to establish peace and justice.

Most ethical discussion of war and peace focuses on two questions:

1 Under what circumstances is it right to declare war (*jus ad bellum*)?
2 What principles should guide the way in which war is waged (*jus in bello*)?

Note

The traditional 'Just War' principles, devised from within Christian philosophy by Aquinas and others, are nowadays also contained in secular agreements e.g. the Geneva Convention on the treatment of prisoners.

The 'Just War' Theory of Thomas Aquinas

It may be just to go to war if:

1 It is done by proper authority (e.g. by a nation, not by an individual).
2 There is a good reason to go to war (e.g. in self-defence, or if an injury has been done to one's own nation or an ally).
3 The intention is to establish peace and justice (e.g. it should never be done for revenge, or for the sake of plundering the enemy country).

To those basic three reasons, others have been added to cover the decision as to whether to go to war and how to fight it. In taking the decision, it is important to consider:

▼ The probability of success (e.g. It is unreasonable to go to war if there is no real prospect of winning, because the suffering inflicted will not yield a positive outcome.)
▼ War should always be regarded as an act of last resort, and only considered once all peaceful means of settling a dispute are exhausted.

While waging war, justice is established in the following cases:

1 The principle of discrimination requires that war is waged against military personnel, not against civilians.

   (Issue – is it ever possible to wage war without civilian casualties, either directly or indirectly? Smart weapons? Economic harm leads to further suffering.)
2 The force used is proportional (e.g. the harm caused should not outweigh what it is hoped to gain).
3 Minimum force should be used in order to achieve one's end (issue of nuclear, chemical and biological weapons).

Hence, following conflicts you may have tribunals to examine 'war crimes'. They try to assess whether particular actions carried out during war should be considered 'crimes against humanity', or whether they are a legitimate part of warfare. In general, events become war crimes if brutality of killing is directed at civilians, or prisoners of war, or if minimum force or appropriate weapons have not been used.

Terrorism v. Warfare

Violence used by terrorists may be considered unjust, since it is not backed by legitimate authority, even if the cause is just. But who constitutes that legitimate authority in today's world? A nation state? The United Nations? Can a religion constitute valid authority?

Since wearing a military uniform implies that your actions are carried out in the name of the nation, terrorism is a **civilian** phenomenon. A military person who discards his uniform but who retains his weapons and continues to fight may therefore be considered a terrorist. Terrorists may, of course, attack either military or civilian targets. Equally, they may claim to represent a people, nation or other group, and therefore argue that they are engaged in acts of war, rather than terrorism. The moral issue is to decide whether they have the degree of authorised backing to justify that claim.

Weaponry

Weapons which affect civilians, or are not a proportionate response to a threat, or which do not represent minimum necessary force, may be deemed wrong.

Nuclear, chemical and biological weapons are indiscriminate in the damage they cause, and are therefore termed 'weapons of mass destruction'.

ISSUE: SELF DEFENCE?
Animals in the wild defend themselves and their own family groups against attack, so it is perfectly natural for humans to do the same. Self-defence is the most straightforward justification for war. But how do you measure a threat before it actually happens? If your information about another country's weapons or its intention to use them is wrong, then you may attack them apparently 'in self-defence' and only subsequently find that they were not in a position to pose a serious threat to you. Who is to blame in such cases?

Figure 11 'Weapons of mass destruction' is a term used for nuclear, biological and biological weapons. Some are 'battlefield' weapons, with limited range and power, but it can be argued that their use may blur the distinction between them and conventional weapons, making the development and deployment of larger weapons of mass destruction more likely. Can such weapons ever represent a 'proportional' response to a military threat?

Notice that it is the *type* of weapon, not the actual numbers of people who may be killed, that determines whether it is a 'weapon of mass destruction'. Some conventional bombs, dropped in quantity, are able to kill as many people as would a small nuclear device. However, the conventional weapons are more predictable than nuclear, chemical or biological weapons.

In the case of weapons of mass destruction, three issues are considered in assessing the threat they pose:

1 The technical ability to create and assemble such weapons.
2 The ability to manufacture chemical or biological agents, or to refine and store weapons-grade nuclear material.
3 The development of delivery systems for such weapons.

This last point is crucial. A lethal chemical cannot be properly considered to be a weapon unless there is some way of dropping it upon your enemy. Until such a delivery system is developed, it remains only a potential weapon.

Note

During the first Gulf War, about 10% of the munitions were 'smart' in the sense that they could be precision guided to their target. The estimate for the 2003 war with Iraq is that 90% of munitions were smart. This applies, of course, to bombs and missiles, not to the ordinary artillery and small arms.

The argument used is that a 'smart' weapon is able to achieve its purpose with as little damage to the surrounding people and buildings as possible.

A smart bomb, dropped from an aircraft, is sometimes referred to as a JDAM (Joint Direct Attack Munition).

Note

Nuclear, chemical and biological weapons are termed 'weapons of mass destruction'. Other weapons are 'conventional'. The largest conventional weapon is the American MOAB (Massive Ordnance Air Burst), a bomb containing 21,000 pounds of explosive and 26 feet long. It is launched from the rear of a transport plane and its blast devastates everything within a one mile radius of its target. Hence the distinction between WMD and conventional weapons is not simply a matter of their power, but of their type.

The use of weapons of mass destruction can be considered wrong on the grounds that the destruction they bring is general, rather than limited to military targets and that the damage done by their use is out of proportion to any good that can be gained.

a) Applying Ethical Theories

How do you balance a utilitarian assessment of results with the intention of the person concerned? In other words, if civilians are killed because a bomb fails to hit its intended military target, does this have the same moral force as the deliberate disregard for civilian life? Does intention matter? Clearly, it is a matter of weighing things up. Was sufficient care taken by those planning the attack etc?

Utilitarian arguments have particular problems when the outcome of military action is unpredictable. For example, it is possible to speculate that, as the result of war waged by one or more western nations against what they perceive as nations that either harbour terrorists or are in a position to aid terrorists, more people may choose to join Al-Qa'ida. They might see such a war as being imposed by western and Christian societies upon Muslim ones, and react accordingly.

But how, in any utilitarian assessment, can you take account of that? It is simply one of a number of possibilities.

It might be easier to revert to the principle that war should only be waged where there is at least a serious possibility that it can have an effective outcome and achieve a just purpose. But how, on a utilitarian assessment, can any war be proved to give overall benefit?

Wars may be fought in response to 'what if' scenarios. What if Saddam had weapons of mass destruction in Iraq? What if he allowed them to fall into the hands of terrorists? What if North Korea sells nuclear weapons to countries sympathetic to terrorism? What if Hitler had invaded and taken control of Britain? What if William the Conqueror hadn't . . . and so on.

> **ISSUE:**
> Is it ever right to assess gain and loss when the destruction of human life is at stake? Can anything compensate for the death of the innocent? If not, then a utilitarian will always oppose war. But what if the result of not going to war is that innocents will still be killed because of internal oppression?

With all such 'what if' scenarios, a range of possible consequences of action or inaction are weighed against one another. The problem is that they can never be proved true or false, because those 'what ifs' are themselves changed by the decision that is taken.

What if Hitler had taken over Europe? What would have happened? Would that outcome have been worse overall, compared with the sacrifices made in the war that stopped him?

What was gained by the USA and Britain going to war against Iraq? Is the world safer now that the regime has been removed? Has resentment and terrorism been reduced or encouraged by such military action? Utilitarian assessments may constantly require revision as events unfold.

Some other ethical theories have already been touched on:

Natural Law might be used to support the idea of self-defence as a natural and rational justification for war.

Kant's criteria for considering actions to be just (i.e. the three forms of his Categorical Imperative) might be used in an assessment of whether warfare is just. So, for example, one could argue that at the point at which I make the decision to respond to a threat by declaring war on the nation that threatens me, that can be something that I am prepared to make universal.

My maxim would be: 'If I am threatened, it is my right to counter that threat by force.' And this might then be considered a universal principle (in effect, it is the same as Aquinas' right of self defence).

Equally, one might argue that, in the same way that individuals should treat others as ends in themselves and not as means to an end – thus preserving their integrity as autonomous human beings – so nations should respect the integrity and autonomy of other nations. In other words, it would be wrong to defeat another country in war as a means of expanding territory, for example. On the other hand, it might be possible to justify intervention in order to 'liberate' an oppressed country, on the grounds that one is then able to treat it as independent and autonomous.

Finally, the third of Kant's principles – that one should act as though legislating for a society of free and autonomous individuals – could guide, for example, the thinking of the United Nations. Each action should be justified as a particular example of those principles that would enable a just system for all nations to co-operate together.

[The Archbishop of Canterbury, Rowan Williams, speaking on 21 February 2003 about the proposal that Britain should join the United States in attacking Iraq]

b) Religious Responses

> I think Christians generally would hold that unless other means of resolution had been exhausted, it would be hard to justify any pre-emptive [military] action. It does not look as if we have exhausted all the possibilities yet.

As we saw above, the general principles of the 'just war' debate in western philosophy were developed within a Christian context by Aquinas, but have been adopted as general secular principles.

Some religious philosophies, particularly Jainism and Buddhism, see the killing of other living things as having very serious consequences for the person who does the killing, as well as for the victim. All such philosophical and moral systems will oppose war in any form. Buddhism, in general, will only accept the taking of life in very exceptional circumstances, e.g. killing an animal for food in order to sustain one's own life.

Jewish Principles of Self-defence

According to the *Talmud*:

▼ Both Jews and non-Jews may kill a pursuer in order to save their own life.

▼ It is permissible to kill an attacker who is threatening the life of another person.
▼ It is obligatory to attempt to stop, and if necessary to kill, a person who is trying to kill another Jew.

These come from the principle of the right to self-defence.

As far as warfare is concerned, it is obligatory to go to war in order to defend Israel against attack, but there is a debate (stemming from Maimonides' interpretation of the *Talmud*) about whether or not it is permitted to use war for the purposes of territorial expansion. In general, however, the Jewish view is that warfare is permitted for defence, but not as a means of aggression.

There is another important principle within Jewish rules on self-defence. One may take action against others only as a way of *preventing* them from doing something, *not* after they have done it. So killing cannot be for the purpose of punishment only – it must have the intention of preventing further harm.

There is also the requirement that restraint should be used in the methods of fighting a war. For example, Maimonides codified the *Talmud*'s instruction that, in laying siege to a city, one should do so on three sides only, never completely. The intention is that civilians and those who do not wish to fight should be given some means of escape. War should not be total.

On the other hand, it is more difficult to justify pacifism within Jewish law, since most interpreters say that a person has a *duty* of self-defence, not just that they are permitted to do so.

Islamic Jihad

In Islam, 'jihad' means 'struggle' and it can take two forms. The Greater Jihad is the spiritual struggle to overcome faults. The Lesser Jihad is the struggle against external threats.

Valid reasons for performing the Lesser Jihad:

▼ To defend the Ummah (the Community of the Islam). If a Muslim country, or the Muslim population within a country, is threatened, jihad against the aggressor becomes an obligation on Muslims.
▼ To fight on behalf of the oppressed against injustice (whether or not the victims of that injustice are Muslim).

However there are restrictions on jihad:

▼ It should be used only as a last resort, when peaceful means fail to defend the community.
▼ It should be carried out with compassion, causing minimum suffering to achieve its aim.
▼ Its aim is to establish justice, not to cause suffering.

The Lesser Jihad should be seen in the context of the general principle that a Muslim is obliged to protect himself or herself and others against injustice, but not to initiate aggression.

[From the *Qur'an*, sura 2: 190–1]

> Fight in the way of God against those who fight against you, but begin not hostilities. Lo! God loves not the aggressor.

▼ ESSAY QUESTIONS

1 a) Describe how Kant's second form of the Categorical Imperative might be applied to issues in sexual ethics.

   b) 'Sex is always exploitative.' Discuss.

2 a) Describe the basis on which a Muslim might justify declaring jihad.

   b) Is it possible to keep strictly to the rules governing jihad? Discuss.

See the 'Further Reading and Websites' section at the back of this book for follow-up work on this chapter.

PREPARING FOR THE EXAMINATION

When it comes to doing well in examinations, there is no substitute for the satisfaction of having taken a genuine interest in the subject, reading as widely as possible around the topics covered, and discussing and debating them with others. By getting to grips with the issues and sharpening up your own views on them, you will have arguments ready to hand when you get into an examination room, and will know how to justify your point of view.

However, the following suggestions are made in order to help you maximise the benefit you will gain from your work, and to avoid some of the common pitfalls.

1 Revising From Your Notes

Remember, your time in the examination is very limited. By the time you have selected your questions, you need to be able to make your case and demonstrate your knowledge within about twenty minutes. In such circumstances, details will only be useful **if they back up your argument**. Everything you include needs to be either **evidence** for the case you are making or an **illustration** of the point you have made.

As you go through your notes, try writing in the margin whether the information you have is likely to be used as evidence or illustration, and **how it might be used**. For example, you might want to write 'Good example of applying a utilitarian argument' or 'Good evidence for a sense of design in the world' or 'Illustration of a miracle of timing'.

Not only will this remind you when to bring in that material, but it will also remind you that – if you do introduce it – you should use 'This is shown by . . .' or 'For example, if . . .' or in some other way link the example to your argument.

Always remember, a list of facts is not sufficient for an essay answer. Everything needs to demonstrate that you understand the material and can put an argument together.

Note

A good way to make sure that you do NOT do well in your examination is to memorise standard answers to what you think the questions might be. Unless EXACTLY the right question comes up, you may be wasting time by writing down things that the examiner will have to ignore.

You get little credit for giving the examiner an overall view of everything you have been taught on the subject, however well you may have understood it. **Always read the question and make sure that everything you say is relevant to answering it.**

2   Checking the Specifications

When you start to revise, get a copy of the specifications for each of the papers you are taking and make sure you have covered each of the topics included. If you want to live dangerously, you may try to guess what questions will be asked, based on past examination papers, and in any case you are bound to be more interested in and know more about some topics than others. However, it would be very foolish to rely on such guesses, so make sure that you know at least **something** about each topic, so that you will not be totally stuck for an answer if the worst possible combination of questions, from your point of view, appears on the paper.

Note

Ignoring topics that have been included in recent papers has the advantage of limiting the amount of work you need to do, BUT, if things do not work out as you planned, you may be in real trouble with a limited number of questions that you know how to answer.

A safer bet is to put topics in some sort of priority order, making sure that you are well prepared for the most likely ones, but still making sure that you have a working knowledge of all of them.

3   Essay Outlines: Advantages and Disadvantages

An examination essay is essentially an argument. It demonstrates your knowledge and shows that you can argue and justify a point of view. It is important that you should know what information is relevant to answering a question, but also that you should understand the arguments involved, along with their strengths and weaknesses.

An essay outline – setting out what you would include and how you would argue your case – may be a useful way of revising topics; it enables you to see at a glance the main points.

However, memorising essay outlines can lead you astray. All too often candidates spot a key word or words in a question and mentally lock on to their memorised essay outline. Some even use mnemonics to help them use all the information included. The temptation then is to reproduce your essay outline, rather than actually answering the question set.

Read the question carefully, noting each phrase (everything in that question is there for a purpose). Then think about how you will present your argument. If it exactly matches the essay outline, fine. If not, concentrate on the actual question **not** the outline.

Hint

It may be more useful to write down outlines of **arguments**, rather than essays. What are the key points in the Ontological Argument? What are the strengths and weaknesses of a utilitarian approach to ethics? If your notes are full of IF, THEN, BUT, SO and THEREFORE, you are likely to remember the flow of the argument.

---

4 On the Day . . . Issues of Space and Time

a) The Paper

Take a good look at the question paper, and be aware of the process by which it has been devised.

First of all, a principal examiner in the subject will have drafted out suitable questions. He or she will have looked back at what has been asked during the last couple of years and will have checked past papers against what is included in the specification. It is, therefore, unlikely, but not impossible, for the same topic to come up in consecutive examinations. Be aware of what is most likely to come up, but also be prepared for the examiner to surprise you.

After that, the examiner will have to devise a mark scheme for the question. This will include the main things that should be included and the arguments that might be used. He or she is required to show that the question gives candidates scope for demonstrating their knowledge of part of the specification, and will include that in the mark scheme.

Ask yourself:
▼ What is this question looking for?
▼ What part of the specification does it cover?
▼ Is it coming at that topic from any particular angle?
▼ What is likely to be included in a mark scheme for this question?

The question will then go before 'revisers' who will test it out to see if it works. It is then presented to a panel of examiners, who will discuss its merits and check it against the specifications to make sure that it is fair, and that it gives scope for candidates of different ability levels to do themselves justice. (After all, there is absolutely no point in making a question so difficult that only the most brilliant will understand it, nor so obvious that everyone will score full marks.)

Positive rewarding

Candidates are generally credited with whatever they write that is both correct and relevant to answering the question.

There may be different ways of interpreting a question, and examiners are always vigilant to spot the unusual but valid answer. If you set out your argument clearly, the examiner should be able to understand how you have interpreted the question. If you absolutely *have* to answer a question and are a bit uncertain about exactly what it is getting at, then **start by explaining what you think it is about**. If yours is a valid interpretation – even if it is different from everyone else's – you should get credit for it. If you are uncertain but do *not* explain yourself, and the examiner may not understand what you are on about, your answer might appear irrelevant, and you will not get the credit due.

---

b) Choosing Questions and Allocating Time

Make sure you check the rubrics on the question paper, so that you are clear about how many questions you are meant to answer, especially if there are 'a' and 'b' parts to questions. Make a mental note of the marks allocated to each part, and make sure that you divide your time appropriately.

Where an examination question comes in two parts, each one will be allocated a share of the total mark, which is printed next to it. For example, most OCR questions will have a first part which will mainly require description and explanation, and a second that may build on this by requiring you to give an evaluation and show relevance. If the first of these is allocated two-thirds of the total mark, it makes sense to spend two-thirds of your time on it. Candidates who skip the first part in order to produce a stunning second part do themselves no favours.

Remember, examination questions are there in order to allow you to show your skills in putting together a reasoned argument, based on what you have studied. If a question looks ridiculously hard or far too easy, think again! You may have missed something.

Hint

If the only way of answering the question is by referring to some obscure article you downloaded from the internet, think again! Examiners do not play tricks on candidates, nor require them to have researched anything obscure. There has to be a straightforward way of answering the question, and the material you need to know to do so will have been in one or more of the books on the reading list.

At AS level you will probably have one hour to answer two questions. Once you are confident that you know what your two chosen questions are looking for, it may be useful (but is not essential) to plan out each essay on paper (you will certainly need to hold the plan in your head and stick to it). Generally speaking, plans and lists of topics are not taken into consideration in giving you a mark for the question – unless, for example, you fail to finish an essay, in which case the examiner may look back at your plan to see what you intended to do.

But remember, it is 'demonstrated' knowledge that is needed – the most your plan will show is that you know the main headings, not that you have detailed knowledge, so that's all you can possibly hope to be credited with. The examiner will NOT give you credit for what he may guess you know, but have not actually included in your essay.

i) Check 'b' Before 'a'

Where you have a question in two parts, the second of them will probably ask for some sort of evaluation or development of the first. Make sure you know exactly how you intend to answer the 'b' part before starting to answer the 'a' part. Otherwise there is the danger that you will already have answered 'b' in the course of 'a', and then find that you have nothing left to say. But, that said, remember to balance the time allocated to each half to follow the marks allocated – little 'a's followed by massive 'b's are a good recipe for a poor grade.

c) No Second Thoughts

Don't start a question until you know how you are going to answer it. Some candidates abandon a question part way through, and then start another one instead. This is a waste of time. Choose only questions that you know you can answer, and then stick with your decision once it is made. Make it clear in the first sentence or two of your answer how you are going to tackle the question and the general line of argument that you will be taking.

Note

Examiners do not have unlimited time to give to each paper. Make life easy for them – set out what you intend to do clearly and then do it. You do not need to start an essay by outlining everything that is going to be in it (that would be a waste of your valuable time), but it is very useful to have an opening paragraph that shows you are aware of the significance of the question.

---

d) Terms

If particular terms are appropriate, use them. As long as you know what 'cognitive' and 'non-cognitive' mean in connection with religious language, then using those terms correctly will not only gain you credit in itself, it will also save you time. Philosophers use special terms in order to be able to set down arguments quickly and clearly, without having to explain absolutely everything every time. But make sure you know those terms. If you get them wrong, you could throw your argument completely.

e) PhDs need not apply!

You are being examined on a specification, and need to show that you understand and can argue about the material convincingly. You are not expected to argue that everyone who has ever written on the subject is completely wrong and that this examination answer is your opportunity to show the world the truth at last! Let your brilliance show in the clarity and precision with which you argue. Your new idea may be interesting, and the examiner may admire your originality, but it may take up too much of your time and not allow you to do yourself justice.

f) No Padding

Don't try to pad out your answer with extra facts or ideas in order to make it look more convincing. All you need to do is to answer the question clearly, justify your point of view, and demonstrate that you know the issues, understand the terminology used in the debates, and have a working knowledge of the topics in the specification. All else is a waste of time. Beyond a certain point (the point at which you are able to put down relevant material concisely and clearly), more generally means worse.

Note

You do not please an examiner by writing *more*, but by writing *better*. If you know how to answer a question, do so as clearly as possible, explaining whatever is relevant. Once you have done that, you are likely to have scored your maximum mark; padding it out does not help, so use your time to best advantage and move on to the next question.

---

g) Check and Add

If you finish with time to spare, go back and look again at the questions you have answered. Ask yourself the same question you did before you started – What is the examiner looking for here? Then read your answer. Have your really covered all that you intended to say?

If you want to add material, just put an asterisk or circled number in the text, or 'Note 1' and then write out the extra point you want to make at the end of the essay. (It's always useful to leave a bit of room between essays so that you can do this.) At this stage, you will not do yourself any harm by additions, and if (but only if) they are relevant, you could improve your mark.

And the best of luck to you all!

GLOSSARY

A posteriori – denotes knowledge that is based on sense experience

A priori – used of knowledge that arises prior to, or is not based on, a consideration of evidence in the form of sense experience

Absolutist – used of moral arguments that suggest that it is possible, in theory, to find moral principles that can be applied universally

Agapeism – moral theory based on the application of love to each situation

Agnosticism – the view that we do not have sufficient evidence to decide whether God exists or not

Ahimsa – the principle of non-violence; used in Jain, Buddhist and Hindu philosophy

Alienation – a state in which people feel themselves to be deprived of personal achievement and satisfaction

Altruism – the unselfish consideration of others

Amoral – an action that, with respect to the person who performs it, is done without reference to any moral system

Analytic – used of a statement whose truth is established by definition (e.g. logic and mathematical statements), rather than by evidence (c.p. 'synthetic')

Applied ethics – term used for the application of ethical theory to specific issues

Archetype – an image through which individuals participate in the common but profound experiences of their society

Atheism – the conviction that there is no god

Axiological ethics – the study of the values that give rise to moral choices, and upon which those choices are based

Behaviourism – the view that mental attributes are a way of describing bodily action (see particularly the work of Gilbert Ryle)

Cardinal virtues – prudence, justice, fortitude and temperance; Stoic principles of the moral life, found in Plato and Aristotle and used also by Aquinas

Categorical Imperative – an absolute sense of moral obligation, which is not related to the anticipated result of an action (c.p. 'hypothetical imperative'). It is particularly used of Kant's criterion for assessing the validity of moral claims.

Charismatic – used of those who claim divine inspiration during worship, being filled with the Holy Spirit

Cognitive language – language that claims to give factual information

Consequentialist – used of an ethical theory that is based on the assessment of results (e.g Utilitarianism)

Cosmological (Arguments) – arguments for the existence of God, based on the fact of the world's existence

Deism – belief in a God, seen as an external designer of the universe

Deontological questions – questions about a person's rights and duties

Descriptive ethics – the description of the social behaviour, related to values and cultures (c.p. 'normative ethics')

Design (Argument from) – the argument that the world appears to be designed, and therefore that God exists as its designer

Determinism – the philosophical view that every act is totally conditioned by its antecedent causes, and therefore that agents are not actually free to make moral choices and any experience of such freedom is illusory

Dharma – this is a Sanskrit word used for 'reality' or 'truth', in the sense of the way in which the world is organised. It is used in both Hindu and Buddhist ethics. For Hindus it means right or appropriate action or duty (i.e. duty that is in line with fundamental reality); for Buddhists it refers to the teaching of the Buddha.

Double Effect, Law of – the principle that an action may be considered right, even if a secondary effect of that action is harmful, or could be considered wrong

Dualism – the view that body and mind are separate and distinct

Egoism – ethical theories that place the human ego as of primary concern

Emotive Theory – the theory that moral assertions are simply the expression of values and emotions. (i.e. to say that something is wrong or bad simply indicates that you dislike it)

Empiricism – the theory that all knowledge comes by way of the five human senses

Epiphenomenalism – the view that the mind is merely a product of the complex physical processes going on in the brain

Epistemology – the theory of knowledge

Existentialism – philosophy concerned with the individual's sense of meaning and existence, and also more generally with the problems of human existence

Final cause – the 'end' or purpose of something; its essence or potential (particularly in Aristotle)

Forms, theory of – Plato's theory of universals, in which particular things share and from which they take their character

Hedonism – the view that the quest for happiness is fundamental to morality

Holistic – describes an approach, argument or view that considers the operations of the whole of a complex entity (as opposed to its constituent parts)

Humanism – a cultural movement emphasising the dignity of humankind and the primacy of reason, as opposed to the acceptance of tradition. In the twentieth century, Humanism was particularly associated with the rejection of traditional religious beliefs.

Hypothetical Imperative – a moral claim based on achieving an intended result: 'if . . . then'

Idealism – the view that reality (or our view of reality) is fundamentally mental rather than physical

Ideology – a set of ideas that can form the basis for a social, political or economic system

Immanence – used to describe God as being found within the world

Induction (inductive inference) – the logical process by which a theory is devised on the basis of cumulative evidence

Interactionism – a general term (in the Philosophy of Mind) for theories in which mind and body act upon one another

Intuitionism – a view that 'good' is a simple term and may not be further defined, but only known through intuition

Karma – 'action' in Sanskrit; used of the idea that actions (good or bad) have an effect on the person who performs them. It is found in slightly different forms in Hinduism, Buddhism and Jainism.

Logical Positivism – an approach to language, developed early in the twentieth century (particularly within the Vienna Circle), which equated the meaning of a statement with its method of verification, saw scientific language as ideal and dismissed religion and morality as meaningless

Logos – the Greek term for 'word', used by the Stoics for the fundamental rationality in the universe and therefore the basis of a 'Natural Law' approach to ethics. Also used of Christ as the 'word' of God in creation.

Materialism – the view that reality is physical

Meta-ethics – the study of the nature and function of ethical statements

Metaphysical ethics – an approach that relates morality to an overall view of the nature of reality

Metaphysics – the philosophical study of the fundamental structures of reality

Natural Law – the ethical theory based on the idea of the 'final cause' or purpose of things, which defines their proper use or goal

Natural philosophy – the branch of philosophy which considers the physical world; a term used for science prior to the eigthteenth century

Naturalistic fallacy – the common error (pointed out by Hume and G E Moore) of trying to derive an 'ought' from an 'is'

Non-cognitive – used of the view that moral claims express the values, emotions and preferences of the people who use them, rather than giving information about the world

Normative ethics – a study of the moral norms or principles that people use to justify action

Numinous – used by Otto to describe the particular sense of awe and dread, associated with religious experience

Obsessional neurosis – compulsive behaviour stemming from repressed trauma

Ockham's Razor – the principle that one should opt for the simplest explanation; generally summarised as 'causes should not be multiplied beyond necessity'

Ontology – the study of the nature of being itself

Panentheism – the belief that God exists within everything (but is not simply identified with everything)

Pantheism – the belief that the whole physical universe is God

Performative utterance – a statement that brings something about (e.g. 'I baptise you.')

Phenomena – those things which are known through the senses; in Kant, it is the general term used for sense impressions, as opposed to 'noumena', or things as they are in themselves

Postmodernism – an approach to culture and philosophy, developed in the latter part of the twentieth century, which emphasises the autonomy of cultural symbols and texts, rather than relating them to a self-conscious author or single authoritative meaning

Preference Utilitarianism – theory based on the satisfaction of the preferences of the individuals concerned.

Prescriptivism – theory that moral statements recommend (or 'prescribe') a particular course of action, i.e. to say something is 'good' is to recommend that you should do it (associated particularly with R M Hare)

Primary qualities – a term used by Locke for those qualities thought to inhere in objects, and are therefore independent of the faculties of the observer (e.g. shape)

Providence – the belief that God, directly or through nature, provides for humankind

Rationalist ethics – used of any ethical theory based on reason

Reductionism – the philosophical approach which sees complex entities as 'no more than' the various parts of which they are comprised (e.g. thoughts are reduced to electric impulses in the brain)

Relativism, ethical – the view that there are no moral absolutes, but that issues of right and wrong are relative to their social, historical or cultural context

Scepticism – a view which doubts any claims to knowledge and certainty

Schematisation – the use of words to understand and describe the 'holy' (according to Otto)

Scientism – the view that science gives the only valid interpretation of reality

Secondary qualities – a term used by Locke for those qualities used in the description of an object that are determined by the sensory organs of the perceiver (e.g. colour)

Secularism – the view that humankind should be concerned primarily with this world, rather than with religious concepts

Situation Ethics – the theory argued by Fletcher in the 1960s that Christian morality should be based on doing whatever is most loving, even at the expense of traditional moral rules

Synthetic – used of statements whose truth depends upon empirical evidence

Teleological Ethics – used of any ethical theory based on the expected end or purpose (*telos*) of an action

Theism – belief in the existence of God

Utilitarianism – an ethical theory based on the desire to achieve 'the greatest happiness for the greatest number', thereby evaluating actions according to their expected results

Virtue Ethics – moral theory based on the development and promotion of qualities and virtues that embody the good life

FURTHER READING

The following books in the *Access to Philosophy* series cover the issues in greater depth than is possible in this single volume, and are suitable for both AS- and A2-level study:

Ahluwalia, Libby *Foundation for the Study of Religion* (for AS level)
Cole, Peter *The Philosophy of Religion*
Thompson, Mel *Ethical Theory*
Walker, Joe *Environmental Ethics*
Wilcockson, Michael *Issues of Life and Death*
Wilcockson, Michael *Sex and Relationships*

The following books in the *Teach Yourself* series also cover these topics:

TY: Ethics
TY: Philosophy of Religion

And for a broad background to the issues, from a philosophical perspective:

TY: Philosophy
TY: Philosophy of Science
TY: Philosophy of Mind

1 Anthologies and Reference Books

For a detailed work of general reference, covering all aspects of philosophy:

Concise Routledge Encyclopedia of Philosophy, Routledge, 2000

Davies, Brian (ed.) *Philosophy of Religion: a guide and anthology*, OUP, 2000

Helm, Paul (ed.) *Faith and Reason*, OUP, 1999
This is one of the 'Oxford Readers' giving a useful collection of extracts from key thinkers in the philosophy of religion, with introductions to each section, setting the context for the passages included. This is a very useful collection for getting students into an exploration of the original texts, and therefore the style of philosophical argument.

Quinn, Philip & Taliaferro, Charles (eds) *Companion to the Philosophy of Religion*, Blackwell, 1999

Sterba, James P (ed.) *Ethics: The Big Questions*, Blackwell, 1998
This is a substantial and valuable anthology for both students and

teachers, covering meta-ethics, moral theories and challenges to ethics.

Johnson, Oliver (ed) *Ethics: selections from Classical and Contemporary Writers* (7th edition), Harcourt Brace, 1994

Introduction to Philosophy: Classical and Contemporary readings, Wadsworth, 1999

2 Other Useful Titles, including titles recommended to me by AS level teachers as useful for teaching philosophy and ethics

Appelbaum, D and Thompson, M (eds) *World Philosophy*, Vega, 2002
This is a large-format illustrated book on philosophy, designed for the general reader but suitable for students. It sets out the issues with illustrations to stimulate an imaginative appreciation of what philosophy is about, and includes sections on the Philosophy of Religion, and Ethics.

Blackburn, Simon *Being Good*, OUP, 2001
An attractive little book, giving a clear and lively introduction to some of the puzzles of ethics and their relationship to fundamental principles and beliefs.

For revision purposes, Greg Dewar's *Religious Studies: Philosophy and Ethics through diagrams*, OUP, 2002, provides a concise but very brief outline of all major topics.

J L Mackie's *The Miracle of Theism*, OUP, 1982, a very interesting critique of the arguments for the existence of God. The title hints at Mackie's general conclusion, namely that it is a miracle that people continue to believe in the God of traditional theism.

MacIntyre, Alasdair *A Short History of Ethics*, Routledge, 1998 (second edition)

Magee, Bryan *The Story of Philosophy*, Dorling Kindersley, London, 1998
This book is particularly useful for getting the background, both culturally and in terms of philosophy, for the various thinkers, with wonderfully lucid summaries of their work.

Pojman, L P. has an anthology and a good number of textbooks suitable for students on a range of issues in ethics (e.g. *Ethics: Discovering Right and Wrong*, Wadsworth, 2001) and philosophy of religion. He comes with the recommendation of several experienced teachers.

Singer, Peter *Practical Ethics*, CUP, 1993
A very influential book; in general Singer takes a preference utilitarian approach to ethical issues.

Singer, Peter *Writings on an Ethical Life*, Fourth Estate, 2002 (a range of extracts from his other books)

Smart, Ninian *World Philosophies*, Routledge, London and New York, 1999

Stone, Martin, 'Philosophy of Religion' in *Philosophy* 2nd ed. A C Grayling (ed), OUP, 1998

Taliaferro, Charles *Contemporary Philosophy of Religion*, Blackwell, 1998

3 Following Up on Particular Chapters in This Book

Chapter 1

Most of the introductions to the Philosophy of Religion given in the Further Reading section give an account of the various terms used.

Extracts from the original texts can also be found in, for example:

The Existence of God, John Hick, Macmillan, 1982

Philosophy of Religion: a Guide and an Anthology, Brian Davies, OUP 2000

For those going on to A2 level, Malcolm's article, which is a very valuable summary of the debate on the Ontological Argument, is found in J Hick, *The Existence of God*.

Those developing work on the Cosmological Argument, especially for A2 level, should include the Kalam argument. For the basics on this see: *TY: Philosophy of Religion*, chapter 4.

The argument is discussed at length in W L Craig *The Kalam Cosmological Argument*, Macmillan, 1979, and an extended extract from Metaphysics by Al-Kindi is included in *Faith and Reason* by Paul Helm.

Chapter 2

Students will benefit greatly from reading selections from the classic texts:

Otto *The Idea of the Holy*, OUP, 1968
Schleiermacher *Speeches on Religion*, CUP, 1996
James *The Varieties of Religious Experience*, Penguin, 1983

Chapter 3

Most standard textbooks on the Philosophy of Religion have sections on the challenges to religion and also on the problem of evil and suffering. See particularly those listed in the Further Reading section.

Chapter 4

Logical Positivism features in most basic introductions to Philosophy, as does Wittgenstein.

Tillich's work (especially in *Systematic Theology*) is readable on the use and nature of symbolic language.

Chapter 5

Controversial (from a religious standpoint) but readable, Richard Dawkins' books (especially perhaps *The Blind Watchmaker* (Penguin, 1990), *Climbing Mount Improbable* (Penguin, 1997) and *Unweaving the Rainbow* (Penguin, 1999)) are always good value. His opposition to conventional religious views is a great stimulus to serious thought.

For more advanced study, *Religion and Science* by Ian G Barbour (SCM, 1998) gives solid and serious coverage of the issues.

Chapter 6

There are many useful introductions to the Philosophy of Mind, but most focus on the modern questions of intentionality, cognition, artificial intelligence and other issues in the broad field of Cognitive Science. At AS level, the issues are specifically linked to traditional religious ideas, and the Philosophy of Mind is therefore best left as background reading. The religious issues themselves are covered at an appropriate level in most of the introductory books on the Philosophy of Religion.

Chapter 7

Students may find it fascinating to dip into Wittgenstein's *Tractatus*, Routledge, 2001 (originally published 1922), if only to be surprised at the way it is set out, and the amazing boldness of its claims.

Ayer's classic *Language, Truth and Logic*, Penguin, 2001 (originally published 1936) would be an interesting challenge for the more able student.

Chapter 8

For a more detailed exposition of all these theories, see *Ethical Theory* in the *Access to Philosophy* series.

George Lord has produced concise and clearly argued booklets on *Utilitarianism* and on *Kant's Ethical Theory of Duty*. These are not available through bookshops, but are sold direct by the author at his various speaking engagements, all monies being given to charity.

A very useful book on Virtue Ethics is Alasdair MacIntyre *After Virtue: a study in Moral Theory*, (Duckworth, 1981).

Chapter 9

Clearly, there has been no scope in a book of this sort to cover any of the details of religious ethics. Most introductions to particular religions include a section on ethics, as do the general reference books on ethics. In terms of AS-level examinations, however, students need to make sure that they are aware of the relationship between ethical theories and religious ethics, and the nature and authority of religious ethics, rather than getting involved with too much detail. They should, however, be aware of examples from the religion they are studying, to be used to illustrate any points they are making.

Chapter 10

Most of the general books on ethics listed above will have sections on freedom and on conscience.

Chapter 11

For those wanting to explore medical and other issues from a distinctively Christian standpoint, try the *ethicsforschools.org* website, provided by the Christian Medical Fellowship (see below) – but be aware of the particular religious origin of this material.

Chapter 12

Within the *Access to Philosophy* series, Michael Wilcockson's *Sex and Relationships* provides further work, and detailed information suitable for both AS and A2 level.

Rawls, John *A Theory of Justice*, Harvard University Press, 1971
A classic text on establishing justice as fairness.

Biting the Moral Bullet (on War, 1997), published by Hodder & Stoughton, covers a range of topics in an imaginative and student-friendly way.

For further information on the Jewish view of war, see:

War and Its Discontents J P Burns, Georgetown University Press, 1996

4 Websites

BBC
www.bbc.co.uk/religion/
This site provides a huge range of material on both religion and ethics, accessible and conveniently arranged, with definitions and arguments clearly set out.

Christian Medical Fellowship
www.ethicsforschools.org
For those wanting to study the Christian perspective on ethical issues, a clearly set out site offers information on a wide range of topics, not merely those linked to medical dilemmas. Students may need to be reminded that this material is written from a specific religious standpoint.

The Internet Encyclopedia of Philosophy
www.utm.edu/research/iep/
Many very useful outline articles, including a timeline of philosophers – valuable for getting a historical perspective on the debates.

Philosophy in Cyberspace
www-personal.monash.edu.au/~dey/phil/
Links to many other sites connected with philosophy. Also useful for anyone thinking of going on to study Philosophy at university, since it gives a global run-down of departments.

Philosophy
www.Eserver.org/philosophy/
This is a valuable site for anyone wanting to look up and search for passages in original classic texts in philosophy and ethics It contains a huge amount of material. Just type in 'Plato' or 'Aristotle' and see what is available!

Philosophy Around the Web
www.ox.ac.uk
Just look up Philosophy of Religion or Ethics as a topic area.

Philosophy Pages

www.philosophypages.com

Just look up a particular historical period and thinker for useful information and background.

For anyone wanting to check details of other books on Philosophy and Ethics by the same author, to ask anything about or comment on this book, or to see additional material particularly suitable for AS and A2 level students and teachers in the United Kingdom, log on to:

www.mel-thompson.co.uk

INDEX